Tamsin Bradley is Principal Lecturer in Anthropology and Director of the International Centre for Community Development, Faculty of Applied Social Sciences, London Metropolitan University. She has published widely on gender, religion and international development, including *Challenging the NGOs: Women, Religion and Western Dialogues in India* (I.B.Tauris, 2006); and (edited with Emma Tomalin) *Dowry: Bridging the Gap Between Theory and Practice* (2009).

LIBRARY OF DEVELOPMENT STUDIES

Series ISBN: 978 1 84885 238 9

See www.ibtauris.com/LDS for a full list of titles

RELIGION AND GENDER IN THE DEVELOPING WORLD

Faith-Based Organizations and Feminism in India

TAMSIN BRADLEY

Published in 2011 by I.B.Tauris & Co Ltd
6 Salem Road, London W2 4BU
175 Fifth Avenue, New York NY 10010
www.ibtauris.com

Distributed in the United States and Canada
Exclusively by Palgrave Macmillan
175 Fifth Avenue, New York NY 10010

Library of Development Studies 2

ISBN: 978 1 84885 427 7

A full CIP record for this book is available from the British Library
A full CIP record for this book is available from the Library of Congress

Library of Congress catalog card: available

Camera-ready copy edited and supplied by
Oxford Publishing Services, Oxford
Printed and bound in Great Britain by
CPI Antony Rowe, Chippenham, Wiltshire

Contents

This book is dedicated to my beautiful daughter Megan
who made a wonderfully nosey research assistant
during numerous fieldwork trips to India.

Acronyms and Abbreviations

BJP	Bharatiya Janata Party
CAFOD	Catholic Agency for Overseas Development
DFID	Department for International Development
ESRC	Economic and Social Research Council
FBDO	faith-based development organization
FBO	faith-based organization
GAD	gender and development
GMS	Gandhian Memorial Society
HIV/Aids	human immunodeficiency virus/acquired immune deficiency syndrome
IDSJ	Institute of Development Studies, Jaipur
IMI	International Monetary Fund
IR	international relations
MDG	millennium development goal
NGO	non-governmental organization
PWDVA	Protection of Women from Domestic Violence Act
RSS	Rashtriya Svayam-sevak Sangh
RUWA	Rajasthan University Women's Association
STD	sexually-transmitted disease
UNIFEM	United Nations Development Fund for Women
UNRISD	United Nations Research Institute for Social Development
VDPJ	Village Development Project, Jodphur
VHP	Vishva Hindu Parishad
VSR	Village Service Rajasthan
WDP	Women's Development Programme
WFR	Water for Rajasthan

Glossary

Adaita Vedanta	the teachings of the final books of the Vedas known as the Upanishads and the philosophy on how to achieve liberation from the bondage of rebirth.
aherent	follower of a specific religious tradition.
atman	the individual soul within each person that connects to the world soul Brahman. The *atman* continues to be reborn until *moksha* or liberation is achieved.
bhajans	Indian devotional songs.
bhakti	Sanskrit word meaning devotion or rather showing devotion to God. It involves devotees expressing their devotion to God through worship and other religious and spiritual practices such as meditation.
Brahman	the world soul or ultimate being in Hinduism.
Brahmin	upper-caste man or priestly caste.
caste	a system of social stratification that divides people into *jatis*, meaning castes. A person's caste is determined at birth, so is passed down through families (lineage).
dalit	person of a low caste or untouchable status. Dalits are a diverse group spread throughout India and different groups of dalits speak different languages.
darsan	Sanskrit word meaning sight or vision, specifically refers to vision of the divine acquired during worship.
dharma	determines a person's duty and responsibilities in life. *Dharma* is gendered but also determined

	by a person's caste. It thus differs from person to person.
ethnocentrism	belief that one's own ethnic and cultural position is superior and an attempt to impose it onto others; measuring and judging all other values and belief system against it.
karma	system of acquiring credit by doing good needs. The amount of *karma* a person generates in a lifetime determines his or her position and status in the next life.
moksha	liberation from the continuous cycle of birth, death and rebirth. It represents the ultimate goal of Hinduism in which the *atman* (individual soul) unites with the world soul (*Brahman*).
neoliberalism	a political orientation originating in the 1960s that blends liberal political views with an emphasis on economic growth.
puja	literally honouring the gods. Hindus perform rituals called *puja* to Hindus, meaning deities.
purdah	cultural practice involving the physical seclusion of women in the domestic sphere.
samsara	continuous cycle of birth, death and rebirth from which individuals seek liberation (*moksha*).
Sanatana dharma	Many Hindus refer to their religion through this term, for it means way of life.
seva	service to god usually through performing charitable acts.
stridharma	women's *dharma* or role and responsibilities in life, which is different from men's.
varna	the four orders of society that represent the foundations of the social stratification system known as caste. *Varna* literally means colour not in racial terms but symbolic denoting a person's spiritual qualities.
Veda	Ancient Indian texts.
Vedanta	last part of the Vedas known as the Upanishads.

Acknowledgements

THIS book would have been impossible without Alex Wright, Joanna Godfrey and Maria Marsh at I.B.Tauris, so thanks to them for believing in and supporting this project. I also thank the Cohens who again took on the task of bringing my manuscript to a camera-ready state. An Economic and Social Research Council (ESRC) postdoctoral grant awarded to me as part of a non-governmental public action research programme directed by Professor Jude Howell, Centre for Civil Society, LSE largely funded my fieldwork. Funding also came from the UK Department for International Development via the Religion and Development Research Programme directed by Professor Carole Rakodi at the University of Birmingham. I thank Jude and Carole for their support and encouragement.

I received mentoring support from Professors Eileen O'Keefe and Jeff Haynes at London Metropolitan University. Their insight and guidance has been invaluable in shaping not just this book but also my career. I acknowledge my inspirational colleagues in the Department of Applied Social Sciences, London Metropolitan University, whose commitment to bridging the gap between research and teaching is shaping the next generation of critical forward-thinking professionals. I hope this book makes a contribution to this venture and gives something back to the academy. I also hope it helps to draw attention to the brave, empowered and often ferocious Indian women with whom I have been privileged to spend time. I hope it highlights the activists and development practitioners who informed my work and whose dedication to their cause is simply breathtaking and awe inspiring. Also, I acknowledge and thank my students who have never ceased to ask me difficult questions, often arising from their own challenging life experiences and without them the constant self-evaluation needed to write this book would have faltered.

Finally, to Donovan, Megan, my mother and father and all my

family, your support is crucial in my achievements, however large or small – thank you.

Introduction

THIS book is positioned within the burgeoning research that examines the theoretical and practical implications of religion for human development. As an applied anthropologist, my intention is to provoke critical analysis of the relationships between competing concepts of development and different dimensions of religion. My work in this area has yielded many more questions than answers, but, as I argue throughout, these are vital questions. At a time when development donors are funding more faith-based organizations than previously and when the activities of religious organizations are becoming increasingly visible and transnational, the value of religion in supporting positive human growth must continue to be debated publicly.

This book is intended to encourage the reader to think about the multiple theoretical approaches to the study of religion and its implications for human development. It is also a call to keep practical matters in focus and to ensure that research on the topic remains loyal to a responsive, bottom-up approach to community development. As a feminist, my concern throughout my research career has been to produce applied anthropological research that will make some kind of contribution towards positively transforming the lives of groups of Indian women who feel they suffer injustice. Religion has been a central part of my work because the women whose lives I have observed were predominantly adherents. Focusing on religion and what it brings to their lives has helped me to hear and witness personal testimonies of joy and pain. It has also provided powerful explanations for the prevalence of gender inequalities in India.

The theoretical basis of this book is a focus on how the disciplines of anthropology, religious studies and gender studies can make more of a contribution to the research and practice of development. Both 'religion' and 'development' are shifting terms that are subject to interpretation and reinterpretation. The approach presented in this book is in part about the critical analysis of how different people understand and use religion and development in varying contexts. A very broad working definition of development is that it constitutes a vision or perception of the world that individuals, groups and agencies aim to create. My specific concern is to understand what part religion plays in this process of creating visions for the future. Religion in the context of development is often regarded as a 'problem' that must be overcome if development visions are to be realized. In faith and theologically-based approaches, religion is presented positively as the vehicle for the creation of an equal and compassionate society. In this book I do not dispute the positive effects of religion but argue that religion can also produce negative impacts on people's lives. I show how a gendered lens opens up analysis into the various intersections between religion and development. By combining anthropology and religious studies I explore how gender feeds into different aspects of the research and practice of development. This book, which is arranged in three parts, covers multiple and gendered links between religion and development. The intention behind each chapter is to highlight the usefulness of an interdisciplinary approach to those engaged in both the theorizing and practice of development.

Religion is important to many people across the globe, including people in developing countries, for it provides secure guidelines for shaping their relationships with one another and towards the world, and provides them with a sense of identity and belonging. Because religion sets a moral code by which to live, it affects decision-making processes and human actions. Religion is manifested in people's lives through a range of institutional and personal spaces. Religious authorities assert their power under the guise of providing guidance on how to face the challenges of everyday life. Religious leaders and teachers interpret the sacred texts with a view to instructing their followers on how to apply religious values, concepts and beliefs to their daily lives. The role of religious teachers and leaders is therefore an immensely powerful one and one that can subvert as much as support the emergence of an equal society.

Religion is also a private affair, for a great deal of a person's religious life occurs internally through dialogue with sacred images and concepts. Rituals are an example of a religious activity that facilitates this personal internal dialogue. Development practitioners often ignore rituals that are important for adherents. Ritual spaces are reflective because, within them, individuals can respond to changing events and express both joy and suffering. Religion, or specifically its experiential component 'faith', is a crucial motivational force in driving adherents towards compassionate pursuits intended to ease the pain of others. In the context of development, faith, spirituality and charitable values produce an energy that seems able to sustain itself as a lasting commitment to the service of the materially poor. This can be seen in the existence of so many religious institutions and organizations from all faiths working towards similar development goals. One can broadly describe these goals as poverty alleviation, improvement in people's quality of life and general wellbeing. The quest to measure the impact of religion on development must be approached at these various levels and with an understanding of how they are linked. In this book I cover the following intersections between religion and development:

- Religion as a personal, private dimension in people's lives, which enables an individual to form his or her own understandings of what development should be.
- Religion as a dominant powerful force, which in many places structures the patterns of everyday life. As such, it has the potential both to obstruct and enhance development, depending on the specific vision being pursued.
- Religion at the community level, which in many instances can determine the shape of the grass-roots organizations that seek to build on local people's development ideals and experiences.
- Religion as shaping the identity of national and international organizations. Some of these organizations donate money to intermediaries who then channel it downwards to support the work of local organizations.
- Religion as highly politicized, so representing a platform or

vehicle that people as well as national and transnational organizations can use to promote their particular development agendas.

Why Gender?

To answer this question, it is necessary to point out that both
religion and development are gendered. In this book I use gender as
an analytical frame with which to evaluate critically the significance
of religion on and in people's lives and on the process of creating and
implementing development agendas. Gender is increasingly being
recognized within religious studies as a vital theoretical position
from which to deconstruct and challenge the production of hegemonic knowledge systems and/or discourses.[1] Gender shapes an
important approach in the study of religion that seeks to understand
how knowledge is formed, by whom and for whose benefit? The
critics of prevailing Western neoliberal development ideals are also
asking this question.[2]

Development too is gendered because it shapes how different goals
are reached by determining who controls the decision making. The
highest ranking leaders of global and transnational agencies are
predominantly middle- or upper-class males.[3] Although there is no
evidence to suggest that this means that decision makers favour
particular groups of people over others for funding, it does reflect a
lack of gender equality within the wealthiest donor institutions that
perhaps bodes ill for the achievement of equality in the developing
world. Jenkins and Alexander[4] not only draw attention to the fact
that white, upper-class male leaders have historically dominated the
World Bank, but they also highlight the lack of development
experience of many of its officers prior to taking up senior positions
in the institution. Second, development affects the lives of different
men and women in a variety of different ways. Scholars now
frequently require acknowledgement of what experiences different
men and women take from development. They ask whose needs
development really meets. Has development been successful in
challenging poverty and inequality and improving human rights for
all people?

As a category of analysis, gender is useful in examining the social,

4

cultural and religious factors that shape relationships within and between men and women. In that much of the ethnographic material I present documents the experiences of individual women who have had to confront oppression and injustice in their lives, this book is feminist. In it I pursue an underlying feminist concern to produce research that challenges the structural factors that inhibit women's life opportunities. My primary purpose is to show the multiple ways in which religion and development converge to produce both positive and negative effects on the lives of women.

I also intend to support those feminists who voice concern about the increasing incorporation of patriarchal religious views into the arenas in which global development agendas are being written. Religion is often homogeneously linked to development. Little debate ensues into what religion really is and how it impacts differently on people's lives. Gender is important as a means of appreciating the complex ways in which religion is experienced and 'lived'. Without the inclusion of gender many adherents find their voices lost while male religious leaders find their status elevated in development circles (see Chapters 2 and 3). Feminists studying religion have consistently argued that religion is inherently patriarchal and exclusionary.[5] The wholesale, uncritical inclusion of patriarchal religion into development deepens inequalities. I show how studying religion and development from a gendered perspective can stop the reproduction of such patterns of inequality. Combining the approaches of the study of religion and gender produces a clearer practical picture of how religion can be used positively in development. It also increases insight into the detrimental impact religion has for those development visions that pursue social equality and human dignity.

The Contribution of the Book
The contribution of this book is that it develops a methodology that allows one to see the intersections between religion and development more clearly and through a single analytical prism. This methodology reveals how development and religion become established as perceptions of reality and how they then impact on the way groups of

people see and act in the world. I believe that religion and development should not be carved up and explored through separate subject disciplines that then pursue detached themes. The failure to adopt an interdisciplinary approach to the study of religion and development can result in individual disciplines, which necessarily prioritize specific research topics, over simplifying the category of religion (see Chapter 2).

Popular research themes include the study of religious or faith-based development organizations; religion's role in peace-keeping efforts; the rise of transnational religious movements; and the role of religion in building a moral framework for development. Although this research is important, it does not convey the full extent of the impact of religion on human development. Although it may seem obvious that studying religion and anthropology should be central to this venture, scholars of theology, international relations and development studies have been more active in producing research on this topic. In this book I adopt a distinctly anthropological approach to the study of religion in development, with gender as the central analytical lens. I hope that other scholars will go on to produce research on this topic that will open up the space these disciplines occupy. This will help produce, within the academy, a wider and more critical debate on the interfaces between religion, gender and development. This will, I hope, influence the more central incorporation of religion and gender in both the practical and theoretical aspects of human development.

What is the Study of Religion?

Scholars of religious studies draw on a number of other disciplines in their work, including sociology, anthropology, philosophy, and textual and linguistic studies. The subject is fundamentally inter-disciplinary. To facilitate complex investigations into religion, many scholars employ research techniques from a number of subjects and move comfortably between different disciplines. I position myself within the study of religion as an anthropologist, but also draw on textual studies and critical post-colonial theory. My particular interest has been in understanding the importance of religion as a

source of strength and courage for women who live in environ-
mentally, socially and culturally harsh conditions.

A second strand to my research emerged as I explored how
agencies and development practitioners respond to these conditions
and try to implement initiatives to transform the lives of women
positively. In my research, some of which is presented here, I found
that many secular and faith-based non-governmental organizations
(NGOs) look upon Hinduism as part of the problem because it
creates a patriarchal culture that regards women as inferior to men.
My own ethnographic studies into the lives of Rajasthani women led
me to a complex and initially contradictory picture of religion. The
Rajasthani women with whom I spoke did not see religion purely in
negative terms, although they recognized its detrimental affects on
their lives. They saw it also as a motivational resource that enabled
them to fight the injustices they encountered.

As stated above, development researchers often isolate the impact
of religion. Because it inhibits certain groups from pursuing opportunities or thwarts peace-building efforts, they either study its
positive benefits or treat it as an obstacle to overcome. For example,
some researchers present the 'faith' or 'spirituality' of the members of
faith-based development organizations as a vital source of drive and
direction. There is a paucity of studies that trace the various intersections between religion and development. In other words, as
outlined above, the impact of religion is usually studied though one
strand rather than as a prism of interlocking strands. Development
approached through the discipline of religious studies reveals the
existence of many levels and points at which religion makes a
significant impact on people's lives and on development outcomes.
The research presented in this volume shows the diversity of the
relationship between religion and development.

Why Take an Ethnographic Approach?
My anthropological training has encouraged me to seek out gaps that
those who work in and study development often ignore. Important
insights can be gathered from within these gaps, which sometimes
reveal visions of development that challenge dominant ideals. These

spaces appear when different development actors meet and interact and they occur at both macro and micro levels. At the macro level, international organizations produce agendas, such as the millennium development goals, which they market globally as the direction towards which all development actors should be moving.

At the grass-roots level, people meet to discuss the problems they face in their daily lives and often build alliances to achieve favoured solutions. These local-level strategies often actively resist the pull of the uniform and impersonal transnational development agenda. Conflicts and tensions might arise when parties disagree over what the development priorities should be and over the best way to achieve them. Ethnography is able to illuminate these moments by leap-frogging over or weaving between the various development relationships and activities. In this book I employ ethnography to place different types of faith-based organizations under scrutiny and to examine critically their relationship to a global neoliberal narrative on development.

The aim of this approach is to understand how religions may or may not support the global agenda of the world's financially powerful development players. Key questions are asked. How do different types of development organizations relate to people at a local level? To what extent do interactions with those directly affected by poverty and other forms of injustice inform their policies? Do alternative visions of development really exist at a local level? Or does the hegemonic weight of donors who want their largely economic visions pursued suppress the creative potential of the individual and group? In other words, is the leverage of these donors too great to allow alternative visions to flourish? Now that many development scholars accept that the people who control the hegemonic process of development planning and intervention do not live in poverty, what chance do local people really have of getting their voices heard? Ethnography is able to highlight the extent to which the various actors at all levels manipulate development outcomes. The conclusions reached in this book offer an optimistic view of local people resisting and negotiating with development processes. I argue that it is important to acknowledge the agency of people at all levels of development because, although money may be channelled hierarchically, people at all points in the prism control the relative success of a project.

How Does Religion Combine with Ethnography?

I challenge the assumption that because an organization is religious it will automatically produce good development results. Although I wholeheartedly support the work of most faith-based organizations and argue that their activities should be supported and positively acknowledged, I believe that the same critical evaluative lens should be applied to the work of both secular and faith-based development organizations. There are cases of religion producing a culturally imperial and Eurocentric approach to development. Religion not only produces a deep conviction based on a compassionate desire to act out charitable sentiments but it also cements a particular way of seeing the world. Brought together these two aspects can construct a rigid tunnel vision that robustly maintains the energy of those working with an FBO (faith-based organization) while adhering to a static picture of the transformation they seek to implement. While compassion can at times bring positive results it can also be negative.

I use an ethnographic approach to highlight the ways in which faith and compassion disempower local development actors by blocking opportunities for actual face-to-face dialogue. Furthermore, the critical application of ethnographic research shows how success is the only possible outcome for some FBOs. The collective imagination of individual members unwilling to face the possibility that their compassionate intentions might fail to bring the good results for which they prayed can hide and mask some organizations' failures. While local people are often considered ignorant and without insights into development, the ethnographic studies presented in this book show that they are actors in their own development and understand how their visions conflict or converge with those from outside.

Furthermore, local actors understand how the macro (national, regional and international) development industry operates and use their agency to gain control over the results of targeted interventions.

Local groups may agree to a project's implementation, but may steer its course to achieve results that are different from those the outside donor envisaged. This view of how the local and international relate to each other produces a more positive and perhaps accurate picture of development. Critics of the neoliberal development agenda may benefit from looking more closely at how local people manipulate the discourse and practice to acquire the benefits they desire. Ferguson,[6] reviewing his own critical stance on neoliberalism, asserts that ethnographers have a role to play in revealing how people happily work within the neoliberal frame to twist and unravel projects according to their own agenda and to create their own visions of development. I seek to make a contribution to this venture by high-lighting how even those considered the most repressed (poor women) adopt an active subject position to shape their own destiny, however limiting the patriarchal structural constraints may be.

The Structure of the Book
This book contains ten chapters arranged into three parts.

Part I: Mainstreaming religion and gender in development
In the chapters in this part I explore the methodological possibilities of combining gender, the study of religion and development. The focus of the first two chapters is on gender as an analytical perspective that enables close examination into who benefits and who loses from development initiatives. This is particularly pertinent because, through effective global lobbying by feminist movements, gender can no longer be left out of development agendas. Gender is also crucial as a lens through which to understand how social and cultural inequalities are produced and sustained, often through the dominance of a patriarchal religious ideology that leaves some groups in any given community with less access than others to material resources and life opportunities.

I begin Chapter 1 with a review of the literature on the interface between religion and development and show how it reveals a paucity of material on gender. I also highlight the overly simplistic treatment of religion by many of the disciplines engaged in this research. As already stated, development studies, sociology, theology and international relations have been the most active disciplines in terms of linking concepts of development to religion. I argue that scholars who study religion and anthropology need to stake more of a claim to research in this area and look at what kind of contribution they might make.

In Chapter 2 I consider how anthropologists working on religion could contribute to discussions on gender, development and globalization. Some anthropological research highlights how power operates through globalization to marginalize local groups. Anthropologists may see religion as a source of identity and accord importance to the rituals through which its adherents express their feelings of exclusion and make sense of the world around them. Within ritual spaces adherents also decide how to respond to and/or act in the world. Both anthropologists and international relations scholars have shown how transnational religio-political movements provide their adherents with a means of resisting and challenging aspects of globalization. Development is understood as working within globalization, hence the need to include a chapter on how ideas about the world are transported across the globe. Combining the tools of international relations and anthropology could cast light on what motivates individuals to join a movement. In turn, such research could provide an explanation for religion's rootedness in the world.

In Chapter 3 I show how the micro/macro methodology I advocate in Chapter 2 works in practice and analyse Hindu transnational organizations from a gendered perspective. The ethnographic data collected on these organizations reveal that recognizable development goals are projected – for example, empowerment of women and poverty alleviation. However, the day-to-day activities of devotees from each organization focus on short-term welfare concerns that support individual visions of spiritual development rather than the structural transformation of the lives of the poor and marginalized.

Part 2: Faith-based organizations and dialogues in development

The chapters in this part demonstrate how, in the critical evaluation of development, combining the study of religion and gender can help unravel the complex power relationships that exist between those with and those without material wealth. These relationships are rooted in the communities targeted to 'receive' aid and through the national and international aid chain they extend outwards to the global development institutions of the World Bank and International Monetary Fund.

Fuelled by an increased interest in the possibility that faith-based development organizations may be more successful than their secular counterparts in delivering effective development, studying religious organizations has become a growing area of research. Questions about how FBOs go about development raise interesting possibilities for the emergence of alternative visions of development from the dominant neoliberal aid chain that structures so many transnational development relationships. Analysing the work of FBOs through a study of their religious perspectives could yield a balanced and critical view of their development work. While this perspective is sensitive to and empathetic with the goals of many FBO workers, it is also realistic about the possibility that the latter can operate independently of the donor leverage of the larger secular organizations. There is a difference here between the study of religion and the theological studies that project a rosier vision of what religion and specifically 'faith' can achieve.

Through an analysis of case studies of various FBOs operating at different levels of the aid chain, in this part I highlight the positive and negative impact these organizations have on the lives of local communities and the individuals within them. In these case studies gender forms an important part of my analysis. Many of the organizations I review focus on transforming women's lives in the belief that they are the most disempowered members of the society. A gendered perspective helps to challenge the stereotypical Third World woman as the victim of patriarchy by revealing her natural agency. My gendered analysis draws attention to the cultural and religious assumptions of members of intermediary FBOs, which in turn separate them from the 'real' lives of local women. The theological ideals of the Western feminists who drive the FBOs fuel an assurance that they understand what liberation needs to happen in the lives of other women. My case studies of grass-roots organizations document more effective development practices that stress the importance of real dialogue between development actors. Religious buildings and rituals are used to forge trust and shared commitment between grass-root organizations and local people.

In Chapter 4 I compare and contrast three groups of faith-based development organizations – community-based FBOs; intermediaries acting as a bridge between the large donors and community organizations; and missionary organizations that work with local communities but see development primarily as religious conversion. This comparison allows clarification of what constitutes an FBO and highlights the variety of ways in which faith intersects with development in the work of different FBOs. The use of two analytical frames assessing the faith of organizations along a continuum and then measuring the position of FBOs within an aid chain, emphasizes the need to acknowledge the diversity of factors that both limit and contribute to the success of an FBO.

In Chapter 5 I focus on a particular type of FBO, the intermediary. In doing this I develop some of the discussion in Chapter 4 about what makes an organization faith-based. I offer a detailed examination of how faith intersects with development in the work of the intermediary organization referred to in Chapter 4. This organization is Christian so I draw largely on the theology of that tradition in my analysis. Also, the FBO is British based and works in rural Rajasthan in partnership with a number of Gandhian grass-roots organizations. Through this case study I explore the extent to which a Christian notion of compassion motivates those who decide to work for Christian FBOs. I want to understand what impact this compassionate motivation holds for effective development practice. This link between the Christian notion of compassion and a commitment to helping the poor is understandable, but is it productive? Do compassionate feelings contribute anything to the alleviation of poverty? In other words, does compassion actually bring results? It is admirable to feel compassion and be motivated by it, but do people who act with compassion do any good?

In Chapter 6, I present ethnographic research spanning ten years, which reveals that in a partnership between a UK intermediary FBO and a community-level Gandhian organization religion acted simultaneously as a binding and a destructive force. At the inception of the partnership 'faith' cemented commitment to a Gandhian vision of development, but in time different theological foundations drove the organizations apart. The FBO sought funds from a secular donor who influenced a change in its direction and approach. The donor promoted a neoliberal model of development, which the FBO absorbed within its own feminist theological vision. The FBO sought to transform women's lives in Rajasthan in line with its feminist, religious values of human freedom and liberty. Money from the donor brought a prerequisite that the organization professionalized its mechanisms for evaluation and accountability. The community organization resisted this change to its operational approach, arguing that it threatened its close and responsive relationships with local people upon which its Gandhian vision of development was centred.

The focus of Chapter 7 is on the work of three community organizations, all part of the Gandhian movement; some details about two of them are covered in earlier chapters. These case studies offer close ethnographic insights into the different ways religion can intersect in the work of community organizations. I argue that although commentators rightly support community-based organizations because they forge close, supportive and effective relationships with local people they achieve this through different approaches. I bring out these differences by adopting a gendered perspective that critically analyses how each organization approaches its work with local women. I also consider the ambiguous Gandhian philosophy on gender. I ask why Gandhi continues to be popular with some feminists working in community development in India despite the patriarchal tones of aspects of his worldview.

Part 3: Religion as a feminist resource
In the chapters in this part I approach religion as a resource for local

14

people, as well as for secular and faith-led development practitioners. Religion is a significant factor in determining how local people respond to development. This is because in many poor communities across the globe it represents an important aspect of both individual and collective identity, though I acknowledge that it may be less significant to some communities or not represent the only factor through which people understand the world. For those who project a strongly religious worldview, however, religion significantly shapes their visions of development. It is a resource on which people draw to understand their world and their place in it.

Ethnographic material on the importance of women's religious activities, particularly their ritual lives, gives insight into how each woman understands the structures that oppress her and works towards finding creative solutions to them. Religion is a resource for many women because, through their ritual performances, they open up social spaces in which they can intersect with others or quietly reflect on their lives and experiences. In the chapters in this part I shall present examples of exclusively female ritual spaces and explore the importance of them for their occupants. I shall also consider the potential of these spaces to do two things – namely to inform development practitioners of the experiences of women and to provide creative forums in which strategies are devised.

Religious spaces refer literally to the physical spaces in which ritual processes take place. Individuals and groups create religious spaces to express and communicate with images of the sacred. The communication that occurs may follow the same pattern each day or may be spontaneously created out of the believer's need to work through a problem or give thanks for a joyous experience. Religious spaces can be formal – a temple, church or mosque – or informal, occurring in private moments when the individual feels safe and secure. Private religious spaces may be occupied by an individual or a group. The private nature of these spaces means that the occupants share the same need to express a specific experience and/or work through a shared problem. In short, when thought of in terms of a series of physical spaces, religion provides a valuable insight into the lives of others. This understanding can feed more effective communication that offers a way of countering the power imbalance that some identify as inherent in processes of development.[7]

In Chapter 8 I explore what positive contribution a focus on physical religious spaces might make to development practice. An ethnographic approach to studying religious spaces can help development practitioners understand the adherents' values and beliefs and thus make it easier for them to forge closer, more empathetic relationships with local people. This approach is particularly useful when listening to the experiences of marginalized groups whose views are more quietly voiced. An example is given of a group of Hindu women who shared stories of domestic violence within a ritual space they created for this purpose. A community development organization offered the women a secure environment in which to perform this ritual. This same organization used religious spaces in its daily practice as sites for communication with local communities and personal reflection.

In Chapters 9 and 10 I show how even secular NGOs might positively and practically bring religion into development practice. In Chapter 9 I show how a focus on religion can highlight how and why violence is so deeply engrained in the lives of women in Rajasthan. At the same time, insights into ritual can clarify those moments when women use it as a source of strength and courage. Interviews with some secular NGOs working towards ending violence against women in Rajasthan reveal their focus on the negative impact of patriarchal religion in sustaining male dominance, thereby sanctioning the use of violence against women. Ethnographic research into exclusively female ritual spaces reveals how religion can act as a positive force for many women by providing them with a social and spiritual space in which to work through their problems both internally and with others. A simultaneously positive and negative view of religion could help outsiders understand how violence can exist alongside supportive, creative and sensitive activism.

In Chapter 10 I compare two projects designed to train groups of rural Rajasthani women as community health workers. Ethnographic research conducted during the training periods of each project highlighted stark differences in their management and structural approaches. The successful project recognized the importance of rituals, specifically *puja*, in the daily lives of participants. Although the managers and trainees of both organizations performed daily rituals to help foster a supportive network, greater sensitivity combined with a wider insight into the practical realities and constraints facing women in rural Rajasthan contributed to the long-term success of the second project. The first project has folded. I argue that a lack of open dialogue and real connection with the participants meant that the project's management was unable to adapt or tailor the programme to the needs and experiences of the women involved.

I conclude the volume by returning to the core argument that studying religion and gender has greater potential than many development scholars and practitioners realize. In effect, religion combined with gender should form a mainstream perspective through which to view and approach development. In development there are many actors all seeking to shape and influence development processes and outcomes. Their pursuits can best be understood through a prism in which religion and gender represent the core strands. Religion and development are shown in this volume to create and direct the course of many other interlocking strands. Woven into this prism is a notion of power that is used critically to unravel the hierarchal chain of aid dissemination. Funds are directed downwards and even when a religious organization represents the primary donor, the money is not given freely but comes with conditions attached to it. However, the analytical prism drawn on in each chapter highlights that these conditions are contested and reshaped as local groups form and lobby against dominant visions of development that do not reflect the way they see the world.

PART I

Mainstreaming Religion and Gender in Development

HE chapters in this part contain more detail than in the introduction of the linkages between religion, development and gender, as well as a methodology for studying them. In the first chapter I review some of the literature on religion and development and analyse the methodologies its authors use to examine these relationships. I also problematize the terms 'development' and 'religion' by challenging their sometimes homogenous or assumed usages. The actual meanings of the terms 'development' and 'religion' are highly contested and shaped by context, discourse and personal experiences. In this book I use these terms broadly to highlight the fluidity of their impact and ever evolving nature. Although such fluidity raises questions about the validity of using these terms to understand people's lives, without them our quest to understand how people personally perceive development and negotiate different visions of their future becomes even more abstract and blurred.

Working Definitions
The exercise of defining terms is not without problems, for it involves simplifying and condensing highly complex concepts into a few sentences. However, I cannot go any further in this book without at least offering some working definitions. *Religion* is used broadly to describe a set of ideas and practices that link to an authoritative

source. This source may be a concept of God or a teacher or spiritual leader endowed with enlightened knowledge about humanity. These beliefs in turn give adherents a firm understanding of the meaning and purpose of life.

Spirituality is an inward process of reflection and growth within which a person focuses on the key goals of his or her religion and seeks a stronger relationship with God, deity or concept of divine. The word 'faith' is Christian in origin but can be used to denote the strength of an adherent's feelings towards the core teachings of his or her tradition, specifically the existence of a divine truth and/or God.

Development is an equally difficult term to define and I refer to it in this book as originating in Western political economic thought. Specifically, I equate the roots of development with neoliberalism, which in turn represents 'a theory of political economic practices that human wellbeing can best be advanced by liberating individual entre-preneurial freedoms and skills'.[1] My analysis considers the extent to which Western and non-Western agencies adhere to neoliberal visions and thus allows for alternative and often contradictory views to emerge, which in and of themselves represent forms of develop-ment. Personal experiences both carry and shape religion and development. The methodology set out in this first section needs to be sufficiently flexible to allow the multitude of meanings, values and beliefs associated with these terms to emerge.

The second and third chapters recognize that transnationalism is part of the relationship between religion and development and therefore should be included in any methodology examining them. The contribution that international relations scholars and anthro-pologists have made to the study of religion is reviewed in Chapter 2. I argue that bringing these subjects together enriches our under-standing of how religious transnational organizations operate, for many of them have political and/or development agendas. In the last chapter I demonstrate how a combined macro and micro approach might go about analysing specific case studies and the benefit this brings to our understanding of how development concepts are res-ponded to and reached.

Chapter 1

Reviewing the Links between Religion, Gender and Development

TO open this part I shall now review the literature on the linkages between religion and development and show that much research fails to utilize a gendered perspective. Many overview texts on development include chapters or references on the lives of women.[1] Gender as a critical lens, however, is rarely used to deconstruct the impact of religion on development. In 2006 the journal *Gender and Development* brought out a special edition on religion. The articles in it collectively highlighted the importance of examining how religion specifically influences women's lives, which in turn has implications for development.[2] Despite such publications, as a discipline development studies still fails to consider gender and religion as central to the critical analysis of development processes. A second gap appears because only a few sources acknowledge the significance of the personal reflective dimension of faith as a vehicle through which adherents express their visions of development. This lack of engagement with what religion is and how it shapes people's everyday lives means that analyses rarely document the full reach of both the positive and negative affects it has on determining the course of a person's life and his or her experience of it.

In this chapter, and in the book as a whole, I argue that, to get to grips with the embedded nature of religion in development, one should conceptualize the relationship as a prism that casts light on the complexities and connections between various visions of development and the role of religion in forming them. To develop such a methodology sensitively and accurately it is necessary to employ a multi-disciplinary approach. In this chapter I look closely at the various disciplines that scholars have used to produce work on this theme and consider what an approach that combines religious studies, anthropology and gender might have to offer. To pinpoint the unique contribution of religious studies to the study of development, it is of course necessary to focus on the different ways in which each discipline treats the category of religion. In doing this I highlight the homogenous and uniform way in which religion is often treated in academic texts. It is commonly evoked in an attempt to understand why so many religious people get involved in development work, but its broader role in shaping and informing people's daily lives is rarely examined. To consider what might be gained from a religious studies perspective I contrast it with a theological approach. It is sometimes assumed that both disciplines are the same, but although their boundaries overlap, each applies a distinct methodological approach to studying religion. As I mentioned in the Introduction, by adopting an interdisciplinary approach I seek to reveal the often subconscious and emotional impact that religion can have on people's lives. The importance of this type of research lies in its ability to deepen our insight into how and why people hold the values and beliefs that they do and that shape their visions of the world.

Before proceeding to examine the differences between theology and religious studies, and to consider what a religious studies approach to development might look like, I shall look at the links made so far between religion, gender and development. I then go on to examine the points of contact between gender, religion and development. In effect, these three features combine to produce a critical and sophisticated methodological base for both the practice and study of development.

Links between religion, gender and development
Early attempts to explore the link between religion and development tended to adopt a macro perspective that largely ignored micro ethnographic approaches and gender as methodological tools. Little

time was spent debating the meaning of the term religion and the focus was essentially on the various ways in which the link occurs. Initial research highlighted the global, cross-cultural impact of religion as a force for influencing and resisting change. In 1980, the journal *World Development* devoted a whole volume to the link between religion and development and, in their introductory article, Wilber and Jameson mention four ways in which religion impinges on development:[3]

- it characterizes and influences the development actors;
- it resists the dominant ideas of development;
- it represents a positive force for development in that it seeks to engage positively with social, economic and political change; and
- it represents institutional transnational actors who often oppose other transnational structures such as the World Bank and IMF.

Some contributors to the journal stressed the need to get beyond seeing religion solely as a barrier that needed to be overcome if progressive economic polices were to be pursued. Instead, they argued, religion should be seen as the moral bias of many societies and consequently development actors must engage with it. Some contributors looked at how religion is manipulated cross-culturally for political and economic purposes. For example, von der Mehden[4] viewed Buddhism and Islam in Burma, Thailand, Indonesia and Malaysia, and Qureshi[5] looked at Islam in Pakistan. Ling[6] argues that Sinhalese Buddhism is responsible for limiting Sri Lanka's economic development because it places greater value on merit and austerity than on the accumulation of wealth.

It has been noted that religion does not disappear once development has occurred,[7] which challenges the earlier assumption of development economists that religiosity diminishes once an economy has been successfully reshaped. Instead, religious beliefs, values and practices adapt and change, but religion remains an important component in the lives of many. Robertson[8] and Beyer[9] identified a trend towards cultural pluralism, but none of these early authors adopted a specifically anthropological or gendered approach.

I look at the benefits of combining macro and micro approaches in the study of religion, development and globalization in Chapter 2. Anthropological research confirms how deeply embedded a religion often is in the lives of its adherents. Globalization does not threaten the importance of religion; on the contrary, it often affirms or strengthens religious identities as a reaction against the pull of secular uniformity.

Eade, Tomalin, Tyndale, and Ver Beek[10] all recognize the reluctance of development researchers and practitioners to address religion. Tomalin feels that the absence of a research agenda on religion in development studies is surprising given the importance of both religion and culture in shaping understandings of human rights. This absence needs to be addressed because human rights discourse is increasingly influencing how development organizations think about poverty reduction. She believes that the Universal Declaration of Human Rights is based on a Western view of rights that ignores, even devalues, indigenous notions of rights. She argues that a perspective shaped by religion will permit indigenous methods of pursuing rights to be both recognized and endorsed.

Although the focus of Eade's edited book *Development and Culture* is primarily on culture, she views religion as a dimension that intersects and shapes cultural processes. She starts by asking 'how do development policies and practices understand or engage with culture?'[11] Her answer is that 'sadly, for the most part they proceed as though all cultures are, or seek to be, more or less the same: development from this perspective is a normative project.'[12] Eade agrees with Tomalin that development dampens cultural and religious diversity, for its objective is to pursue a universal set of aims involving the singular transformation of the developing world. Eade goes even further by arguing that development practitioners often look upon culture as the problem. Echoing Tucker's views,[13] she describes how development officials regard culture as an obstacle to overcome if successful projects are to be implemented. She states that if they persist in ignoring culture as a fundamental dimension in shaping people's visions of their world, communities in the developing world will continue to resist the projects.

Eade does not, however, acknowledge the importance of religion as distinct from culture, which means that she misses the extent to which religion acts as the motivating energy behind the actions of adherents. Tyndale[14] stresses that development practitioners often ignore the spiritual dimension of people's lives. According to her, religious people often view poverty as a lack of spirituality rather than purely a lack of wealth. Tyndale's case studies of religious community-based organizations across the developing world show that they all focus on nurturing spiritual growth because they believe that material improvements will follow spiritual development.

These authors agree that development based on Western secular values fails to acknowledge and respond to the perceptions and beliefs of religious people in the developing world. Unless development practitioners engage with the cultural and religious aspects of people's lives they will be unable to communicate with them effectively. This lack of communication will alienate the development practitioners from the very people with whom they wish to work. Consequently, projects will be founded on a conceptual framework that conflicts with the religiously influenced cosmology of many communities in the developing world. In short, religion must be brought more centrally into a methodology for the analysis, evaluation and practice of development.

A greater variety of more rigorous research links are, however, now being made between religion and development. The UK Department for International Development, for example, has funded a Religion and Development research programme at the University of Birmingham,[15] which consists of five projects, each of which is broken down into a number of different components. This research programme represents a systematic attempt to unpack the various and multiple ways in which religion and development intersect.[16] However, despite such programmes, religion is not automatically included as a strand in the analysis of development research and practice. Focus is placed on one area in which religion and development meet. For example, religions have an impact on economic growth.[17] Research into the growth and structure of religious movements and organizations[18] shows that religion is a soft power that shapes the processes of globalization.[19] Some sources consider religion as a platform for peace building.[20] Theological research identifies and responds to the inequalities caused by globalization.[21]

Some scholars have made concerted efforts to demonstrate the significance of religion for development policy and practice.[22] They argue that religion is a permanent force that is unlikely to disappear and decision makers must therefore find a way of incorporating it into both policies and the processes through which they are constructed. Scholars like Alkire[23] and Deneulin and Bano[24] have analysed the multiple ways in which religion intersects with development. Deneulin and Bano go a step further in their book by comparing development and religion in both the Christian and Islamic traditions. They present a methodology that draws on theology, philosophy and economics to analyse the implications of these religions on human development.

Within development studies, or specifically the anthropology of development, Philip Quarles van Ufford, who coedited a book with Schoffeleers called *Religion and development: towards an integrated approach*, was the trailblazer of the linkages between religion and development.[25] In that book Quarles van Ufford proposes that development should be treated as a quasi-religious phenomenon. He claims that the sheer determination of development workers and their organizations to push through certain changes, combined with an almost evangelical commitment to a neoliberal development ideology, are similar to the core characteristics of many organized religions. Models of development contain promises that if 'faith' is placed in them they will deliver miraculous transformations. These models acquire an almost sacred quality in that they cannot be doubted and are ultimately authoritative.

A second relationship between religion and development is identified in the book, with both editors making the point, which I pick up and develop in Chapter 2 that, in the developing world, religion constitutes 'an essential medium through which development is mentally digested by those at the receiving end.'[26] Quarles van Ufford holds that treating development as a religion makes researchers, practitioners and onlookers more aware of the ideological content of development. Furthermore, a focus on religion helps our understanding of how local people respond to development because it is flexible enough to be used as the vehicle through which they articulate and make sense of change. Often the views expressed at the local level are highly critical of development initiatives and they seek to manipulate and refocus interventions to achieve different goals.[27] Religion is therefore useful in studying the impact of development. However, to record and reveal how local people use it in this way, a micro or ethnographic research focus is vital. The anthropological background to this book also serves to show how important ethnography is in studying the various intersections between development and religion.

In a similar way to the theological material reviewed above, Quarles van Ufford argues that the moral foundation of religion highlights the need for development, or the practice of it, to be aware of its ethical obligations to others. The strong religious underpinnings of many development agencies and organizations reveal a contemporary shift in how morality is theologically understood, at least within Christian traditions. God, through depictions of Jesus, is often described as pursuing social justice. Emphasis on God giving out punishment for past sins has been replaced by a stronger assertion that Christian morality and actions must be directed towards the achievement of social justice.[28] This emphasis on morality can be seen in texts that take a theological approach to development, which will be reviewed shortly. Also working from within the discipline of development studies, Clarke[29] makes similar arguments to those of Quarles van Ufford. Clarke talks of how religious values become embedded in development discourses and visa versa. He argues that the sheer number of FBOs that now exist means that the relationship between faith and development is firm. He claims that the way in which these core values are expressed within development means that they can sit easily alongside other worldviews, for example the secular humanistic perspective. Sentiments such as valuing 'human dignity' are shared by everyone committed to development work and can be understood in faith-led or secular terms. I explore the fluidity and flexibility of central development values such as equality, dignity, freedom and empowerment more closely in Chapter 6. In this chapter I show how the development agenda of a faith-based intermediary is able to exist comfortably alongside that of its powerful secular donor. Because these neoliberal values can be interpreted in both religious and secular terms, neither organization has to compromise its core beliefs.

What these sources fail to do, however, is incorporate a gendered perspective alongside religion. When gender accompanies religion it produces an even more sophisticated methodological lens through which to examine and support development processes. With the exception of Tomalin, who successfully incorporates gender into a religious studies approach to development, most scholars fail to appreciate the critical insight that gender can bring to debates on development and religion. This means that their research fails to appreciate what very different impacts religion and development can have on the lives of people, even within one community.

By expressing concern that in the rush to include religion in development, only the dominant view of religion is being heard, Pearson and Tomalin[30] make a compelling argument, for the dominant view excludes women's voices and unique expressions of spirituality. Many of the texts that examine religion and development tend to assume that religious traditions speak as one voice. Pearson and Tomalin, citing the World Bank's interfaith paper on the millennium development goals (MDGs), highlight how the view of particular male religious leaders comes to represent the views of all adherents from that tradition. Male religious leaders represent traditions and typically marginalize and essentialize women's roles. In other words, Western development institutions are giving religious leaders a platform on which to represent and further promote their essentialist views about women. As the authors explain: 'this danger is particularly acute in countries and contexts where the political rise of both fundamentalist and conservative religious forms has challenged the movement towards the acceptance of universal rights for women.'[31]

The resurgence of religious identities across the globe is often played out through women's lives, emphasizing the need for them to return to their traditional role of reproducers and nurturers. Those that emphasize the need for women to return to this traditional mothering role attack the women's rights agenda.[32] This in turn seriously undermines the significant inroads that gender development activists have made into promoting social equality.

Although the scholars reviewed above acknowledged both the positive and negative influences of religion on development, few researchers argue that adherents of the same religious tradition can have starkly different experiences of it. Religious values and beliefs translate into social realities for members of a community in diverse ways. Gender is a crucial analytical lens through which to examine this diversity and to appreciate the various layers through which religion impinges on people's lives. As I argue below, in the third section of this chapter, a gendered perspective helps create a sophisticated lens through which to appreciate how religion shapes people's lives and also provides answers to the question of why people remain religious when their lives are ridden with injustice and suffering. Pearson and Tomalin show how important it is to ask this question. They state that women living in a particularly harsh patriarchal atmosphere and in material poverty draw on aspects of their religious tradition for strength to challenge their gender inequality, even though religion is part of the problem. They cling to their tradition for the sense of dignity and motivation they gain from it. Before I explore in more detail what a combined, religious studies, anthropological and gendered approach to development would look like I need to distinguish between how theology and religious studies treat development.

Theology and Religious Studies: Differing Approaches to Development

Theological approach
Scholars who take a theological approach are usually, but not always, positioned within the faith tradition they study. In other words, theologians usually practise the religion they research and

write about. A wish to understand their own faith more clearly and to help it adapt and respond to a changing world motivates their academic work. Theologians wishing to pursue political goals, particularly when these touch on issues of social justice, assert that religion has a significant role to play in shaping resistance to national and global power structures. The liberation theology movement is an example of how personal religious beliefs are used as a vehicle to mobilize a wide-scale agenda for change. This agenda in Latin America was directed at transnational religious actors and the institutions of the worldwide Catholic Church.

A theologian's approach to research on development would be to challenge the underlying structural inequalities that shape the world. A core concern in the theological literature is to expose the harmful effects of the secular, materially-driven values of globalization. Secular approaches to development, in which solutions to problems are measured materially in terms of what people lack, fail to acknowledge the importance of faith and spirituality in many people's lives. As Tyndale[33] points out, people belonging to a religious community may not feel poor in a holistic sense because their faith gives them a positive sense of self. Their self belief derives from living in a stable community defined by its faith and from their spirituality, which motivates them to act when injustices have been done.

I argue that a grass-roots approach encourages alternative concepts of development[34] that challenge the globally manufactured goals of many development agencies and organizations. By identifying eight dimensions against which inequality can be measured and fought, the millennium development goals represent a global attempt to address material divisions. The very fact that millennium goals exist at all reflects a positive aspect of globalization, suggesting that nations might work together to achieve shared objectives. Theologically driven work supports this programme, but stresses that the only way to bridge material gulfs will be through a moral transformation in the consciousnesses of the rich. Linden,[35] for example, holds that the only hope for a harmonious global society lies in the adoption of a universal moral code.

Such a code would draw on religious teachings and use a shared language to analyse the roots of conflict and injustice, thus enabling, in his words, 'mankind' to look forward to a future committed to the eradication of poverty. He stresses the importance of civil society movements in pushing for human rights and a universal common good. Religious communities also possess the resources to shape a new politics.

Like Linden, Alkire and Newell, Harper, and Tyndale[36] also stress the need to use faith and spirituality as the basis for development practice. All these authors agree that globalization is based on a rational, technocratic approach to development, which, by measuring progress materially, overlooks the valuable sense of peace and fulfilment that spirituality offers. Tyndale[37] argues that life founded on a quest for spirituality (as distinct from religion) encompasses a drive to live in harmony and equality with others. Harper believes it is possible to be both spiritual and scientific. She believes that a balance between a spiritual quest for peace and harmony and technical solutions to the world's resource problems, offers a new transformative approach to the practice of development. Alkire and Newell wish to challenge the disempowering effects of globalization that leaves individuals feeling helpless in the face of extreme material inequalities. Alkire and Newell stress that, through positive actions, an individual can make a difference, and they lay out a set of Christian responses and actions to be taken to achieve the millennium development goals. White and Tiongco[38] adopt a similar theological approach in documenting the injustice in the lives of the poor in Bangladesh. Other scholars[39] have incorporated Sen's capability approach into their analyses of religion and development. Sen[40] describes human development in terms of nurturing human capabilities and such capabilities can only grow in communities of freedom. Researchers who combine religion with Sen's approach argue that faith holds the potential to shape and nurture communities of freedom.

As my review highlights, Christianity is the dominant force behind motivating these authors to stress a message of unity between people who should in turn produce a shared sense of moral responsibility towards each other. Development actors need a clear purpose or vision towards which to direct their energies and this must, at its core, stress the importance of cultural/religious diversity. It must also be open to the possibility that religion can and does produce inequalities. Theological approaches contain an implicit assumption that faith is the only way forward, which excludes those who do not choose to follow a religious path through life.

Replacing a secular discourse with a faith-inspired approach does little to challenge the underlying power structures that sustain inequalities. The World Bank-funded world faith dialogue sought to forge an approach that capitalized on the moral foundation of religions respecting all faiths by stressing that much can be learnt from each. However, interfaith dialogue often translates into a drive to find commonality. This drive to highlight how all faiths are at some levels the same, perhaps unintentionally but nonetheless problematically, points towards a quest to unify us all behind a common cause. Even when the common cause is as worthy as an end to global poverty, differences must be encouraged to ensure that individuals, groups or communities have the freedom to respond to inequalities on their own terms. As Pearson and Tomalin state, the inclusion of a gendered perspective is also crucial to ensure that programmes such as the World Bank's 'World Faiths Development Dialogue' do not prioritize the views of male leaders but allow men and women to express their differing concepts of development and to negotiate a vision flexible enough to reflect an array of needs.

All theological approaches to development regard religion as an active and potential energy that not only drives social, political and economic change but also displays resistance when change threatens deeply held values and beliefs. Clearly, those engaged in development work cannot ignore religion, but theological approaches often fail to analyse the local experiences of global development programmes. The analysis should identify other concepts of development that may in turn challenge the tendency for global initiatives to be shaped and imposed outside the experiences of those positioned as 'beneficiaries'. An important contribution in this local approach could be made by micro, anthropological research that focuses on documenting how religion forms a platform from which people articulate their concerns and visions of development. A combined macro/micro methodology is set out in Chapter 2, bringing together international relations as a discipline primarily concerned with macro-level processes and anthropology.

A religious studies approach

As stated before, the study of religion is interdisciplinary. The interdisciplinary nature of religious studies has the potential to show how religion interfaces with development in even more complex ways than other subjects currently acknowledge. The lines between theology and religious studies are blurred. The study of religion, however, is largely thought to be a secular or neutrally focused discipline. The personal faith (or not) of the scholar should have no impact on how he or she studies, analyses and writes about different religious traditions. The core objective of most scholars of religion is to explore the various levels of each tradition – institutional, mytho-logical and doctrinal, right through to the lived aspect of the religion. The contemporary study of religion also engages in the critical post-colonial analysis of how different discourses and regimes represent and often distort religions at different points in history.[41]

Religious studies and development neatly combine in academic research because development can also be studied at these various levels. Development has been examined through its institutions[42] and through mythology in terms of the utopian vision it projects.[43] Devel-opment is also doctrinal in the sense that it projects a set of core ideals and values.[44] The anthropology of development has helped to highlight how people live and experience development through its impact on the structures of their daily lives.[45] Many development scholars pursue a critical post-colonial line that challenges the ways in which those determined to assert power over the lives of others construct and control development discourses.[46] Religious studies and development studies marry in many useful and insightful ways that could further explore both the practical and analytical possi-bilities of relating religion to development.

What is the value of a religious studies approach to development?
At its core, development focuses on social, political and economic change; and these changes have an impact on the individual. Religion shapes its adherents' view of the world and their perceptions of where they fit within it. It determines how they respond to change, which includes curbing processes that work against personal or community interests. I argue that an anthropological perspective on religion shows its impact on people's lives. This insight could give development researchers and practitioners located outside the communities they wish to affect a better understanding of the lives and experiences of those living within them. This understanding could bring more effective communication, and with better communication comes recognition of the views of others. The final result could be a more effective partnership between all involved in development.

A model based on responding to the needs of others could replace the development practitioners' tendency to disregard local knowledge.[47] Although this criticism of development riding roughshod over local culture and contexts is old, it is still thought to be one of the main barriers to a truly responsive and ethical approach to development.[48] The prevailing ideal is to build on local knowledge and incorporate the creative strategies that people already practise in handling their problems.[49] As I demonstrate later in Part III, religion could provide an important dimension to such an approach.

Following on from Quarles van Ufford, the methodology I suggest takes a micro-focused view of religion. If religion is viewed as a series of physical spaces, each fulfilling an important function in the believer's life, a practical methodology becomes possible. The anthropology of religion literature shows that religion encompasses more than just faith in a god.[50] Religion is also a space to which people turn to understand the world and their place in it, and they do this over and over again as they try to work through their problems and seek answers. Religious spaces can give development workers a chance to gain insights into the self-perceptions of different members of each other's communities. This insight could then lead to a more fruitful dialogue between everybody involved in the development work. A religious studies approach could make two important contributions to development.

First, some scholars argue that there are insufficient ethical guidelines for development work,[51] which is problematic because it means that practitioners are not accountable to a set of professional codes of conduct or moral principles. However, since a moral and ethical framework underpins religious traditions, a study of how religious ethics guide those working for FBOs may reveal the potential role of religion in helping to construct a moral framework that different secular organizations could adapt.

Second, critics of development also stress the lack of real communication between development partners.[52] In Chapters 8, 9 and 10 I argue that practitioners working with religious communities should heed the centrality of faith in the lives of many local people. Acknowledging the religious identities and lives of others is a first step towards building sensitive dialogue. Silently witnessing others express their faith could be taken as a sign of respect for them. It could demonstrate the outsider's willingness to engage in and understand the lives of others. In return, it may stimulate a reciprocal feeling of empathy and engagement in groups of local people who realize the potential of the friendship that an outsider could bring to their lives.

The Relationship between Gender, Religion and Development

Pearson and Tomalin neatly sum up a combined gender and religion approach to development:

> A critical gender analysis from a religious perspective should also engage with ways in which this inequality can be challenged; it should integrate the internal dynamics of religious institutions and traditions which resist any changes in this situation and should join forces with those voices within such traditions which are challenging the status quo and working for reform and change from within faith communities.[53]

A gendered perspective on religion and development simultaneously draws out the aspects of religion that are problematic for women while also pointing to its importance in many of their lives. Specifically by revealing the patriarchal foundations of many, if not all, religious traditions, a gendered perspective can highlight the ways in which women find themselves disadvantaged and marginalized. Also, observing religion from a gendered perspective allows us to see how women draw on aspects of their tradition to fight the injustices they experience. Tomalin[54] presents an example of this in her research on a movement in Thailand that is pressing for the *Bhikkhuni* ordination of women into Thervada religious orders. Its members hold that it is necessary to challenge the patriarchal values of Thervada Buddhism not only to enable women to enjoy equal religious status, but also because there is a direct relationship between women's low status in Thai Buddhism and their low status in wider Thai society. The latter leaves women vulnerable to a range of abuses, including domestic violence, sex trafficking and increased risk of HIV/Aids and other STDs. Questioning the patriarchal assumptions inherent in Buddhism is seen as an essential first step towards achieving the development goals of bringing women equality and human dignity.

The importance of focusing on religion as a link between a patriarchal religious tradition and women's daily lives is also evident in the work of Rew,[55] who undertook ethnographic research in North Orissa, India, on the goddess rituals that Hindu women perform. He describes how women from a village form processions in honour of Kali and then link up with other such processions in the surrounding area. Not only is this ritual religiously symbolic in that it celebrates the power of the female goddess, but it also offers women opportunities to sustain and broaden their social networks. Women from different social castes are thus provided with a rare opportunity to mix and to share their ideas and aspirations. Out of these networks a stronger political voice is generated through which to challenge patriarchy. The social networking opportunities that religious rituals present to women are also discussed in Chapters 8, 9 and 10, in which I explore the concept of female empowerment, which some feminist scholars have extracted from the otherwise patriarchal tradition of Hinduism.[56] Their feminist reinterpretation focuses on the ferocious side of the Hindu goddess whom they describe as possessing immense energy or life force, *shakti*.

Tomalin is clearly in agreement with Peach[57] in stating that 'institutional religion can legitimize values and rules that disempower women; the importance of religion in the lives of millions of poor women across the globe means that secular feminism is often perceived as lacking cultural relevance.'[58] Women do not reject their religion in response to patriarchy but develop different types of religious feminism. The movement within Thervada Thai Buddhism pushing for female *Bhikkhuni* ordination is an example of a type of religious feminism. If their religion is important to them, women in pursuit of political empowerment will tend to reinterpret its core values rather than draw on secular concepts and models of development. Tomalin sounds an important word of caution when she states that we must be careful not to assume that all non-Western women are religious or that oppression is exclusively caused by religion and/or culture.

Conclusion

In summary, in this chapter I have reviewed the work of various researchers interested in the impact of religion on development. At the start of the chapter I argued that the interface between religion and development is like a prism in that the shifting local, national and global environment creates multiple and forever changing linkages. Authoritative figures attempt to control and influence the way we live through the religious and development discourses they propound. The institutional mechanisms through which religious and developmental ideas are articulated are patriarchal and male dominated. As I show in Chapter 3, religious ideas about individual responsibilities are heavily gendered in that they separate men and women according to biology.

Through my review of the literature, in the first section of this chapter, I drew attention to a marked absence of gender studies, anthropology and religious studies in many works focusing on the relationship between religion and development. In the second section I considered what religious studies might have to offer research on development in contrast to theology, which stresses the importance of religious values as a foundation for ethical development. I noted that researchers examining the complex ways in which religion shapes people's lives, including the emotional experiential aspects of spirituality and faith, are usually secular. In the third and last section I explored the importance of gender. Theoretically and practically, gender needs to be central to any study of development and should be used as a critical lens through which to unpick the power relationships that influence our lives.

Chapter 2
Understanding Global Development through Religion and Gender

THIS book is partly about developing a new perspective for the study of gender, religion and development. In the previous chapter I explored the various ways in which gender intersects with religion and development by reviewing past and current approaches and by drawing attention to the potential benefit that gender and religion can offer a critical analysis of development. In the Introduction I referred to religious studies as an interdisciplinary subject. I described my positioning as an anthropologist studying religion and stressed the importance of gender in understanding the social inequalities that affect the lives of men and women. With its micro focus, anthropology is ideally suited to revealing insights into people's everyday experiences of poverty and injustice and the local strategies they employ to challenge and reverse oppression.

The purpose of this chapter is to highlight the potential of anthropology's gendered ethnographic research methods for examining and analysing the impact of global development policies, as well as the influence of transnational political religious movements and the processes through which new religious networks are formed and grow. While anthropologists have been relatively slow to move from the micro to the macro sphere, disciplines that traditionally focus on the broader canvas have been reluctant to recognize the potential of a micro–macro partnership. The rise of transnational religious political movements and the current global preoccupation with the security risks that the growth in fundamentalist ideologies and radicalization pose, highlight the need to find new ways of working across subjects that draw on each other's strengths and insights to fill in gaps that might otherwise have been missed.

In this chapter I hope to show what a valuable contribution a gendered anthropological approach can make to any macro study of the role of religion in development. Although I stress the importance of looking closely into people's lives to ascertain the role of religion in shaping their responses, most literature, including some reviewed in the previous chapter, places the emphasis on religion as a global force. Because most scholars at the forefront of research on the macro relationships between religion, globalization and development are in the field of international relations (IR), I shall now shift the focus to that perspective. From the outset I not only acknowledge the huge contributions of other social science disciplines to the micro analysis of globalization, but I also draw attention to a tendency to underplay the importance of gender in analyses of how patriarchal hierarchies shape and propel particular religious ideologies and discourses.

Sociology and religious studies scholars have taken an active interest in globalization for some time, with Beyer's[1] work frequently cited in discussions on religion and globalization. Sociologists tend to look at the intersections, or meeting points, between globalization, development and religion. They note how each point of contact leads to the creation of new boundaries, which in turn reveal new social formations and relationships.[2] To examine the impact of globalization on religious traditions, religious studies scholars frequently adopt a comparative cross-cultural approach, which will also cover the role of religion in peace-keeping efforts.[3] Alternatively, scholars might focus on a particular tradition, often combining history, sociology and religion to document the rise of social and political movements within that religion.[4] Sociologists of religion have also paid close attention to the impact of globalization on gender and religion.[5]

Anthropologists working on religion, by contrast, have been relatively slow to stake out the ground in this important contemporary area of research. One aim of this chapter, therefore, is to suggest what contribution anthropology might make to work on religion, development and globalization, with a view to developing a partnership between anthropology and the macro discipline of international relations. Because they commonly study communities and cultures with strong religious identities, anthropologists make valuable contributions to research on religion and globalization, whereas international relations scholars tend to focus on macro relations. The inclusion of religion within the framework of IR research is largely limited to seeing it as a global force in the founding of transnational politico-religious movements. Anthropologists, on the other hand, see religion not as an exceptional phenomenon but as something that is deeply embedded in the lives of the people they study. Religion as a category in ethnographic research is used to understand the ways in which people live and experience religion on a daily basis. In this chapter I take a close look at how anthropologists study religion and demonstrate the value of this work for IR scholars, as well as for the wider field of development.

In short, IR scholars should take on board the anthropologists' suggestion that they raise the profile of marginalized voices in their analyses of global power relations. A dialogue between IR scholars and anthropologists could produce a dual application of the category 'religion', one that recognizes the collective and personal ways in which non-Western adherents turn to religion to make sense of their world. I begin this chapter with a review of the IR literature on transnational religio-political movements. Critical analysis of this material acknowledges the important contribution it makes while also highlighting the understandable gaps/questions it leaves unanswered. The second section contains a more detailed review of the work of anthropologists of religion and of their treatment of the sacred and divine.

The Value of Cross-disciplinary Dialogue

With the anthropologists' micro analysis filling some gaps invariably left by the IR scholars' macro focus, I believe that a dialogue between anthropologists and IR scholars could yield a useful analytical framework. First, IR scholars who study religion recognize it as a permanent global force, but find it hard to say 'why' this might be. Macro work is insightful in mapping and commenting on global patterns and relations, but one needs micro research to find out 'why' these patterns or relations form. Other social scientists who examine the micro areas of people's lives to address global questions could benefit from the ethnographic research of anthropologists of religion. Anthropologists see religion as playing a fundamental role in determining how its adherents relate to and understand the world.[6] Since anthropology is essentially the study of human behaviour, the link between belief and behaviour is primary. Ethnographers document how people relate to their world and respond to internal and external changes. Religion is a popular category of analysis among anthropologists because it is within sacred, ritual spaces that people often seek answers to their problems and concerns. Furthermore, for those who possess a strong faith, religion is a vital aspect of their identity, one they seek to project in all spheres of their lives. The embeddedness of a religion in the lives of its adherents explains its endurance as a global force. If IR scholars were to look into the anthropology of religion, their macro analysis could explain why secularism has failed to replace religion.

However, as I repeatedly stress, religion is gendered. A patriarchal gendered ideology fundamentally shapes religious movements, institutions, practices, values and beliefs. None are neutral, yet IR scholars have been reluctant to integrate a gendered analysis into their work on religion and development. This means that much of the analysis reproduces the dominant male perspective, which has been at the forefront in shaping transnational movements and promoting the legitimacy of particular fundamentalisms. The absence of a critical gender dimension means that the differentiated impact these movements have on people's lives goes unnoticed.

The second question on which a dual IR/anthropological perspective could shed light is why is religion so prominent in the construction and rise of transnational political movements? The personal, emotional dimension of religious actions and spaces allows those who study them to identify feelings and experiences that could turn into defiant actions. Those who study transnational movements recognize that the motivation for individual membership is likely to relate to their religious identity and life experiences. Religion functions in two ways. First, the growth of a movement is linked to the construction of a religious identity that reflects and empathizes with its members' experiences and, to ensure that it resonates with them, it may be necessary to manipulate history and/or reinterpret religious discourses. Second, religion operates at a private personal level. Sacred spaces create a safe environment in which an adherent can communicate with the divine. Personal feelings are expressed here and actions determined that may not be articulated in any other sphere of life.

In employing an anthropological approach, Pratt[7] shows how political movements begin with the formation of a specific discourse that becomes emotionally charged as it draws on a wider membership. Religion provides emotional and spiritual dimensions to its adherents' lives. The use of religious narratives to tap into these personal experiences provides a strong base from which political identities and movements can be built. However, this process of building authoritative narratives about the world also acts to exclude groups. For example, anthropologists employing a gendered perspective show how women are particularly vulnerable to marginalization within political and social movements.[8] Processes of exclusion and inclusion are central to how religion is enacted, interpreted and lived. They highlight the need to view religion and power as inextricably linked. Narratives change as the world of which they try and make sense alters. Since transnational movements are founded on narratives about how the world is and how it should be, religion tends to unite those who share the narrative but exclude those who do not or who only partially see their experiences in it. Anthropological material on liberation theology and on Hindu nationalist movements shows that this process of marginalization also occurs in movements to isolate members who may at the start have supported the narrative but later find their needs are not being met.[9]

Anthropology has a further contribution to make to IR. According to Benthall,[10] as well as Edelman and Haugerud,[11] discussions on globalization should incorporate an anthropological critique of power. As the literature cited above on gender and transnational movements shows, anthropologists use their micro focus to seek out the unheard voices of those who are usually hidden from view in macro focused studies. This perspective highlights how global processes produce marginalizing effects at the local level. It also reveals how people display resourcefulness in how they respond to repressive situations. For adherents, religion is an important part of the process by which they make sense of change and decide on the best course of action.

IR and Transnational Politico-religious Movements

IR scholars study the operational structures of transnational politico-religious movements at a macro level. Research has shown how religion gets firmly embedded in a movement's structures, but a movement's growth is determined largely by how well it taps into the globalization processes. Haynes[12] believes that, with transnational terror groups such as Al-Qaeda able to take advantage of global communications networks, globalization has facilitated the rise of transnational politico-religious organizations and movements. He stresses that religion should continue to act as a lens through which to view shifts in global relations, especially power relations, and argues that religion manifests itself in a variety of ways globally, each having an influence on shaping the world. For example, religious fundamentalism has become a means of exercising power; furthermore, religious power is now being used in conflict resolution and peace building. In funding the world faith dialogues programme, the World Bank was recognizing the contribution of religion to peace building.[13] In effect, globalization has drawn more and more of us into extensive networks and new layers of regional/global governance. Through subscribing to these networks, individuals are able to express their feelings about aspects of globalization. The collective weight of these views creates a global civil society capable of challenging hegemonic discourses on a number of issues ranging from human rights to poverty alleviation.[14] Religion provides a unifying platform from which adherents can project their worldview.

Fox[15] argues that the inclusion of religion in IR research is long overdue, but he sees it as just one more dimension alongside politics and economics that leads to the formation of transnational movements. He misses the extent to which religion encompasses and enacts political and economic processes and influences people's reactions to globalization. This is acknowledged in the work of Thomas who calls for greater interdisciplinary engagement in understanding the role of religion in shaping the world. His analysis of the rise of religious movements acknowledges that 'religion often helps to constitute the very content of a social movement's identity, and religious values, practices, traditions and institutions really do shape their struggles, encourage mobilization and influence their type of social or political action.'[16] In his interdisciplinary approach, Thomas draws on international relations, economics, religious studies, sociology of religion and theology. He calls for more debate within IR on what it means to be religious and on the implications of each individual's beliefs for global processes of development.

As already mentioned above, the anthropological perspective has much to offer research that seeks to get to the core of how religion shapes human responses to the world. Anthropologists, drawing on other micro disciplines, could help build an analytical bridge between religion's macro impact on shaping transnational movements and the more experiential aspects of religion that motivate individual action. Anthropologists are well positioned to determine what specific experiences provoke adherents to propel their feelings onto a global stage, for religion has a dual function as both a site for the personal expression of marginalization and powerlessness and as a platform in the pursuit of power (see Chapters 8 and 9).

Such a perspective could make a useful contribution, not least because what is intentionally absent from macro focused literature is an appreciation of how individuals, often those whom structures of power marginalize, experience and enact resistance. Juergensmeyer[17] argues that radical ideologies have become the vehicles of rebellions against authority linked to social, cultural and political grievances. People's everyday experiences of living with marginalization and injustice are, however, what shape these ideologies and anthropologists of religion are the people who document individual accounts of injustice and exclusion. Witchcraft, spirit possession and shamanism, for example, are commonly studied in anthropology and often involve recording feelings of anxiety and concern over unwanted occurrences or traumatic experiences.[18] Anthropologists use these themes to record how communities and individuals explain shifts in the status quo. Religious figures such as shamans are turned to for help in taming forces of change that disturb the desired rhythm of life.[19] Work on spirit possession shows that distress and resistance are often articulated through the act of being possessed by a spirit.[20]

Radical ideas are expressed and explored during the assumed safety of a trance, for external forces rather than the individual in question is held responsible for what transpires.[21] Similarly, transnational religious movements provide spaces within which individuals are encouraged to vent their anger and frustrations at the forces that oppress them. At the micro level, adherents create physical spaces in which to express their faith. Global and national movements offer people opportunities to affirm their religious identities through the expression of the core values that shape their perceptions of the world. Transnational movements merely amplify the beliefs and grievances expressed at a local level. A combined micro/macro approach casts light on how religion becomes the vehicle through which these feelings become embedded in the structures of transnational movements.

Haynes states that 'there is a growing awareness in international research of the importance of religion as a transnational actor in the context of globalization'[22] and there is a mounting body of evidence to back this point of view. Studies of international movements conducted within IR, and anthropological accounts of the role of religion in shaping individual and community identities, provide convincing evidence that religion is a permanent force in the world today. However, these two discourses are as yet unlinked by a single analytical thread.

Anthropology of Religion

Where or how does religion interface with globalization? 'Religion' entails dialogue with a sacred image or images, or with a notion of the divine. This dialogue then motivates and directs people's actions and perceptions of the world. According to its theorists, globalization is penetrating virtually all parts of the earth and is introducing change in even the remotest areas. It is likely that those with religious beliefs will respond to and make sense of this change through their religion. At a macro level this is clear in the rise of global religious movements such as Pentecostalism and funda- mentalist religions. At a local level too, individuals privately and collectively articulate and understand change by working through their responses to it in a religious domain. Religion has been studied at a local level in the subdiscipline of anthropology of religion. Anthropologists like Aigbe, Akinnasi, Angro, Barber, Bennett, Gold, Gottlieb, Hirschkind, James, Knauft, Lambek and Swantz[23] highlight religion as a source of beliefs and values that structure everyday life. The anthropology of religion literature shows that religion encompasses more than faith in a god. It is also a space to which people turn for an understanding of the world and their place in it. Anthropologists of religion look at how religious beliefs, specifically a notion of the sacred, inform and determine everyday life.

There has been a notable output recently of edited books on the link between anthropology and religion[24] that stress the fluidity of religion and urge scholars to move away from viewing it purely through a Western Judaeo-Christian lens. The amount of time devoted in these texts to defining 'religion' reveals an absence of IR input on the subject, for IR scholars spend little time critically evaluating the term. Mandir[25] is critical of Juergensmeyer's[26] usage of the terms 'religion' and 'power' on the grounds that they reflect an overly narrow view of the former. Juergensmeyer sees religion simply as a reactionary force set in opposition to secular global processes of change. Mandir, writing specifically about Indian religions, wants to see religion reclaimed from its colonial roots. If this fails to happen, Mandir warns, non-Western adherents will be forced to articulate and express their epistemological perspectives through a limited Western-derived concept of religion. A fluid understanding of religiosity more accurately portrays the freer more responsive way in which Indians use religious spaces to negotiate with the rest of the world on their terms.

In the introductory statements of the key anthropology of religion texts cited above, religion is placed at the heart of life not only in terms of its impact on human relations, politics, economics and cultural identity, but also with regard to its role in shaping world-views and beliefs. Religion is understood as providing beliefs relating to a spiritual or supernatural sphere. The source of these beliefs is a concept of the sacred. The sacred origins of ideas and values ensure that they possess an authority that restricts the degree to which they are challenged. The believer experiences the sacred, which is often described in terms of a relationship with a divine being or spirit. Claims to understand the sacred give a religious group and/or leader legitimacy; it therefore follows that the leaders of a transnational movement must show their members they have a close relationship with the divine by proving that the sacred has directly inspired their actions. The role of religious leadership in the formation of the Hindu nationalist movement is seen in McKean's[27] ethnographic research and is examined in the next chapter.

Anthropologists regard religion as an experiential concept rather than one that can be understood through mapping out a series of behaviours. In her overview text on religion and anthropology, Bowie[28] defines religion in terms of a supernatural realm to which people look for explanations for why and how human life came to be. She describes religion as the arena through which spiritual and practical guidance is offered to people.

Asad[29] links the personal dimension of religion to the formation of national power bases. He is interested in how power and discipline impact on people's everyday lives. Highlighting the links between religion and power, he argues that religious symbols are not only intimately linked to social life but also support or oppose the dominant political power. His views resonate with those of scholars positioned at a macro level. For example, Reychler and Paffenholz[30] argue that faith is often presented as a soft power shaping the discourses that describe how the world should be, driving people to act according to that vision. Anthropologists such as Asad support this view, claiming that because religion affects how people perceive their role in life, it influences their actions. Although Asad does not write specifically about transnational movements his work offers explanations about how and why religion is such a pervasive element in the formation of transnational movements. Religion becomes the authoritative platform on which transnational movements are built. Asad acknowledges that religious beliefs and practices are not static but change with history. The authority of religion is ensured through the adaptation of beliefs and practices to suit the needs of a new emerging order. His work offers ethnographic historical evidence to support IR scholars who argue that religion has not and is unlikely to subside as globalization persists, but it also pinpoints a concept of authority at the heart of religion that allows for the assertion of counter hegemonies.

Adherents give authority to religious worldviews that both reflect their cultural identity as well as offer explanations and direction at times of crisis. In other words, they seek out authoritative voices from within their own tradition that seem to empathize with their experiences. Religious movements must adapt their beliefs to reflect the concerns and anxieties of their 'target' membership. It is this ability to adapt that determines a movement's pervasiveness.

In the next chapter I consider more closely what anthropology can offer our understanding of how religion impacts on the formation of transnational movements. On the whole, anthropologists of religion seek to understand how people view their world, how they react to changes from outside, as well as to changes that individuals and communities initiate from within. Ethnographic studies frequently contain primary evidence of people joining movements precisely because of their experiences of marginalization and exclusion. Movements offer the powerless an opportunity to challenge the authority of others. Anthropologists interested in politics and religious identities tend to focus on the emergence of militant or radical religious identities. Such identities are often formed as political and emotional reactions to globalization, which is blamed for causing marginalization.[31] Asad, for example, advocates adopting a historical approach to ethnographic research to see how communities are responding to the impact of globalization. Other anthropologists of religion[32] show that religious subjectivities often underlie political mobilization and result in certain national and ethnic identities gaining prominence as they react to change.

Conclusion

The objective of this chapter was to highlight the contributions of two different bodies of literature to the debate on religion, globalization and development and to argue in favour of encouraging these approaches to intersect. Multi-disciplinary research has given us a comprehensive picture of how globalization, development and religion overlap in the formation of transnational movements, but anthropology has not made a prominent contribution to this debate.

The anthropological perspective could enhance the micro work of sociologists and scholars studying religion and I have identified two key questions that ethnographic research could help to answer. First, why has religion remained such a prominent force in the world today? Second, why is religion such a central element in the formation of so many transnational political movements? IR scholars could use anthropological studies to highlight how local people react to processes of change that challenge their status quo. These studies show how religion makes an impact at a personal, emotional level and also operates as a vehicle through which resistance can be mounted. IR scholars could use this material in their analyses and produce an even more dynamic picture of globalization as a negotiated set of processes – one in which all actors, to varying degrees, have a stake in determining its cause and direction.

The leaders of movements manipulate and reinterpret religious narratives and even rituals to create a common, popular identity that supports their agenda. Those who feel marginalized by this discourse may, however, turn to religion to express these feelings and consider what strategies of resistance they can employ. A combined gender, anthropology and IR perspective leaves one in no doubt that the concepts of power and authority are central to the formation of a successful movement, but it relies heavily on a claim to 'know' the sacred. In other words, religious insight must be claimed if the movement is to achieve a growing membership. In addition, because religion is experienced at a personal level, leaders must influence the intimate spaces within which adherents express their spirituality. Van der Veer's work[33] shows how Hindu nationalists achieve this by reaching into the spaces where private rituals are performed. IR scholars show how movements can use global technologies to extend their claim to knowledge beyond their community and culture. A chain of processes and events is more clearly revealed through the intersection of IR and anthropology. Strengthening the relationship between these two disciplines could, if combined with other micro disciplines, yield even more important links between global hegemonic structures and people's lives, making audible individual responses to globalization and drawing attention to the platforms people create to articulate their dissent. Furthermore, activists could use this work to shape their responses to these voices by supporting the direction of change they demand. Finally, ethnographic research shows that religion is a vital part of many people's lives and is unlikely to diminish, not least because it is from religion that many people gain a sense of their world and place within it.

Chapter 3

Gender, Mothering and Development: Case Studies of Three Hindu Transnational Movements

THIS chapter is about the teachings, operational structures and development activities of three large transnational Hindu organizations – the Ramakrishna Mission, the Guru Mata Amritanandamayi Mission and the Sadhu Vaswani Mission. The study combines fieldwork conducted in Pune, Maharashtra, between November 2008 and October 2009 with a review of the literature. The objective of these case studies is to show how much insight ethnographic gendered research can amass. Through analysis of these case studies, I demonstrate how the combined macro/micro gendered approach described in Chapter 2 operates and the type of analysis it produces. All three organizations, which attract mainly middle-class followers, emphasize the importance of serving the poor as a means of achieving individual spiritual progress. I selected them because they are among the largest religious transnational organizations operating in Pune with mainly international financial support.

Although I describe these organizations as Hindu, it should be noted that the Sadhu Vaswani Mission refers to itself as 'secular', defined in Indian terms as the observance of more than one religion.[1] My ethnographic research inside this organization in Pune contests the secular view it holds of itself, for I recorded a significant daily emphasis placed on Hindu worship, practices and ideas. Before going into detail about these organizations' beliefs and operational structures, I need to identify the main Hindu concepts and beliefs to which each of these organizations adhere and on which their philosophical and spiritual practices are founded. The use of the term 'Hinduism' is itself highly problematic. Hinduism is a hugely diverse tradition reflecting the geographical and cultural plurality of the Indian subcontinent. The history of the term 'Hinduism' highlights the artificial and overly simplistic nature of the label.[2] The section below is therefore intended, not to present Hinduism as a homogenous and uncomplicated set of religious beliefs and practices, but merely to pull out key concepts that devotees of the three organizations I examine share.

Commonly shared Hindu beliefs

All three organizations share three key concepts identified through a review of their literature – *karma*, *samsara* and *moksha*. Life is considered to be an endless cycle of birth, death and rebirth (*samsara*). Humans must try and live according to the karmic law and pursue their *dharma*, or duty, in order to acquire merit that will see them reborn into a 'better' life the next time. *Moksha* is the end goal that involves unity between the individual soul, *atman*, and the world soul, *Brahman*. *Moksha* represents the end to the cycle of rebirth (*samsara*) and releases the *atman* from the toil of rebirth. What constitutes a 'better' life is rooted in the caste system, a hierarchy that ranks people's status and role in life according to how close they are perceived to be to achieving *moksha*. High-caste men who live ascetic lives completely devoted to God are thought to be more likely to achieve *moksha* than a person of a lower caste. Gender also plays a part in privileging men as the most likely to achieve the spiritual goal of *moksha*. Women, by contrast, who find their religious lives tied to their domestic roles, have little time for ascetic practices. The term *varna*, which is closely associated with caste, refers to a person's occupation and ranks people according to their levels of 'purity'. Certain occupations are considered impure, for example street cleaners and leather workers.[3] Not one of the organizations rejects caste, largely because they fail to associate it with the *varna* system that labels people untouchable according to their occupation.

All three organizations talk about Hinduism being founded on a unifying central concept of God or *Brahman*. Because the world soul, *Brahman* is considered too complex and all encompassing to worship directly, many different gods and goddess have evolved and developed over time, all of which represent aspects of *Brahman*. Two Hindus may worship different deities while still conforming to the overarching beliefs and principles of the tradition. Anthropological research across India suggests that adherents are drawn to deities whose stories, as told in the religious texts, reflect aspects of their own lives. The relationship between an adherent and a deity is personal and often involves the worshipper recounting parts of his or her own life experiences that seem to overlap with particular textual or oral narratives.[4]

Hindus access religious teachings from a number of sources, texts, television adaptations of epics such as the *Ramayana*,[5] local temple priests, gurus and swamis. Hinduism has a tradition of gurus, sadhus and swamis who offer religious and spiritual guidance. The organizations I studied in Pune utilize a variety of mediums through which to promote the religious teachings of their central figure. The methods of communication do not vary hugely, and will be discussed shortly, but each organization has packaged the teachings in terms of key messages to make the guru stand out. Without this packaging and marketing, the differences between the founding philosophies of each organization would be less obvious. Before I review each organization and consider what the key messages for each are, I need to examine in more detail the influence guru figures have over the beliefs, values and actions of devotees. Analysing this relationship will allow me to say something about how big an impact each of my case study gurus, through his or her organization, has on shaping the perceptions and worldviews of his or her devotees in Pune.

The role of gurus, sadhus and swamis in Hinduism

Mlecko[6] describes how gurus in India work as religious teachers and are simultaneously the focus for worship. Gurus as religious teachers have, according to Mlecko, played an important role in the transmission and development of the Hindu religious tradition. Hindu worship involves *darsan*, which is the process by which the devotee looks at the deity but it also occurs when a devotee looks at a guru.[7] The deity in the image looks back at the devotee who lies within and experiences his field of power.[8] My observations of *darsan* in the middle-class organizations I studied reinforce Eck's description of hierarchy shaping the relationships between devotee and guru. Devotees in all three organizations described their awe and subservience to their guru whom they certainly perceived as divine. *Darsan* in the cases we observed operates to enforce and ensure the guru's superiority as godlike; and his authority is unquestioned because of his divine connection. Spatially, the guru's picture is central in the main prayer and the spaces of other deities are marginal in relation to it. There are, for example, huge photographs of Guru Mata Amritanandamayi and Sadhu and Dada Vaswani prominently placed where people worship in their complexes. In turn, this authority influences people's attitude towards development focusing on the obligation of each individual to perform *seva*. *Seva* in the work of these organizations has been translated into the provision of welfare and basic services such as primary health care, emergency relief and a commitment to education for boys and girls. However, as I shortly show, the specific type of education advocated is shaped by, in the case of the Ramakrishna Mission and Sadhu Vaswani Mission, patriarchal gendered ideology.

These three organizations, like many transnational Hindu organizations, rely on the centrality of a religious figure thought to possess divine qualities. A focus on the religious teachings of these gurus in each case represents the organization's founding philosophy, which, as already mentioned, has been marketed, transported, even 'sold', through transnational diasporic networks of Hindus and foreign devotees. This process of packaging and selling the teachings of a guru is enabled by the mechanisms of globalization.[9] The internet has helped these philosophies to reach larger and wider audiences. That numerous video clips of Guru Mata Amritanandamayi and Dada Vaswani can be found on YouTube[10] and on social networking sites means that devotees can be connected to each other and to the central ashrams of their guru. These ever more sophisticated means of marketing and selling the guru's messages have broadened the sphere of influence each one has by drawing in more and more devotees. Although these organizations may influence the worldview of many people, this does not necessarily translate into clearly defined visions of development. Devotees may follow the teachings but not take part in any development activities.

In Pune, Dada Vaswani and Guru Mata Amritanandamayi are prominent living gurus. Vivekananda is influential but his legacy lives on through the work of his Ramakrishna Mission. The Ramakrishna Mission, the Guru Mata Amritanandamayi Mission and the Sadhu Vaswani Mission serve, to differing degrees, poor and untouchable communities, but most of the devotees do not come from the dalit (meaning untouchable or outside the caste system) or low castes. I shall begin these case studies by summarizing at least some of what is known about the origins and development of these organizations and give details of their operations in Pune. I then identify each organization's key messages and distinctive features before analysing, in each case, how goddess imagery, gender and mothering represent core elements of its ideology. The analysis then moves on to look at the impact this focus on women as mothers has for the type of education each organization offers girls. The section ends with a cross-organizational analysis designed to highlight the differences and similarities in how they use their religious teachings to shape ideas about development.

The Origins and Philosophy of Each Case Study

The Ramakrishna Mission

The Ramakrishna Mission, which can be described as moderately Hindu in orientation, represents the charitable arm and partner of the Ramakrishna Math, which focuses on monastic life. People such as Beckerlegge[11] have used the word 'movement' to describe both the Ramakrishna Mission and the Math because of their combined transnational profile. The Pune centre is just one in a network of 42 across the globe. The movement is divided into different branches to fulfil its various functions, which are primarily to offer religious guidance based on the teachings of Vivekananda but also include welfare and education. Its main headquarters, Belur Math, are in Howrah district near Calcutta. Though a subsidiary of the main organization, the complex in Pune is still of significant size comprising a large main temple open to the public, an ashram for the residing monks, a clinic, an administration block and a bookshop. Unlike the other two organizations under consideration, the Pune operation has no school. Nevertheless, the mission holds strong beliefs and ideas about education and runs many schools elsewhere in the country and abroad. The movement has 23 centres in India and 19 outside. One of its central aims is to spread Vivekananda's message.[12]

Vivekananda founded the movement, which is named after his teacher Ramakrishna who was born in rural Bengal to poor Brahmin parents in 1836. As a young boy Ramakrishna followed his elder brother to Calcutta to study, but on becoming preoccupied with the question 'is God real?' pursued an ascetic path living alone in virtual starvation. He was joined first by a *Sannyasini* (female renunciate) who helped him recover his health and taught him about religion and then by a *Sannayasi* (male renunciate) who read the *Vedas* with him. This period in his life as a young ascetic shaped his teachings, which can be summed up in the following sentence taken from a local Ramakrishna publication: 'Religion does not mean words, or names or sects, but it means spiritual realization.'[13]

In contrast to Ramakrishna's poor upbringing, Vivekananda was born into a rich family in Calcutta in 1863. He pursued spiritual knowledge and practice from a young age and Ramakrishna, his guru, taught him *Adaita Vedanta*, or service to God. Vivekananda used his experiences of Western cultures to develop the teachings of Ramakrishna and to promote his philosophy outside India. Most famously, Vivekananda raised the profile of Hinduism outside India as a result of a speech he delivered to the Parliament of World Religions in Chicago in 1893.

The main difference between the approaches and teachings of Ramakrishna and Vivekananda revolves around how they viewed the concept of service, or *seva*. For Ramakrishna it was a focus on realizing God that was of most importance. The creator in his view was both distinct and superior to creation. Knowing God was equal to knowing the world. In his teachings, by contrast, Vivekananda stressed that service to man was in fact the highest service to God. Showing compassion and concern for others was for him the primary route through which the individual would get to know God.

People who follow Ramakrishna and Vivekananda describe themselves as *Vedantists*, or followers of the *Vedanta*, the central goal of which is spiritual enrichment and enhancement. The term *Vedanta* originally refers to the Upanishads' part of the ancient Indian scriptures known as *vedas*. Later, however, the term was used to describe a philosophical and spiritual approach aimed at achieving self-realization or knowledge of God (*Brahman*). The movement is also described in scholarly literature as *bhakti*, or devotional, because of its focus on worshipping and honouring God. The term *bhakti* characterizes the religious practice of this organization, which centres on the worship of *Brahman*, the supreme-being in Hinduism (see section above for more details).

Core teachings: spirituality and service

The movement believes that its message about the importance of spirituality is a global one and it seeks to spread it beyond India. It regards serving the poor as an integral part of its religion but does not pursue it to realize any specific development goal or vision. Tomalin describes the movement today as 'a socio-religious welfare organization that is still active in development and humanitarian work'.[14] In my research on the movement in Pune, I found that the welfare dimension of its work functions as a tool, or rather a means by which to achieve the central goal of enhancing personal spiritual growth. Members of this organization conceptualize development as spirituality and the provision of charity or welfare. This picture of serving the poor as a means of reaching spiritual enlightenment was expressed both in the conversations I had with monks at the centre in Pune and in the local literature the movement published in India.

The goddess, gender and mothering

The conceptualization of a supreme being in Hinduism often focuses on the mother goddess with references to the connection between the goddess, earth and life-giving energy. The 'Holy Mother' is projected as a role model for both men and women because of her complete devotion to Ramakrishna and the deep spiritual knowledge she is thought to have gained because of her devotion. Ramakrishna is said to have had a vision of the 'Divine Mother' – 'he was consumed with a thirst to have it constantly.'[15] His mother decided it was time her son got married and arranged him a match with a young woman in his home village of Kamarpukur; her name was Saradamani.

After their marriage Saradamani became known as the 'holy mother'. Her loyalty and wifely devotion to Ramakrishna are well documented and presented in terms of her fulfilling her duties as a wife. Her devotion expressed through daily domestic tasks to ensure the wellbeing of her husband is what indicates her divinity. In addition to serving her husband she is thought to have acquired detailed insights into his teachings and philosophies, thus making her the disciple closest to Ramakrishna. Saradamani is often depicted alongside Ramakrishna, thereby projecting an image of unity and partnership. This partnership is obviously gendered and although all Ramakrishna followers replicate Saradamani's devotion, the specific nature of her service is the preserve of women. This delineation between the roles and responsibilities of men and women is emphasized through the specific educational programmes the Ramakrishna movement prescribe for boys and girls, which I discuss below. The Holy Mother is also worshipped separately as a divinity in her own right; she was elevated after her death to the status of goddess. However, she is regarded as a goddess because of her nurturing qualities, which in turn make her a symbolic mother.

Women and education
The movement has brought out a number of publications on the issue of women and stresses the importance of seeing men and women as equally important. Education is regarded as vital for ensuring that Ramakrishna's teachings are passed on to future generations[16] and is considered crucial to the development of both boys and girls. However, careful attention is paid in the literature to

the specific nature of girls' education, which must equip them to take on the role of mothering in later life. For Ramakrishna, mothering and womanhood is one and the same thing. The movement exalts motherhood and the reverence directed towards women as mothers is presented as proof that it opposes the subjugation of women:

> The ideal woman in India is the mother, the mother first, and the mother last. The word woman calls to mind of the Hindu motherhood; and God is called mother. ... In the West, the woman is wife. The idea of womanhood is concentrated there as the wife. To the ordinary man in India the whole force of womanhood is concentrated in motherhood.[17]

Women must become mothers to fulfil their religious roles and education must support them in this process. The focus is placed on the following subjects – religion, arts, science, housekeeping, cooking, sewing and hygiene. According to the organization, these represent 'the simple essential points that ought to be taught to our women. It is not good to let them touch novels and fiction.'[18] This stress on girl's education as a means of preparing them for motherhood is seen also in the teachings of the Sadhu Vaswani Mission and is picked up again below and in the third section of this chapter.

Guru Mata Amritanandamayi

Guru Mata Amritanandamayi, or Amma (the common name for Guru Mata Amritanandamayi meaning 'mother'), like the Ramakrishna organization, belongs to the *bhakti* devotional tradition of Hinduism in which individuals seek spiritual salvation through personal devotion to God – in this case through the devotion of a guru. It can also be described as a moderate Hindu organization. Guru Mata Amritanandamayi, or Amma, is globally known as the 'hugging mother' because she hugs devotees during audiences as a means of healing them. She was born to a poor fishing family in a village called Parayakadavu, near Kollam in the southern state of Kerala. Stories of Amma's early life describe how she displayed immense compassion and spent hours in a spiritual trance. She became noted by those around her for possessing divine qualities, which in turn led to her acquiring guru status. In 1980 Amma founded her main ashram in Kollam; the Pune centre is one of 22 regional centres around India.[19]

Core teachings: spirituality and service to others

Warrier[20] describes how Amma encourages her devotees to worship God in whichever form they can relate to best, but most worship her directly as a living goddess. Local literature collected from her ashram in Pune written by a long-term Western female devotee describes how Amma offers her devotees 'Devi Bhava *darsan*'.[21] Amma is documented as describing Bhava *darsan* as:

> All the deities of the Hindu pantheon, which represent the numberless aspects of the one supreme being, exist within us. One possessing Divine power can manifest any of them by mere will for the good of the world. Krishna Bhava is the manifestation of the pure being aspect, and Devi Bhava is the manifestation of the eternal feminine, the creatrix, the active principle of the impersonal absolute.[22]

The devotee and author of this text, Swamini Krishnamitra Prana, described her own relationship and experience of Amma. In one passage she recounts a dream: 'Amma often appeared to me in my dreams at night in the form of Devi, glaring at me as if to say "Aren't you going to wipe my face for me?"'[23] This passage reveals the superiority of Amma and the constant concern or preoccupation devotees have with not upsetting or displeasing her. Her authority is unquestioned and her divinity marvelled. Amma has become a huge transnational figure and commands large donations. She emphasizes in all her texts the notion of *Sanatana dharma* or the real Hinduism translatable as eternal wisdom/law.[24] Her teachings emphasize 'love and compassion for all', in a similar tone and manner to which these values are expressed by Sadhu Vaswani in his texts (see below). Guru Mata Amritanandamayi's charitable activities are very important and social welfare is a central dimension in her teaching, thus representing how her values are translated into everyday practices.[25] However, as I discuss later, the Pune centre devotes fewer of its resources to welfare than the main ashram in Kollam. Devotees in Pune focus more intensely on their own personal spiritual journey through expressing devotion to her rather than by serving the poor. Development is individualistic and internalized in the lives of at least some of Amma's followers.

The goddess, gender and mothering

The heavy use of feminine symbolism is significant and in particular the stress on the concept of mothering. Jones speaks of how Amma incorporates mother–child symbolism in her teachings, which 'builds on Indian understandings of the family and relatedness, feminine 'essence', discourses on love and selflessness, and concepts of the Mother Goddess.'[26] The concept of motherhood is central to her discourse and motivates her charitable activities. She stresses that just as a mother loves and cares for her children, so it is the responsibility of each individual to reach out to those who are less fortunate. The main difference in how Amma uses feminine symbols and imagery in her teachings compared with the Ramakrishna movement and Sadhu Vaswani Mission is that she does not then translate these images into separate gender roles for boys and girls. She does not state that it is the responsibility of women to mother but instead claims that men and women should act in a motherly/compassionate way towards everybody. In Amma's teachings femininity and mothering are conflated and presented as the ideals of compassion and love that we should all emanate.

In fact, elements of Amma's teachings on women reflect at least to some degree a Western feminist concept of empowerment:

Woman is *shakti* (power). She is much more powerful than man. Though it may be difficult for a woman to have a determined mind, once she does, no power can stop her. She cannot be defeated then. …

Many people live with the misconception that women are only supposed to give birth and raise children. These same people might also think that men are the only ones who can rule and command. Both ideas are wrong. A woman can rule as well as a man if she brings out the dormant masculine qualities within her. And a man can be as loving and affectionate as a mother if he works on that unmanifested feminine aspect within him.[27]

This passage advocates that women should be free to make their own decisions about their life path and not be influenced or controlled by men, specifically their husbands. Her statement above is a radical departure from the usual patriarchal teachings of many Hindu gurus and certainly from the views of Dada Vaswani and Swami Vivekananda.

Women and education

Amma runs schools attached to her ashram complexes. Often, as in her ashram in Kerala, these schools are specifically aimed at educating the poor. In Pune, however, the school is targeted at the middle-classes with only a few scholarships awarded each year to able students whose parents cannot afford the fees. In Pune the school is relatively new and was still under construction at the time of research. It educates around 1500 pupils and is run by a *Sannyasini* whom Amma dispatched from Kerala to become school principal. The curriculum combines religious and academic classes with heavy investment, particularly in science laboratories and computer suites. Daily sessions are run to teach students about Amma's philosophy and spiritual practice. Amma's image is highly visible throughout the school and there is a huge picture of her in the main hall where students congregate for daily assemblies. All the teachers are female. While this may not be unusual given that it is regarded as a female profession, it also reflects Amma's emphasis on promoting the positive benefits of female qualities in both men and women. The teachers with whom I spoke expressed their immense respect and admiration for Amma and the majority claimed to be devotees. The pupils and their families were not necessarily devotees but the level of exposure to her teachings during their education was likely to result in a least some becoming lifelong adherents. The principal believed that many of her pupils continued to follow Amma after graduation.

Amma places a great deal of emphasis on education and has published a series of volumes in which she talks about her key teachings in a format thought to be accessible to school-age children. Amma has written five books, often recounting journeys she has taken with her devotees whom she regards as her children. The devotees are taught through a combination of questions, watching her in spiritual practice and practical demonstrations. Her teachings are less prescriptive than those of the Ramakrishna Mission and Sadhu Vaswani Mission in terms of detailing the different roles of men and women. However, she is clearly concerned that pupils adopt her values and beliefs in their daily lives. These core values focus on the achievement of non-duality, whereby the individual body is no longer experienced as separated from *Brahman*, the eternal soul. The achievement of non-duality involves nurturing compassionate feelings for other people and the ability to empathize with and respond to the suffering of others – hence, the importance of *seva* or service as an integral part of a person's daily activities. Amma teaches that one best develops empathy and compassion for others by serving people who live in need.

The Sadhu Vaswani Mission

In Pune other Hindu organizations use their social welfare agenda to push a nationalist agenda and ideology. Before going into detail and offering a case study of one such organization, clarity is needed about what I mean by Hindu nationalism. McKean writes, 'the Hindu nationalist movement is by no means a monolithic entity. It is supported by a spectrum of leaders, groups and individuals whose ideological positions range from moderate to militant and whose projects vary from charitable work and religious education to political power, hatemongering and communal violence.'[28] The best-known and perhaps largest organization identified as nationalist is the Rashtriya Svayam-sevak Sangh (RSS). Tomalin outlines how K. V. Hedgewar, a Hindu Mahasabha member, formed the RSS:

The RSS is not a political party and instead considers itself to be a cultural organization with an emphasis upon militaristic style training for men, women and children. M. S. Golwalkar, successor to Hedgewar, took a broader understanding of 'who is a Hindu'. He distinguished between culture and religion, taking religion to be a 'private' matter. Thus, although the public culture must be Hindu, people's private faith was a matter of religion.[29]

Today the RSS is one 'wing' of the so-called *sangh parivar* ('family of organizations') alongside the VHP (Vishva Hindu Parishad) and the BJP (Bharatiya Janata Party founded in 1980). The VHP (founded in 1964) is a religio-cultural organization that strives to achieve a universal Hinduism. Various scholars have written that the nationalist discourse is centred on conservative gendered ideals about women's potential as the saviours of the Indian nation fulfilled through their conformity to a domestic, mothering role.[30] Although many secular Indian feminists see nationalism as a worrying barrier to female empowerment and gender equality, many women across castes subscribe to the discourse.[31]

The Sadhu Vaswani Mission is not an overtly nationalist organization and I certainly cannot prove its link to more prominent nationalist organizations such as the RSS, which, according to many of my informants, has a strong presence in Pune. What I can argue is that aspects of its teachings, operational structures and the focus of its activities reveal a conservational, right-wing philosophy in line with elements of the Indian nationalist discourse. There is less research published on Sadhu Vaswani Mission than on either Amma or the Ramakrishna Mission. For this reason I concentrated a greater proportion of my field research on this organization. Through interviews with approximately ten employees of the organization and informal conversations with many more devotees I pieced together a picture of how this organization operates on a day-to-day basis.

The Sadhu Vaswani Mission, as detailed below, is a prominent Hindu organization with headquarters in the city. It is smaller and less well known internationally than either the Ramakrishna Mission or Guru Mata Amritanandamayi, and has fewer centres outside Pune. It does, however, have centres in the UK (London), the USA and Southeast Asia. According to an interview with a senior employee, it receives support from the Hindu diaspora communities in these countries. The mission is founded on a lineage that began with Sadhu Vaswani, who was the uncle of the current leader 'Dada' Vaswani. Dada received his mantle as Sadhu Vaswani's successor after his uncle recognized that he possessed divine qualities.

The mission complex is large and is situated on Sadhu Vaswani Road with a huge statue of the founder positioned on a roundabout at one end. The main mission complex contains a kindergarten, a primary and secondary school for around 1400 girls, huge meeting halls, an administration block and Dada Vaswani's residence. The mission also has its own publishing house (Gita Publishing) located in the administration block. The mission's educational activities extend beyond this central complex and include Mira College and a nursing college. In total, the mission claims to be educating about 4000 girls at any one time. The mission is planning to extend its educational provision through the construction of a college of commerce, again exclusively for girls. There is also a large Sadhu Vaswani Hospital, which is where nursing students carry out their practical training and where many of them later find employment. The hospital is private and local informants told us that they felt it to be very expensive. The hospital offers a small amount of free treatments and operations each year for the poor.

Core teachings: nationalism, spirituality and service
The mission, perhaps deliberately, prominently projects its social welfare activities and highlights its work empowering girls through education. It does not openly claim to be pursuing a politically-oriented goal of uniting India through a singular culture and religion. The organization's insistence on being called secular further obscures this second goal. As already stated, the term 'secular' here refers to a commitment to all faiths (see introduction to this section for details). The most senior figure I interviewed in the organization, one of the executives, insisted that Sadhu Vaswani Mission was secular because

it 'served all faiths'. Even when probed he refused to admit that the organization was predominantly Hindu, claiming instead that it worshipped and celebrated all faiths. He also claimed that the mission was active in interfaith dialogue and collaboration. As proof of its interfaith credentials, he mentioned that the Sadhu Vaswani Mission organized a huge gathering in October 2009, which the Dalai Lama attended. Office screensavers showed pictures of the Dalai Lama and Dada Vaswani holding hands and showing affection to each other.

This senior informant refused to couch the organization's core principles in religious language, but said, 'we use the word "love" to describe our actions in serving the poor.' In response to a question about where God fitted in, he said, 'God is love. You do not need a separate word.' The image this organization markets publicly is secular, yet spiritually oriented. In his literature, Dada stresses the importance of serving the poor, challenging human suffering and working to achieve world peace.[32] The mission runs various daily welfare or *seva* programmes to feed different groups of poor people at various times during the day.

Most of the local people interviewed outside the organization in Pune endorsed its image of 'secular spirituality'. Sadhu Vaswani's *samadhi* (place where ashes are buried) at the heart of the ashram complex depicts him with one of his forefingers raised, indicating that we are all one. This image of Sadhu Vaswani is how he is most commonly depicted and informants described him as promoting the mission's interfaith agenda.[33] However, in my review of the organization's literature and after hearing Dada Vaswani speak, I felt that the raised forefinger and stress on interfaith served in general to highlight the similarity of all religions and in particular to point to the inclusiveness of Hinduism as a faith that can embrace all others. In other words, the purpose of the underlying message was to promote Hinduism as the one all-encompassing religion to which all Indians should belong.

With close study and enough time I was able to draw out an underlying agenda that reflected a more nationalistic and conservative ideology than the organization at first presents. An examination of its literature reveals more clearly the organization's nationalist sentiments projected through its insistence on preserving a singular Indian culture and religion. As I document below, in audiences Dada Vaswani talks about the need to emancipate India from the clutches of British colonialism. The mission concentrates on educating women as the bearers and nurturers of Indian culture and religion, and stresses the need to heal India by strengthening its spiritual foundations. Scholars of Hindu nationalism recognize themes that advocate a singular Indian culture and religion, that lay stress on women as the bearers of culture and religion, and that express anti-British sentiments as common to the discourses of many organizations.[34] As I discuss later, the exclusive focus on educating girls to achieve this vision of a united India is unusual, for most organizations mobilize both men and women in their approach.[35]

The passage cited below details the origins of the movement outside Maharashtra in Sind and offers a reason for the nationalist tone that runs through its discourse.

> What we know as the Sadhu Vaswani Mission today was started by Sadhu T. L Vaswani in 1929, at Hyderabad (Sind).
>
> Kumari Shanti Maghanmal was a devout disciple of Sadhu T. L Vaswani. At her behest, her father offered a hall where Sadhu Vaswani could hold his *satsang* (fellowship meetings). In those days it was known as the *Sakhi Satsang*.
>
> In the early days of the *Sakhi Satsang*, it was largely composed of women. For in an age when the woman's place was considered to be largely confined to the kitchen, Sadhu Vaswani was a visionary who believed that women had a great potential – a great *shakti* – which could be utilized for the betterment of the society and the nation.
>
> Sadhu Vaswani believed that service and sacrifice were the most vital aspects of the spiritual life. Under his guidance the *satsang* was a dynamic organization, rendering service to the community of Hyderabad – Sind.[36]

As detailed in this passage, the mission emerged in Sind primarily, so the literature claims, as a religious cum social-welfare organization focused on educating girls. Its founder, Sadhu Vaswani, was a teacher by profession who wanted to rectify community concerns about girls' education being considered of secondary importance to that of boys. Sadhu Vaswani felt that because women are the primary nurturers and educators of toddlers, educating girls would result in a higher level of attainment in their children. In other words, education is a part of 'nurturing'. History, or more specifically partition, also shaped this organization in that when the British carved up the Indian subcontinent into religiously defined regions Hyderabad became part of Pakistan.[37] Also, Sind was the site of the Indus Valley civilization, from which the Indian religion that subsequently became known as Hinduism is thought to have originated.[38] Its geographic heritage might thus partly explain why, as I show later in this chapter, the experience of partition remains so strong in the organization's collective memory, for its supporters are united in their belief that a unified and culturally homogenous India is vital to the nation's future strength and prosperity. The following quotation from one of the mission's publications is indicative of the organization's sense of heritage. 'Ancient is the history of Sind. The Indus Valley civilization is at least 7000 years old. The Sindis are a highly civilized and cultured people – enterprising, hardworking and industrious, full of the spirit of faith and courage.'[39] Although the mission does not describe itself as Sindi, its regional identity is evident because in Pune it largely serves the Sindi community, many of whose members moved to the city from Gujarat. Key employees, such as the headmistress of the secondary school, are Sindi. The mission's sponsorship programme concentrates on serving the poor Sindi community in Pune, offering means-tested scholarships to worthy cases.

The goddess, gender and mothering

The Sadhu Vaswani Mission places the emphasis on the behaviour of women, in contrast to the stress on masculinity seen in the operation of the RSS.[40] In my conversations with the organization's devotees and employees, the subject of masculinity, as a gendered construct, never arose. Although the highly visible and central figure of a male leader suggests strong patriarchal male dominance and authority, the organization's literature focuses almost exclusively on the importance of the women's role and responsibility in unifying India.[41] This focus on girls seems driven by a desire to embed a sense of appropriate female behaviour and pursuits into the mindsets of young girls who by the time they graduate from the Mira system may well be happy to comply with its underlying patriarchal gendered ideology. This, for example, can be seen in the quote from Dada Vaswani:

> Now woman gets her chance. She is called upon to build a New World. She is a symbol of *shakti* in the Hindu scriptures. And *shakti* is not a force. *Shakti* is integration. This includes intelligence. Education, more education, is needed. But it must be education of the right character.[42]

The mission believes that the stability of the Indian nation depends on women's willingness to embrace motherhood – hence the statement by a senior devotee that appears in the mission's literature: 'educate women and you educate the whole country', which is a core Sadhu Vaswani Mission teaching.[43] Passages throughout the locally published literature reinforce this overtly patriarchal conception of gender relations, conflating womanhood with motherhood in a similar way to that of the Ramakrishna movement.[44]

Although claims are made on its official website and by the members I interviewed that the Sadhu Vaswani Mission is dedicated to empowering women, its conception of empowerment is far from any Western secularist model. Western notions of empowerment equate the term with equal opportunities for boys and girls, whereas the mission stresses that the roles for which education must prepare women differ from those of men. It is difficult to fathom what concepts of gender and equality really mean to the members of this organization because they use Westernized words like empowerment to describe their core objectives. The tone of the mission's declaration that it is committed to helping women fulfil 'their potential as liberated beings'[45] is reflective of the Western feminist concern to see women freed from male oppression. Nevertheless, the mission's sentiments are all highly worthy, as are its spiritual values of love and compassion.

The conservative and nationalist side of the organization's ideology came to the fore during an annual questions and answers session for students held with Dada Vaswani at the Mira College for girls in Pune on 20 November 2008. The observations I made on this occasion clearly brought home the extent to which the girls are being taught to absorb and pursue a specific gendered role that prescribes their place in the world as mothers and home makers. The country is still 'emasculated by the British'. 'It is your duty to complete India's emancipation.' 'We are not yet truly free' and, in seeking to achieve his vision of a united and free India, Dada Vaswani focuses exclusively on girls and women. During this audience with him I sat at the back of the hall and observed the students around me. Although the female employees from the Sadhu Vaswani Mission office had told me that the silence in the hall was so complete when he spoke that 'you could hear a pin drop', I noticed that many were not giving him their full attention. I witnessed a lot of whispered chatting throughout Dada's audience. In addition, I could see that many of the students did not even attend the session and were sitting in and around the college grounds. This raised questions about the extent to which the girls were sent to Mira College because of the high standard of education it provided rather than because of Dada Vaswani and his teachings. Or perhaps the parents rather than their children were the Dada Vaswani devotees. Whatever the explanation, the influence of Dada's teachings may be less long lasting than the mission hopes in terms of shaping the roles girls pursue in life.

Women and education

The Mira movement for girls, which supports schools and colleges across India, delivers the education programme. As Sadhu Vaswani explains, the Mira movement is associated with 'the great Indian saint – St Mira'.[46] The mission describes her as a religious woman who turned her back on her wealthy upbringing in Chitor,

Rajasthan to devote her life to Lord Krishna. The mission emphasizes her loyalty and devotion to Krishna and upholds her as a role model for students, describing her as the 'representative of the very soul of Indian culture, the very spirit of Indian wisdom'.[47] The first Mira school opened in Sind in 1932 and the next in Pune following partition. The first Mira College in Pune was established in 1962.

The mission believes that it offers its pupils a unique blend of spirituality and academic classes. It claims that 'social service and community development are an integral part of the Mira education system.'[48] Sanskrit and Sindi lessons are included in the curriculum and martial arts are thought to be desirable to help girls develop the physical techniques needed to defend themselves. This stress on developing girls' physical strength is reflective of the RSS approach in its schools where physical and mental agility are developed simultaneously. In fact, the RSS holds that physical strength is even required to defend Indian culture.

On numerous occasions informants inside the mission asked me if I had seen other organizations adopt a similar approach to education. In the subsection below I compare the approaches to education that each of our three organizations took and conclude that the way in which the Sadhu Vaswani Mission integrates spirituality, or more specifically religious instruction, into its mainstream academic curriculum is not unique. However, the precise content of what they actually teach in their religious programmes is different. As already mentioned and as stated in the mission's literature, the exclusive focus on girls is deliberate:

The Mira Movement has chosen to concentrate on educating girls because it was Sadhu Vaswani's firm belief that women would play a vital role in shaping India's destiny in the future. 'Woman-soul shall lead us upward, on!' he asserted emphasizing the spiritual *shakti* that women represented. The Mira Movement is, in effect, aimed at the empowerment of women – emotional, intellectual and spiritual.[49]

According to the female devotees and graduates with whom I spoke, the Sadhu Vaswani Mission not only offers a high academic standard of education but it also disseminates the organization's teachings. For example, in daily sessions called 'sanctuary' the students are taught about Indian culture and the important role women play in preserving the unity and stability of Indian society. The reproductive and nurturing role of women is stressed during these sessions and by activities such as bird feeding and nature walks. Some of the girls with whom I spoke described the sanctuary as their favourite part of the day. According to the mission:

> The sanctuary period, where all the children meet every morning, is the focal point of education. Here in the atmosphere of purity and prayer the girls recite *bhajans*, hear stories of sacrifices and services of the great men of India and elsewhere and also do meditation. The idea is that during the most impressionable years of their lives, the girls realize that life is more than passing examinations. All the activities, throughout the day, are permeated by the atmosphere of sanity, serenity, goodwill and high idealism generated in the early hours every day. The school lays special emphasis on all-round personality development and character building of its students.[50]

The seven pillars of education the mission cites are:

- Reverence for all life;
- Reverence for Spirit of Education;
- Life and Nature;
- Character Building;
- Spiritual Unfolding;
- Love of Indian Ideals;
- Living for Others.[51]

These dimensions highlight the extent to which shaping the character of each girl is considered to be of primary importance and this in turn is orientated towards the preservation of 'Indian ideals'.

Cross-organizational Analysis: How Do Religious Teachings Shape Concepts of Development?

Poverty and the act of seva (to give)

Many Hindu organizations refer to their welfare work as acts of *seva*, the Hindu word for 'to give'. According to Jacobsen,[52] the concept of *seva* has its origins among worshippers of Vishnu, which dates back to the *Vedas* and basically means serving Vishnu by helping in his temples and worshipping God from a place of intense love. This love can be expressed not only through songs and rituals but also through serving others to alleviate their suffering. Vivekananda institutionalized the concept of *seva* during his lifetime, making it a central part of a monk or nun's obligations, regardless of which god they followed and thus gave it a new social expression. Gandhi's use of the term also promoted its use and it is now central to modern Hinduism.[53]

A closer look at the concept of *seva* reveals that the practice of 'giving' requires someone to 'give to'; a power relationship is implicit in this act. However, the word means 'service' not 'gift'. *Seva*, as Vivekananda and others such as Gandhi developed it, is directed to people in need and it is in this context that a power relationship emerges. Vivekananda identified the poor as God: 'the poor, the illiterate, the ignorant, the afflicted – let these be your God.'[54] Also, as Swami Vivekananda puts it in the following passage:

> I see what they call the poor of this country and how many there are who feel for them! What an immense difference in India! Who feels therefore the two hundred million of men and women sunken for ever in poverty and ignorance? Where is the way out? Who feels for them? They cannot find light or education, who brings the light to them – who will travel from door to door bringing education to them? Let these people be your God – think of them, work for them, pray for them incessantly – the Lord will show you the way.[55]

Calling the poor God assigns power to them but at the same time the very process of identifying them as poor and in need of the help of others renders them powerless and awards the giver power. The process of *seva* as an act of service is paradoxical in the teachings of Vivekananda. In the case of Amma and Dada Vaswani it is straightforward in that the poor are not given a divine status; their position in life is seen in karmic terms.

> Poor children. Mother is deeply wounded in Her mind, seeing these people's suffering. Who will take care of them? People talk about helping the poor, but no one seems to be doing anything for them. Children, compared to the suffering of these people, our suffering is nothing. God has provided us with food, clothing and shelter. But these children have nothing. Let us use our God-given faculties with utmost discrimination. We must not cheat him by misusing them. These children might have misused such gifts in their previous births, and that is why they are suffering now. Still it is our duty to have compassion for them. In fact God created the rich to help the poor, the healthy to assist the unhealthy and normal human beings to help and serve the mentally retarded and physically deformed.[56]

Although Amma stresses that no one should live a life of poverty and suffering, she believes that people's past acts determine their position in life. She stresses the importance of daily spiritual practice, which essentially includes the expression of compassion for everyone. Amma's devotees have to find someone poorer and worse off than they are on whom to focus their compassion and thereby display to her their ability to generate empathy. 'Charity given from a guru to people who are not necessarily devotees can also be said to create a social obligation from the receivers of charity towards the guru.'[57] Jones describes a process by which, to establish the foundations of authority, the guru combines Indian understandings of family relations and love with gift giving and hierarchical practices. The authority thus acquired enables the guru to suggest that the receivers of their gifts show gratitude by becoming devotees. This allegiance may not increase the organization's finances but could help to build political support if, in the case of Dada Vaswani's mission, the organization is simultaneously pursing a political agenda.

The obvious question then is 'can acts of charity claimed to be altruistic also be understood as strategies to obtain social dominance?' Appadurai[58] describes how the symbolism of gratitude and the language of hierarchy are closely connected. Rather than verbal thanks, gratitude is expressed by making the appropriate promise to the guru of future return and an acknowledgement of the social relationships between giver and receiver, for example praise. Mauss[59] likewise talks of the gift exchange as one that implies reciprocity, placing the receiver in a position of indebtedness if she or he cannot then repay the gift. Similar criticisms have been applied to the way in which mainstream development operates.[60]

The different approaches to and conceptualizations of *seva* found in the literature of these organizations also came through in discussions with their followers. Devotees at the Guru Mata Amritanandamayi Mission were keen to stress their commitment to Amma and less eager to talk about the observance of *seva* as charity. When asked what *seva* was about they did not give a clear explanation apart from saying that it means displaying devotion to Amma. For them, devotion to Guru Mata Amritanandamayi did not entail direct charity work with poor communities, but was expressed through other actions such as volunteering to help run the centre, for example in the gift shop. Through these activities they still felt themselves to 'be giving' or specifically performing *seva*. This focus on serving Amma is linked to an individualistic vision of personal spiritual development. 'Love' and 'compassion' are important values that Amma teaches should be strengthened through spiritual practices of devotion. For our informants, charity was not seen as a primary tool with which to achieve this. These conversations differed from those we had with devotees of Dada Vaswani who strongly emphasized their daily *seva* activities of feeding the poor. Informants from the Ramakrishna mission also talked about their work feeding the poor and providing daily medical support in the slums located near their complex. In both organizations informants conflated *seva* with their own personal spiritual journey, seeing these acts of charity and welfare as a means for them to grow in their devotion and service to their guru and through them to God.

The geographical locations of these organizations seem to have a bearing on how their devotees approach *seva*. The Sadhu Vaswani and Guru Mata Amritanandamayi missions are located in exceedingly prosperous parts of Pune, whereas the Ramakrishna movement is in an ordinary middle-class area. In all three cases, however, the devotees are middle class and those towards whom they direct their *seva* are not, which suggests a power imbalance between those in a position to 'give' and those selected to 'receive'. The process of selection is significant because organizations do not randomly choose a community to serve, but rather 'give' to the people who live in the slum settlements nearest to where they are located. The Guru Mata Amritanandamayi and Ramakrishna missions go into the slum settlements they serve, whereas the Sadhu Viswani Mission invites poor people into its more modestly located complex to receive food twice a day. In all cases, a process of selection determines who will receive their charity and organizations seem to manage to avoid targeting the same communities.

The language of service is one of supplication, but this does not in fact mean that the server will show subservience. Given the highly politicized environment of Pune and the small amount of ethnographic data on the politics of slum settlements, the process of selecting who to serve is unlikely to be wholly apolitical, or at least devoid of political implications in the future. None of the people to whom I spoke at the organizations could detail a long-term development plan or vision. None of the organizations based their *seva* operations on a concept of economic and social transformation with poverty alleviation as an end goal. The absence of this long-term vision meant that *seva* maintained a relationship of dependence in which the poor must continuously come and receive rather than look to a future of self sufficiency. The *seva* activities of these organizations also stand in stark opposition to the visions of the future expressed by local people in the slum settlements who wanted to see themselves achieve a socially respected and economically stable existence.[61]

Reactions to the caste system

In the last section I portrayed *seva* largely as the pursuit of middle-class Hindus who regard development as the charitable work they do to help them along their personal spiritual journey. This view stands in stark contrast to how poor Hindus and the organizations to which they belong understand development. For the poor, economic prosperity, political agency and human rights are core goals and religion the tool with which to achieve them, either through the utilization of religious spaces as political platforms[62] or in the hope that religious practices might bring prosperity. The attitudes of poor Hindus to caste are revealing insofar as they highlight how Hinduism is either used to fight poverty and injustice, or rejected because it serves the needs of the middle classes and promotes hierarchy rather than equality.

The recent increase in Buddhist organizations in Pune is because large numbers of Hindus have come to recognize the injustice of the caste system. The rise of the dalit movement results partly from a rejection of the brahminical Hindu ideas of social organization that the Ramakrishna, Guru Mata Amritanandamayi and Sadhu Vaswani missions promote. To a certain extent the growth of the Shiv Sena movement in Pune was an ideological reaction against the brahminical strand of Hinduism, which it holds responsible for the treatment of low-caste Hindus. By rejecting what it saw as the elitism of the religion's dominant strands, the movement sought to reinvent Hinduism as a religion committed to social justice and social equality. Shiv Sena promotes militant Hindu symbols and deities to drive home its vision of social transformation.[63]

Although all three of the organizations presented here direct their welfare activities towards dalits and do not condone the kinds of marginalization and injustices to which they are subjected, none of them campaigns for the total abolition of the system. The primary reason for this is that these organizations believe that the caste system provides social stability in that it enables each person to understand and find his or her place in the world. For example, as Swami Vivekananda states:

We believe in Indian caste as one of the greatest social institutions that the Lord gave to man. We also believe that though the unavoidable defects, foreign persecution, and above all, the monumental ignorance and pride of many Brahmanas who do not deserve the name, have thwarted in many ways, the legitimate fructification of this most glorious Indian institution, it has already worked wonders for the land of Bharata and is destined to lead Indian humanity to its goal.[64]

The above passage, taken from a contemporary publication produced and sold by the organization in Pune, as well as conversations with devotees, reveals an absence of any rights discourse in the organization's teachings and activities. The belief that caste contributes something positive to people's lives, however, could be read as a political statement opposing the anti-caste message of Shiv Sena and other dalit organizations, both Hindu and Buddhist. All three of the organizations examined here see caste as an important way of supporting individuals' personal religious journeys by establishing their *dharma* according to their position, status and gender. The problem, according to Vivekananda, occurs when people in superior positions exploit the system to subjugate the lower castes for their own benefit.

Gender and dharma

The specific way in which an organization understands and talks about *dharma* influences how its members conceive of development as spiritual growth, welfare and charity. In the three organizations I studied, each individual's *dharma* is to grow in spiritual awareness; the act of giving is one way of making that happen. Because it is through *dharma* that religion intersects with development, the emphasis is on the individual's personal spiritual journey and part of this involves *seva*. Although, as already stated, the simplest definition of *dharma* is 'duty', a person's *dharma* will differ according to his or her caste, gender, age and stage in life. *Dharma* is gendered and a woman's duty is traditionally depicted as fulfilling her domestic obligations as wife and mother. Gender roles are in turn reinforced through texts like the *Ramayana* that present Rama and Sita as the ideal role models for men and women.[65] In the *Ramayana* women are not assigned a spiritual or religious path in the same way as men are. Sita is expected to concentrate on her domestic role of looking after her husband and later her children. A woman's duty is defined through the term *stridharma*, which positions her squarely in the domestic sphere. Marriage is endorsed within many Hindu texts as a rite of passage that cements a woman into her socio-cultural role.

Scholarly interpretations of religious texts and ideas have now expanded to include more nuanced socio-cultural and gendered understandings of the prescriptive roles assigned to men and women.[66] My analysis of the Ramakrishna and Sadhu Vaswani missions in Pune certainly supports this link between text, religious teachings and a patriarchal gendered ideology that separates the roles and responsibilities of boys and girls. In the literature of all three organizations *dharma* is central and the importance of each person fulfilling his or her duty is emphasized. The Ramakrishna and Sadhu Vaswani missions divide *dharma* into responsibilities for men and women. As discussed in the first section, the Ramakrishna Mission has published books on the role of women. In addition, both organizations demonstrate *stridharma* practically through using characters who have been longstanding devotees of the main male guru as role models. In the Ramakrishna Mission, the figure of the 'Holy Mother' as the consort of Ramakrishna is celebrated and worshipped alongside Ramakrishna and Swami Vivekananda. In the Sadhu Vaswani Mission the female figure of a long-term devotee of the first Sadhu Vaswani acquired divine qualities as a result of her devotion. Both these female figures are honoured as mothers because of the way in which they nurtured and supported the main male guru.

Amma's concept of *dharma* is to some extent gender neutral in that it is considered the same for both men and women. Her description of *dharma*, however, is highly feminized in that it focuses on qualities she believes to be innately womanly, for example love and compassion. Although men should aspire to emanate them, women are more likely to be successful.

Education

Religion has a significant role in determining who has access to education and the type of curriculum followed. In my research I found that this process is gendered in both the Ramakrishna and Sadhu Vaswani missions. The curriculums these organizations follow distinguish between education for girls and boys based on the belief that each sex has differing *dharma* to fulfil and therefore needs to be prepared differently. As reviewed in the first section of this chapter, the religious teachings of both the Ramakrishna and the Sadhu Vaswani missions equate femininity with reproductive and domestic roles for women, or *stridharma* effectively conflating motherhood and womanhood. The curriculum reinforces this message in a number of ways. Both organizations view education as a means of empowering women, but the concept of empowerment is understood as the achievement of *dharma*, which in the case of women means fulfilling a traditional domestic role.

As already noted, the concept of empowerment that Amma conveys in her teachings endorses an identifiably Western notion of gender equality. She urges women to free themselves from the grasp of male authority and to make life decisions on their own. For the teachers at Sadhu Vaswani's schools, empowerment describes the purpose of education, but their understanding of the concept differs from that of the Ramakrishna Mission and Amma's teachings. They see empowerment for girls as having the strength and courage to withstand the pressures of a modern secular life and remain true and loyal to Dada's teachings. As previously outlined, girls are encouraged to acquire mental and physical strength to the point of receiving regular self-defence classes. Although the Ramakrishna Mission's literature rarely touches on empowerment, the devotees with whom we spoke equated it with *dharma*, which, as already mentioned, is inherently gendered. In other words, a person is empowered if they are able to fulfil their *dharma*.

The low-caste untouchable Hindus with whom I spoke in the slum settlements, by contrast, saw education as a route out of poverty and marginalization. Empowerment was the end goal that education would help them achieve. These slum dwellers saw education as equally important for boys and girls because it was a route to economic advancement and a higher social status. Interviews with NGO workers, however, revealed that although people may claim to support education for their daughters, in reality girls are often taken out of school because they are needed at home to help look after their younger siblings.

As noted, the Ramakrishna, Guru Mata Amritanandamayi and Sadhu Vaswani missions all fund and support kindergartens as well as primary and secondary schools. The Sadhu Vaswani Mission only supports the education of girls, but it does so through to college level and beyond. The Ramakrishna and Guru Mata Amritanandanmayi missions claim to support the education of girls and boys to an equal extent. In all three cases, a limited number of places are free or subsidized, depending on the child's circumstances, but not many students come from very low-caste or untouchable families. While all the organizations regard education as a vital part of a child's socialization, whether girl or boy, they do not think it should tackle caste inequalities. The Ramakrishna Mission describes education specifically as a way of spreading the teachings of its guru.[67]

Both the Ramakrishna and Guru Mata Amritanandamayi missions combine academic classes with religious instruction and the school day begins with prayers directed towards the central guru. The Guru Mata Amritanandamayi Mission invested heavily in developing the school site and extensive building work was underway when I conducted the research. The organization's educational dimension seemed to be of the highest priority. The huge investment in school buildings contrasted starkly with the somewhat paltry amount of welfare the organization supports – feeding the poor once a day in a nearby slum and supporting a travelling clinic once a month. This rather undermines Guru Mata Amritanandamayi's underlying teachings, which lay particular stress on the importance of serving those who are less fortunate than oneself. The guru's main ashram and centre in Kollam, Kerala seems to run a more diverse and extensive range of development activities than the Pune branch supports.[68] The scale of the school development is perhaps because it is through educating the next generation of Guru Mata Amritanandamayi devotees that the organization's future can be assured. Also, the schools are privately run and therefore generate revenue.

Conclusion

To conclude, these three middle-class organizations link their spiritual philosophies to notions of personal development that require acts of material charity. However, in each case, the relationship between spirituality and development produces only short-term results in terms of addressing deep-rooted patterns of poverty and social exclusion in the wider communities in which they exist. For the Sadhu Vaswani Mission, religion is also a means of achieving a political vision of India, which again should not be confused with a development agenda committed to rectifying structural inequalities.

The purpose of presenting these three case studies was to highlight how effective a combined ethnographic and gendered approach is in the study of religious organizations. Furthermore, the kind of critical analysis that anthropological research produces helps create a more complex insight into how differing concepts of development emerge and become embedded in the devotees' worldviews. These concepts and views of the world are then transported through transnational networks that influence the religious and political beliefs of people outside India. A combination of this type of ethnographic research with the macro theoretical perspective of IR has huge potential to further unlock insights into why religion continues to be such a powerful foundation for global movements, while also helping us to understand how individuals may experience the religious discourse in their everyday lives.

PART II

Faith-based Organizations and Dialogues in Development

THE focus of this part of the book is on faith-based organizations (FBOs), in other words on the intersection between religion and development. The term 'FBO' emerged in recent years from attempts to examine the identity, character and approach of faith-based organizations.[1] It is now widely used in the study of religious organizations engaged in broadly defined development activities, which can be welfare focused or can concentrate on pursuing a political or human rights agenda. Clarke[2] was one of the first scholars to define the term FBO and he did so through a typology that is summarized in Chapter 4.

Other literature explores the specific impact of faith on shaping distinct organizational characteristics[3] and goes on to consider whether these create very different approaches to development compared with their secular counterparts. To date, no overall conclusion has been reached on the relative benefits of FBOs. Despite a burgeoning literature on them, there is no overwhelming evidence to suggest that FBOs are any better at development than secular NGOs. In fact, most academics, and I include myself here, tend to avoid answering that question. As with NGOs, FBOs vary so greatly in size and ideology that the task of evaluating their effectiveness is both challenging and ethically fraught. FBOs often shift their identities and recreate themselves to present a more favourable image to prospective donors. Seeking out the 'real' agenda is often a pointless objective because organizations are not static and constantly alter both their identity and their objectives.[4]

I shall consider why FBOs have generated such interest and review some of the approaches developed for studying them. Part of the discussion involves a critical analysis of the usefulness and accuracy of the category FBO. During my fieldwork in Pune, Maharashtra, I came across organizations that were clearly identifiable as FBOs, yet shed that label if they felt that it failed to serve their objectives. While undertaking research on new Buddhist organizations in Pune, Ramsay and Bradley[5] came across one organization that consciously maintained a dual religious and secular identity. It claimed to be a religious or faith-guided welfare organization to those who supported its Buddhist foundations, especially its main Buddhist donor, yet employees of a subgroup operating within the organization's head-quarters to promote primary health programmes for women described themselves and the project as independent of any religious tradition. It received funds from a long chain of secular health donors, including the Gates Foundation. Clearly, the leverage of donors has an impact on determining how local community organiz-ations present themselves, but this example highlights the agency that FBOs exercise at the local level in altering their outward image to attract much needed funds.

The complexities associated with how organizations, or rather the people in them, identify themselves are covered in this part and obtained from ethnographic fieldwork and analysis. Gender is central to this analysis as a means of piecing together these identities and the approaches of the organizations under study. Much of the case material presented here comes from work I have conducted with various Gandhian community organizations and a UK intermediary organization that channels donations to them.

My overall objective in this part of the book is to urge funders, practitioners and academics to move beyond their current obsession with defining FBOs, to prove their worth or otherwise, to a more complex and critical approach to analysing the work of all development organizations. This critical analysis should include gender and religion irrespective of whether the organization professes to be secular or faith based, for the impact of each, as the chapters in this part show, are far reaching and complex. With at best the line blurred between what makes an organization religious or secular, ethnographic research that incorporates both religion and gender can produce a more sophisticated awareness of how a web of interlocking factors shape all development organizations. These include the dominant religious or secular discourses on which an organization is founded and that shape its self-identity, relationships to sources of funding – often a mixture of faith-based and secular donors – as well as the local, national and transnational political, economic and cultural contexts in which these organizations exist and operate.

Chapter 4
What is a Faith-based Organization?

T HE aim of this chapter is to compare and contrast different types of faith-based development organizations, shortened in this chapter to FBOs, to understand more clearly the various ways and degrees to which faith shapes their work. The objective is then to explore how the work of FBOs may be critically analysed to ascertain the impact that 'faith' may or may not have on development practice. Because of the huge variation in the character and practices of FBOs, their disparities must be acknowledged critically to distinguish organizations that are 'good' at development from those that are not. I understand good practice to mean adopting a personal approach in communicating with local people and being responsive to the wide range of needs in any one community. Where faith is an important aspect of people's lives, development practice must recognize that material and spiritual needs may be intertwined.

In all development organizations, whether secular or faith based, power is key in determining the effectiveness of the work they do. Power plays a part in the relationships between different FBOs. It divides those that have money and can decide what to do with it from those that depend on others for funding. Power is also apparent in FBO relations with local communities at the grass roots level, for the faith-led identity of an FBO affects its style of practice and how close it gets to meeting the needs of local people. As I argue in this chapter, in some instances faith enhances local-level relationships; in other cases, it stands as a barrier to dialogue. Faith carries good intentions, but the processes through which it may bring positive results are complex and fraught with the same power issues that secular development organizations have to face.

I use two interlocking analytical frameworks. The first is a continuum along which to place FBOs according to how faith shapes their identity and influences their practice. At one end of the continuum are secular NGOs in which faith is of minimal significance, though individual members may have a faith. At the other end are denominational or faith-led organizations in which religion determines their members' perception of the world and what actions they take. The continuum shows that some FBOs more than others will assert their religious identity and faith as a motivating force for their work. The degree to which faith steers and directs the work of an organization will differ. My use of a continuum shows that organizations may find themselves in the same category as an FBO but have very little in common in terms of how they incorporate faith into their work. In short, FBOs vary widely in character and identity.

My second analytical framework is designed to show how diversity in identity translates into diversity in practice. In considering the efficiency and effectiveness of a development organization I argue that it is important to acknowledge how aid is disseminated. A hierarchical structure positions an organization at some level along a chain of aid. A series of power relationships produce this hierarchy. The agencies that hold significant power are those with the most money and the ability to decide which organizations to fund. The power of donor leverage is well documented.[1] By positioning different types of FBOs along this aid chain I show that the 'faith' of an organization carries little weight against the monetary power of the organization on which it depends for support in its work. Although 'faith' may shape an FBO's identity and understanding of how development should happen, its actions may be limited because it has to conform to its donor's agenda.

Each analytical framework has a contribution to make to the debate on FBOs. The development community recognizes the potential of faith-based development organizations to deliver long-term sustainable development, which is borne out by the amount of research funding being allocated to examining the work of FBOs.[2] Much of the research is geared towards finding out if FBOs approach development differ-ently from their secular counterparts. There is an underlying feeling that some FBOs may provide a safe, secure way to deliver development initiatives. Yet, there has been very little research into what an FBO actually is and which ones, if any, are good at development. Because many different types of FBO exist, more research is needed to assess their work comparatively. I hope to contribute to this venture by reaching a clearer understanding of what makes an organization faith based and considering the impact of FBOs on development.

To begin, we shall consider the various definitions of an FBO. I outline three groups of organizations that represent a broad con-tinuum – grass-roots organizations motivated by spirituality and a desire to relate closely to local communities; denominational organ-izations that use their religious affiliation to raise money; and missionary-driven FBOs inspired by a zest to achieve religious salvation for all. Although some local people may support such a goal, in poverty-stricken areas it is unlikely to be a priority for the majority. I then go on to focus more directly on the analytical frameworks I employ to explore the differences between FBOs and to analyse practices. These frameworks are then used in the remainder of the chapter to examine case examples from each of the three groups of FBOs identified.

What is an FBO?

Before going any further I must give a broad working definition of an FBO. In this chapter I understand an FBO to be an organization with faith embedded in its organizational structures, thus producing a range of approaches to development practice. In some cases, faith provides a platform for close partnerships at the community level, which might allow concepts of development to emerge that challenge the hegemony of Western models. Other FBOs find their religious worldview compromised by the need to fulfil the secular policy objectives of global donors. In yet other organizations, faith acts as a mechanism for bringing 'others' into a power relationship in which the FBO presents itself as offering salvation to the suffering of people at a local level.

91

Clarke considers what is unique about FBOs. He views them as agents of transformation characterized by a culturally inclusive and non-materialistic view of wellbeing that resonates with the concepts of development held by the local faith communities. According to Clarke, 'faith is an analytical lens through which the poor experienced and rationalized poverty and through which the well off empathized with their struggles and provided practical support.'[3] It is clear from the extensive research that Clarke has conducted on the faith/development interface that he sees the relationship as potentially fruitful. He also cautions that not all FBOs share a vision of culturally sensitive development practice. Greater critical analysis is needed into the work of FBOs to prevent funding being directed towards FBOs that proselytise and/or denigrate other faiths.

Clarke[4] identified a need for researchers to be more specific when outlining the type of organization to which they were referring, so he devised a vast typology of the various faith-based organizations, of which faith-based development organizations formed one strand. Many faith-based organizations do not engage in conventional development work at all. Much of the material on religion and development refers generally to faith-based organizations. I argue that the development sector's interest in religion should not include the work of all FBOs, but should instead focus squarely on the work of those engaged in development activities. Since the only organizations under scrutiny here are engaged in development, I use the terms faith-based organization (FBO) and faith-based *development* organization (FBO) interchangeably.

Although a broad range of organizations engage in 'development', many faith-based organizations exist that have no development mandate whatsoever. A tighter definition is therefore needed if researchers are to examine the development work of religious organizations critically and assess how well they are carrying it out. Not only is the attempt to define FBOs a thankless task in that the differences between them are endless, but the characteristics of any one organization are also subject to constant changes and influences. Rigorous attempts to define these organizations at the very least entails acknowledging and exploring these difficulties, which in turn sheds light on the complex field of FBOs and the cultural, social and political worlds in which they operate.

Clarke's typology of FBOs contains five main groups:[5]

- Faith-based representative organizations or apex bodies that rule on doctrinal matters. These organizations govern the faithful and represent them at state and global levels.
- Faith-based charitable or development organizations that mobilize the faithful in support of the poor and other social groups, and that fund or manage programmes that tackle poverty or social exclusion.
- Faith-based political organizations that deploy faith as a political construct and mobilize social groups on the basis of faith identities to pursue broader political objectives. See Chapter 2 for an example of this type of organization in the Hindu nationalist movement.
- Faith-based missionary organizations that seek to convert non-believers.
- Faith-based radical, illegal or terrorist organizations that promote radical or militant forms of faith identity and justify the use of violence on the grounds of faith.

These categories highlight a wide range of different FBOs of which many pursue some kind of development work or agenda. I would add to this typology a sixth category.

- Local or grass-roots organizations that seek to support and enable their individual adherents to reach a better understanding of their faith and openly share their spirituality with others. Examples of this type of group are bible or scriptural study groups or prayer meetings, meditation and/or yoga classes.

To analyse the intersection between religion and development, a narrow or more specific typology is needed that will draw from this larger picture the specific development activities in which different FBOs engage. In my work I use the category faith-based development organization to help pinpoint and critique the different ways in which organizations work in development.

I identify three main groups of FBO. These by no means represent the full array, but they offer a starting point for understanding the variations between them. My case studies are mainly Christian, but one is a Gandhian (largely Hindu) FBO. My first set of examples is positioned on my continuum as being spiritually driven. Faith is deeply embedded in the identity and work of these organizations and creates a spiritually inspired response to community-level initiatives. For these organizations, development is about more than alleviating material deprivation; it is also about the need to find a balance between the spiritual and monetary aspects of life. With responses to poverty indigenously rooted in the geography and cosmology of the local community, these FBOs try hard to resist being subsumed into a global development agenda. However, their position at the bottom of the aid chain means that, as community organizations relying on donations from larger organizations, they are continually forced to negotiate against other concepts of development that conflict with their own locally-grounded initiatives.

The second type of FBO is placed in the aid chain as an inter-mediary. These are still FBOs because their membership comes from a specific religious tradition. On my continuum they are denomin-ational because their primary concern is to raise money from within their religious community, though some money also comes from national governments and global development agencies such as the World Bank or International Monetary Fund (IMF). The way in which money is disseminated and allocated through local partner organizations reflects the bureaucratically accountable systems that most secular agencies use. Faith drives their commitment to raise money, but unlike the first group of community-level FBOs, their work is not spiritually rooted in specific locations. In other words, 'faith' does not spur intermediaries to live alongside the poor. Faith is an important source of motivation for fund-raising activities but it does not shape a distinct development practice. Faith used solely as a vehicle for fund raising, rather than to form relationships with local people, can produce problematic results in practice. The example I give of an intermediary organization highlights how its position in the aid chain above the community level prevents it from achieving locally responsive practice. The faith of the membership drives a desire to raise money and to help the rural poor of Rajasthan, but so focused are they on this quest that their faith constructs an unhelpful, homogenous image of a poor Rajasthani. Faith, in this case blocks inclusive dialogue at the local level.

My last group raises some important questions about how to evaluate the development work of faith organizations. Some religious organizations work in poor communities but resist the FBO label. In the example I give, PEACE Plan members refuse to acknowledge that their activities are development driven, yet they work in poor Rwandan communities. Furthermore, this organization seeks to change the lives of poor people by ending social inequality (a goal many NGOs and FBOs share). However, their approach to development is grounded in the belief that faith in a Christian god is the only way for the poor to achieve salvation. In its focus and practice, this is clearly a missionary organization. Conversion is seen as necessary if individuals are to access material goods. On my continuum, 'faith' shapes the identity and practice of this group, placing it, on first consideration, in a similar position to the first group of spiritually driven FBOs. For some mission groups, however, faith shapes a different type of practice from the locally responsive approach so central to the work of community embedded FBOs. Strength of religious conviction drives this organization towards pursuing its goal of extending the Kingdom of God. Although some members of their 'target' community may share this goal, it is likely to exclude and marginalize many more. The lack of a mechanism to identify needs through consultation and dialogue means that a power relationship is clearly evident in the practice of this FBO. In terms of where it fits in the aid chain, PEACE Plan seems to lie outside my framework. It donates directly to local communities, which means it experiences little or no conflict with other donor agencies that could influence its agenda. It is potentially well placed to respond directly to local needs. However, faith, as in the case of the intermediaries, blocks the possibility of sensitive, personalized development practice.

The analytical frameworks

Two criteria determine where on the continuum an organization is placed, namely the degree to which a collective 'faith' is central to the organization's identity and the extent to which 'faith' shapes and drives its practice. This helps one to make comparisons between FBOs that may display these criteria in different ways and to varying degrees. Also, by increasing the visibility of faith as a point of comparison between secular NGOs and FBOs, one is better placed to enter the debate over what constitutes an FBO. The continuum is useful in pinpointing just how much faith an organization needs to qualify as an FBO. Faith is present to some degree in many organizations. It has played an important part in motivating individuals to work in development and might even have been essential in the foundation of some secular development agencies. For example, Canon T. R. Milford of the University Church was a founding member of the Oxford Committee for Famine Relief (now Oxfam), which met for the first time on 5 May 1942.[6] It is likely that his Christian principles played a fundamental part in his decision to help create Oxfam. However, Oxfam is a secular organization because faith is not part of its collective identity and can not be seen as a dimension in its practice.

Amnesty International is a further example, like Oxfam, of an organization founded on Christian principles but professing a secular identity. It was launched in St Paul's Cathedral and its early newsletters contained prayers directed at the suffering of 'prisoners of conscience'. Although the organization no longer describes its activities as motivated by faith, its internationally recognized image of a candle wrapped in barbed wire alludes to Christ's suffering.[7] According to Hopgood, many Amnesty employees subscribe to the Christian values on which the organization was founded, but according to my continuum Amnesty is secular because faith is not a collective aspect of its identity and does not in any way fuel its practice.

These examples show that, to qualify as faith-based, faith needs to be embedded in the organization's operational structures rather than just existing as a source of personal motivation for individual employees. The use of a continuum helps one to understand the different ways in which faith structures and shapes an organization. For example, faith may stimulate fund-raising by encouraging those who share a faith to contribute. An FBO might target religious institutions, congregations and communities in the hope that their shared faith will motivate them to give generously. Faith may, however, also determine what development priorities are pursued or practices adopted. It may act more powerfully as a guiding force to steer an organization towards a particular concept of development. Religious teachings and leaders may be consulted in setting development agendas.[8] For these organizations, faith is not just an emotional drive that motivates them to act, but also a source of inspiration and knowledge. Faith may become embedded in an organization's everyday practices, with the FBO setting aside distinct religious spaces to use for collective and individual reflection.[9] Some FBOs incorporate time for prayer and meditation to allow individual members to reflect on the benefits their actions bring. In these examples, faith is a strong dimension in both the conception and practice of development.

Once the impact of faith on shaping an organization's identity has been examined, the next step is to consider if these differences lead to different practices. One way of analysing the translation of faith into action is through the visual representation of where individual FBOs lie within a wider aid chain consisting of multilateral agencies (World Bank, International Monetary Fund), secular NGOs, national governments, field agencies and community-based organizations. Morse and McNamara[10] have devised a useful conceptual framework for this purpose. Following the distribution of funds from governments, the World Bank and IMF, different types of organizations are located in different parts of the aid chain. The domain of the donor agencies includes secular NGOs (organizations operating outside direct government control like Oxfam and Save the Children), faith-based organizations (like CAFOD, Christian Aid and World Vision) and government organizations. Aid flows to 'field agencies' consisting mainly of NGOs and FBOs, which are positioned as intermediaries between donors and the final strand of development organization, 'the beneficiaries'. Intermediary organizations may be national or international. Oxfam and CAFOD, for example, set up field agencies

in countries where national organizations do not exist. The beneficiaries are located in the public domain and consist largely of
community-based organizations, some of which will be faith based
(for example church groups), but they can also be individuals,
households, communities and companies, all of which are potential
recipients of donor funds.

As the language used to separate donors 'with money' from
beneficiaries 'without money' suggests, power is deeply embedded in
the aid dissemination system. Power affects the relationships that
emerge from this chain and makes equal partnership unlikely.
Despite Morse and McNamara's visual depiction of a sideways chain,
aid clearly flows downwards from global organizations such as the
World Bank and IMF. Neoliberal economics determines the development agendas of the World Bank and IMF.[11] The other links in the
chain, regardless of 'faith', have to negotiate against this hegemony.
As my case studies show, power limits the effectiveness of organizations at every level. I shall now examine three groups of FBOs
whose work can be located at different points on the chain. By
positioning each organization along this wider chain, I can consider
the constraints and limitations of the work they do while highlighting how faith gets embedded in the FBO's organizational structures.

Community-level Organizations

Tyndale claimed that spiritual organizations brought a unique and
successful approach to development work.

> Spirituality is used here in the sense of the dynamic, life giving
> energy that can arise both collectively and individually in
> connection with a personal quest for the true purpose,
> meaning or reality of life. It refers to an existential experience
> that is described in many stories as 'personal transformation'.[12]

Tyndale highlights the spiritual component of their work as the
unique characteristic distinguishing them from their secular counterparts. Clashes between local FBOs and Western donors often revolve
around alternative concepts of what development means. Tyndale

argues that for these organizations development is perceived as a lifelong process of nurturing spiritual growth. As a result of focusing on the spiritual dimension of life other forms of development will evolve, including economic, political and social.

Tyndale's case studies of spiritually-grounded FBOs provide a convincing twofold critique of Western development practices. She states that spiritually-inspired FBOs offer a stark alternative to many NGOs caught in a Western Eurocentric approach to development. Certainly, many critics of Western models of development[13] note the common practice of measuring outcomes against universally conceived and implemented development objectives. The release of new donor money is dependent on the successful achievement of these goals. Some anthropologists of development[14] argue that development projects designed outside local contexts fail to respond to local needs and are not supported by 'target' communities (a critique much of the research in this volume endorses).

In her case studies, Tyndale noted a deliberate resistance to being drawn into a scientific evaluation and preconditioned process. Western donors lean on successful community-level FBOs to 'scale up' their activities, which the latter experience as further pressure.[15] Tyndale expressed concern that if the projects were to be replicated elsewhere the distinctness of their localized identity would be lost. In her presentation of community FBOs, however, she focused on the philosophy of the organizations rather than offering clear empirical evidence that faith translates into effective development practice. The location of these community-focused FBOs in the aid chain suggests, at least at times, that they must receive money from donor or intermediary organizations. It is therefore unlikely that they are able to sidestep the pervasive nature of how power operates through the chain. In other words, to receive money they have been positioned as beneficiaries (regardless of whether they see themselves as such). Money may not always be given to them without preconditions.

What these case studies show is that local FBOs often have a strong sense of the importance of beliefs and values for people living in material poverty. A shared cosmology cements collective identity, which in turn preserves a much needed sense of dignity. Collective identities bind communities, thus enabling them to act together at times of crisis and suffering. This collectivity may offer an alternative to Western development models. In other words, pulling together and sharing whatever resources they have in order to help each other through a time of crisis does not rely on external aid. Self-reliance allows communities to resist being pulled into a subservient role as beneficiaries of someone else's money. Local FBOs at times provide the direction and momentum for collective action.

The case study I present below corroborates Tyndale's assertion that communities often welcome and support locally-rooted FBOs motivated by spiritual convictions. These organizations forge fruitful partnerships at the community level of the aid chain, even though donor demands at times constrain their practices. Many community-based Gandhian organizations in India can be described as spiritually inspired because at heart they remain committed to a philosophy that perceives of life as a spiritual journey that involves building communities founded on equal, respectful relationships. In writing about the influence of the Gandhian movement on Indian grass-roots development, Kumar[16] refers to FBOs that stress the importance of living according to Gandhi's core ideal of *gram seva* – village service. In fact, service is the driving force behind the actions of those who work for Gandhian organizations. In serving poor communities they gain satisfaction from knowing that they have fulfilled their *dharma* or duty. Humility and mutuality shape the development approach and emphasize the centrality of reciprocity. Those who work in the service of others receive as much as they give. *Gram seva* connects followers to Gandhi's vision of social equality, the achievement of which is the duty of every individual regardless of his or her social position (caste), faith and material circumstances.

The Village Development Project, Jodhpur (VDPJ) is a specific example of an organization firmly rooted in the rural communities of Jodhpur district, Rajasthan whose members live according to these principles. VDPJ was founded in 1983 and is based on the Gandhian philosophy of self-reliance. It works towards rehabilitating drought-affected marginalized rural communities through village ownership and control of the environment, institutions and relations. One VDPJ member described its work to me as follows:

VDJP is a voluntary organization that takes a Gandhian approach to rural development by working with the poor of the desert to enable them to help themselves. Since its inception in 1983, VDPJ has worked with over 50,000 desert families across 850 villages in Rajasthan, and has established over 300 Village Development Committees.

VDPJ has achieved notable success in a variety of projects from water harvesting and irrigation to community health initiatives. It believes that 'hard work, spirit of service and commitment earned them the trust of the rural community that was necessary to implement their ideas.'[17] My ethnographic research of the organization conducted during a field trip in 2003 revealed a visible connection between the spirituality of VDPJ members and their approach to development work. The organization's members, who would live and work in field centres for periods of time before returning to their families, followed a daily schedule similar to that of a religious ashram.[18] While inhabiting the centre they would follow a strict daily routine that began and ended with a period of quiet meditative reflection. During these times members were urged to share their thoughts and feelings about the work they were doing. This time was used critically to evaluate the work of the organization, but it also acted to deepen spiritual and emotional commitments to the communities alongside which they lived.

Since local people are employed wherever possible, the organization is deeply embedded in the geography of the place. This embeddedness has over time won VDPJ the support of local people, who participate in the decision-making processes at regular village-level meetings at which projects are planned and discussed. Although it cannot be proved empirically that this approach is unique or more successful than others in achieving development outcomes, this case highlights how faith generates commitment, which in turn results in a deep connection between the FBO and local communities.

Community members recognize this commitment and respond respectfully. They become receptive to the development views of the FBO. The FBO workforce can then use this platform to present project ideas and concepts of change.

The respect that VDPJ commands explains the success of its community health-care projects.[19] A travelling medical team of doctors and nurses supports local women in the field who are trained in basic primary-health practices. The community health team includes numerous Rajput women, many of whom practise strict purdah[20] and whose high-caste identity often marginalizes them from employment opportunities and excludes them from public spaces. The VDPJ was able to target this group of women for employment as community health workers because the respect it commands from local people meant it was able to persuade reluctant husbands that the role of a community health worker was appropriate for their Rajput wives.

Clearly, the Rajput women's participation in the community health-care programme in no way challenges the patriarchal system that gives husbands the authority to sanction their wives' movements. But, as employees, the women now have access to credit schemes designed to increase their economic decision-making power. In turn, these schemes provide them with a degree of financial freedom, thus loosening some of the control their husbands have over them. Although other secular NGOs may be able to claim similar successes, the VDPJ's approach is spiritually rooted, with motivation sustained twice daily through collective prayer and individual contemplation. This shows that faith is deeply ingrained in the day-to-day structure of this FBO, shaping its identity and practice.

As detailed below, tensions arising during negotiations with its donor, a denominational fund-raising organization in the UK, challenges the ideal practice described above.[21] The fraught relationship that ensues highlights how the realities of power affect the work of at least some FBOs.

Intermediary Organizations

FBOs such as Christian Aid and CAFOD (there are many more) often take on the role of intermediary agencies. On the website for each organization Christian principles are emphasized as the source of motivation for the work they do. Such organizations offer Christians and non Christians the opportunity to give money to those perceived to be materially less fortunate than they are. Secular donors may feel that giving money to these organizations increases the likelihood of it being put to good use. In other words, the religious aspect in the identity of these organizations creates an image of altruism and moral discipline. This is visible in these organizations' mission statements. 'Underpinning CAFOD's work is a deeply held set of values that are central to the organization's ethos and identity. We act based on principles of compassion, solidarity, stewardship and hope.' CAFOD goes on to describe itself as 'the international aid agency of the Catholic Church in England and Wales, sharing in the Church's task of transforming the world to reflect the Kingdom of God, through solidarity with the poor and action for justice.'[22]

Christian Aid articulates similar sentiments through its website:

We believe that all people are created equal, with inherent dignity and infinite worth. Individual human needs must always come first, ahead of dogma, ideology or political necessity. We know that each one of us, in all our diversity and varied talents, can make a real difference in the battle to end poverty and injustice. Poverty is a condition created by an unjust society, denying people access to, and control over, the resources they need to live a full life. So we take the side of poor and marginalized people as they struggle to realize their civil, political, economic, social and cultural rights.[23]

Both organizations stress that they work through partnerships with locally-based organizations. Morse and McNamara[24] examine how partnership works between various levels of Catholic agencies. The chain of partnership begins at the level of national governments and international donor institutions, which in turn give money to Catholic donor agencies such as CAFOD. CAFOD then funds projects that Catholic field agencies manage and that channel resources into community-based organizations, which are often attached to churches. In highlighting how aid flows along a chain, Morse and McNamara show the hierarchical nature of development practice and starkly relate resources to decision-making power. Money is not given at any level of this chain without preconditions. These often reflect global and/or national development priorities and do not always support local-level concerns. Morse and McNamara focus on relationships at the starting point of this chain and expose how tensions arising when non-Catholic donors subcontract projects to Catholic donor agencies. The conditions of the subcontract often disrespect the religious worldview of the Catholic donor agency. Agencies such as CAFOD are forced to work differently, making it hard for them to fulfil their vision of working in 'solidarity with the poor'. Working in solidarity requires close partnerships at a community level. Yet CAFOD, according to Morse and McNamara, is forced to align more closely with the interests of the national donors in order to secure the funding needed to carry out its work. Furthermore, compliance with a secular approach to project planning and evaluation is a necessity. If analysed against my continuum, intermediary FBOs tend to have a strong denominational identity, but the faith of their members does not always create a close, locally responsive style of practice.

In the next chapter I analyse the work of a UK donor/intermediary FBO by focusing on its relationships with communities and specifically with the local partner organization it funds (VDPJ). I argue that its development activities make both positive and negative contributions to the lives of the Rajasthani people with whom it works. Faith is a strong motivating force behind its work. The organizational structures rely on donations from church groups (all denominations) across the UK and also the UK government through grants awarded by the Department for International Development (DFID). Individual churches work with this agency to set up specific projects in rural Rajasthan. Groups are then encouraged to visit project sites to see the fruits of their efforts. Often donors are acknowledged for projects, such as building a well or school, through the ceremonial unveiling of a plaque. These actions embed visible links between church groups, individual donors and the local beneficiaries of money given in accordance with the Christian concept of social justice. In this way, channels are maintained between the various parts of the aid chain that link individual donors (church-goers) to faith-based intermediary agency, to partner community organizations in rural Rajasthan and on down to local Rajasthani villagers. This chain is effective in getting money to drought-stricken communities that lack welfare services, health and education.

Prayer plays an important part in sustaining relationships between the different levels of the structure, but the sheer physical distance between the faithful who give the money and the people on whom they believe it will have an impact renders the relationship problematic. To sustain the link they rely on a created image of a destitute Rajasthani villager, often a young veiled woman pictured in the middle of dry cracked earth with a water pot on her head. My ethnographic studies into the lives of Rajasthani women[25] and research conducted by Gold and Raheja[26] challenge this bleak view of women's lives in this area. Such a narrow, one-sided depiction of Rajasthan gives a biased impression of community life in the area. In fact, fixating on fictitious images can only blind the onlooker to the complex array of experiences and views present in any location.

The lack of physical face-to-face dialogue means that the power relationship between the intermediary and the 'recipients' goes unnoticed and unchallenged. The intermediaries believe their money is having a positive benefit, yet, in the absence of communication between them and those they describes as their 'partners', it is more likely that they are making decisions on behalf of 'others'. This aid chain disempowers the community organization, in this case VDPJ. Rather than respecting and supporting the close relationship VDPJ has with local communities, an external agenda is imposed. The intermediary FBO experiences pressure from its largest secular donor, DFID, which expects money to be spent in the areas it prioritizes. Furthermore, the intermediary must report back to DFID with clear evidence that development objectives have been achieved. This process of aid dissemination is rigid and stands in the way of the 'faith' of the intermediary creating an open dialogue through which shared goals may be reached with VDPJ.

Both VDPJ and the Rajasthani communities with which it works are rendered passive and subservient in this chain of development aid. If the 'targeted' Rajasthani communities experience the FBO's approach as disempowering, they are unlikely to cooperate and the intermediary's efforts will fail to bring good results. In fact, there was a breakdown in the relationship between Water for Rajasthan (WFR) and another of its Gandhian partner organizations Village Service Rajasthan (VSR). As described in Chapter 6, after 20 years of partnership, the relationship between VSR and its UK intermediary was ended. VSR declared that it would rather go without funding than conform to a development agenda that was unresponsive to local needs. Although WFR and VDPJ are still working closely, the story of the breakdown of another WFR partnership reveals the fragility of development relationships.

Missionary Organizations

Comparing the first two groups of FBOs with the last gives us a clearer picture of why some FBOs make a more positive contribution to development than others. The leaders of PEACE Plan are reluctant to allow the organization to be viewed as an FBO. In fact, they do not believe its work conforms to mainstream 'development' because its focus is on encouraging people to join the Kingdom of God rather than on improving their material wellbeing, as is clearly stated in the organization's objectives.

> The peace plan is a massive effort to mobilize one billion Christians around the world into an outreach effort to attach the five global, evil giants of our day. These are the world's biggest problems, affecting billions, not just millions of people: spiritual emptiness, corrupt leadership, poverty, disease and illiteracy.
>
> These big global giants ravage the lives of billions of people worldwide and all work together to constrain them and cut them off from knowing the saving grace of a loving God who sent his son, Jesus Christ, to die for their sins allowing them eternal hope and security. There is no organization or govern-

ment that can effectively eradicate these giants. The only successful solution is the global church of Jesus Christ.[27]

I emailed the organization for clarification on how it understood its identity and purpose. I asked about its approach to development: 'PEACE is not an organization or an agency. It is a model of how to do church missions that our church, Saddleback, teaches.' I then asked: 'I understand that you are not an aid agency, but am I correct in thinking that part of your mission does involve development work, that is tackling issues related to poverty? The reply came back:

> In a sense it does. Our church is working on solutions to these problems; however, our focus remains training churches by giving them a broader more general approach that mainly deals with the rethinking of strategy. If you came to our event you would hear much about overall strategy in terms of mobilization of the congregation, looking for best principles when dealing with doing mission work, but nothing really specific on how to address each of the giants (poverty, spiritual emptiness, corrupt leadership, pandemic disease, and illiteracy).
>
> The training revolves around what is PEACE, why is it best as a model for missions, the tools we give to implement PEACE, and mobilizing the membership to engage in PEACE. The content and material is specifically addressed to church leaders and pastors who are thinking of doing PEACE in their congregations. If you think that this would be beneficial for you and your studies then please come by all means.

The responses confused me. PEACE is clearly a church-based organization that believes it has devised a successful approach to mobilizing its followers into action. Once generated, this energy can then be directed at tackling the global giants identified above, the first being spiritual emptiness. The mobilized reach out beyond their church community in an attempt to draw others in and to fill their spiritual void. This approach to religious mobilization has been packaged and marketed to other churches and leaders, and seems to follow similar patterns to those used by the early colonial mission organizations.[28]

PEACE understands mobilization as the act of persuading others to join the mission through the adoption of Christian values and principles. I include PEACE in a third group of missionary organizations, but acknowledge that not all missionary organizations pursue conversion practices and many in fact concentrate on material development through a more culturally sensitive approach than the one PEACE adopts. My continuum needs to include a group typified by the term 'missionary' because several FBDOs observe problematic development practices. Clarke[29] alerts us to the fact that proselytizing organizations can benefit from being aligned with culturally and religiously sensitive FBDOs. The above statement relays a clear desire to see more people convert to Christianity. It goes on to state that it is from within this religious identity that the world's biggest development problems can be challenged. 'Conversion' characterizes PEACE's development objective and strategy.

The 'ideal' definition of development given at the start of this chapter sees it as a material and spiritual process requiring culturally and religiously inclusive practice. Inclusive practice can be seen successfully in the work of many community-based FBOs, but, as stated, pressure to fulfil their donors' agendas compromises the work of many locally-rooted FBOs. PEACE Plan locates itself in the heart of poor rural communities and brings with it funding that it is free to use to achieve its objective. As such, it is not constrained by the chain of aid in the same way as other FBDOs. Furthermore, this organization clearly believes in the importance of spiritual development out of which material benefits may follow. On the face of it, PEACE Plan seems to share many of the VDPJ's characteristics and objectives. A close comparison between the two organizations allows one to make an important critical contrast. PEACE Plan is a missionary organization because its sole emphasis is on Christian spiritual development. VDPJ supports an autonomous spiritual journey in which individuals follow the path best suited to them. This view is influenced by Gandhi's humanistic and interfaith perspective. Furthermore, VDPJ acknowledges material wellbeing as a vital part of spiritual growth. Because spirituality needs to be nurtured by a healthy body and mind, material development is given high priority. Although some Rwandans may welcome the conversion experience PEACE offers them, the approach taken excludes those who wish to preserve a different cultural and religious identity. Whenever an approach excludes some, a power dynamic is constructed.

Conclusion

My aim has been to compare and contrast different FBOs. I wanted to understand what 'faith' brings to development and to assess whether the faith/development interface is always positive.[30] I have argued that 'faith' does have a positive contribution to make to development. It motivates adherents both to give generously to the poor and to strive in their actions towards eradicating inequalities and, for many communities, it shapes the way people view the world and how they understand their place within it. These perceptions of the world also influence people's notions of how the world should be, which in turn affects their concepts of development. In this chapter I have argued that some faith-based development organizations appreciate and respect the angle that faith creates and from which adherents can view the world. Many FBOs are also sensitive to the different visions of development that emerge from different faith perspectives. As stated throughout this chapter, ideal development practice should be responsive to culturally and religiously rooted visions. Practice should be flexible in meeting the needs that emerge locally and should not be rigidly committed to achieving goals set by donors who are far removed from and culturally insensitive to life in the community. As an analytical focus, faith allows close relationships to form between development agencies and local people. Reciprocal dialogue then becomes possible and the possibility of reaching a consensus about development priorities becomes more likely.

The objective of this chapter has been to discern how faith may or may not translate into a distinct practice. I argued that while faith has the potential to yield good results, it can also marginalize local people and disregard their views and perceptions of development. I sought first to clarify what makes an organization an FBO and then critically to assess the work of different organizations. It became clear that FBOs vary widely in both their structures and operational approaches. Power limits the effectiveness of many organizations either because FBOs at the bottom of the aid chain are forced to negotiate with intermediaries and donors with a vision of development that does not reflect local needs and concerns or because some FBOs deliberately seek to impose their own agenda on others through their proselytizing mission. They wield power by promising salvation and a better life to the poor if they embrace their organization's religious identity.

Through my case example of an intermediary FBO I showed how faith can block fruitful dialogue between intermediaries and community-based FBOs as well as between intermediaries and local people. Through prayer and quiet reflection the members of the intermediary FBO in question conjured up the image of a destitute Rajasthani woman to represent the kind of person they wished to help in rural Rajasthan. Dialogue with this fictitious image removed the need, in the minds of the intermediaries, to forge physical relationships with local people. Furthermore, they were so sure that they 'knew' and understood this community's development needs that they disregarded the knowledge and insights the local FBO had gained from years of loyal commitment to local villagers. The situation, however, is even more complex. The intermediary is put under pressure by its secular donors who want to see targets met and evaluated according to preconceived agendas and assessment grids. The FBO is pulled into a secular way of working that perhaps limits the positive impact its 'faith' can have on its practice. In this case, the combination of hierarchical pressure from within the aid chain and lack of locally responsive practice meant that faith failed to bring positive results.

Employing two analytical frameworks to compare a range of FBOs allowed one to see their variations more clearly. I assessed the differences between three groups on a continuum. The first group, community-level organizations, were shown to be more likely to achieve culturally and religiously sensitive results than the other two groups. Here, faith both motivated them to do the development work in the first place and shaped the distinct practice the organization adopted. The second group, the intermediaries who work with both donors (who are often secular) and community FBOs, are in a tricky position and are rarely able to deliver the kind of practice they intend. The intermediaries' faith directs their denominational fund-raising activities and motivates individual members in this regard, but it does not provide close insight into the lives of others. In the third group, the mission-led organizations, faith has an impact on the organization's practice but fails to produce reflective or responsive development.

My analysis of the variations between FBOs through the aid chain shows that faith impacts differently on the identity and practice of FBOs. It also shows that the powerful dictates of donor agencies at the top of the chain can constrain FBOs as much as much as they do secular organizations. To conclude, faith can bring positive development practices, but caution, clarification and constant evaluation are required to ensure that the factors that inhibit the success of FBOs are curbed. This venture is even more important if FBOs continue to become ever more prominent in the development business.

Chapter 5

Can Compassion Bring Results? Reflections on the Work of an Intermediary FBO

I N this chapter I focus on a particular type of FBO – the intermediary. As described in the previous chapter, the intermediary in question, referred to by the pseudonym 'Water for Rajasthan' (WFR), is Christian, British based and operates in rural Rajasthan in partnership with a number of Gandhian grass-roots or community-level organizations. I shall explore to what extent a Christian notion of compassion motivates people who choose to work for Christian faith-based organizations. I want to understand the impact of compassion on effective development practice. A link between the Christian notion of compassion and a commitment to helping the poor is not surprising, but is it productive? I shall ask if compassionate feelings contribute anything to the alleviation of poverty. In other words, does compassion actually bring results? It is admirable to feel compassion and be motivated by it, but do people who act with compassion do any good?

I begin by developing the discussion from the last chapter, which sought to define an FBO and take it further by comparing WFR with its secular counterparts. I take a close look at one FBO with a view to extracting its unique non-secular features and highlight the distinct characteristics of many Western faith-based development organizations that operate as intermediaries to channel money from individuals and institutions to community-level organizations. I present a balanced critique of this organization's work, claiming that it avoids the usual short-term approach that many development organizations adopt. I argue generally that FBOs frequently display long-term commitments to local communities. This commitment, development critics argue, is missing from the work of many secular NGOs. Potentially, FBOs could solve at least one problem that other NGOs face – lack of long-term commitment. Through my case study I pinpoint compassion as the source of this commitment and trace its biblical origin. I introduce a critical perspective by arguing that compassion does not automatically result in effective poverty alleviation. An analysis of the workings of WFR show how in the context of this example faith can result in a blindness that prevents its members from really seeing the local people they claim to help.

Critiques of Development Practice

In this chapter I compare the practice and vision of WFR with the commonly expressed critiques familiar now to both practitioners and researchers of development. There is much in the references cited in this book about the limitations of Western NGOs to bring about positive social development.[1] These scholars hold that NGOs are so anxious to fix problems resulting from poverty that they often put projects together in haste without adequate reflection. NGOs often bypass consultation with target communities to reduce the time scale and thus reduce costs. In *Whose Development? An Ethnography of Aid*, Crewe and Harrison[2] present a bleak picture of a deteriorating improving situation in the developing world. These scholars highlight the over eager and brash approach of NGOs, stating that projects fail because community participation in project planning and implementation is overlooked. The knowledge local people possess about their own environment is ignored.

Development as it currently stands is failing to achieve the kinds of results we should expect, considering what huge budgets many of the larger NGOs command – clearly something is wrong. De Sousa Santos states: 'suffice it to recall how the great promises of modernity remain unfilled or how their fulfilment has turned out to have perverse effects.'[3] He lists statistics that reveal an ever widening gap between the rich and poor.

Various attempts have been made to explain why, despite the financial input, NGOs have failed to reduce this gap. Pottier[4] suggests that a large part of the problem is the reluctance of NGOs to make long-term commitments to the communities they 'target'. In their eagerness to see the impact of aid maximized with quick, cheap results, donors put pressure on NGOs to replicate the same projects in one region after another. Sustained development, however, is expensive and requires extensive time commitments; effective development responds to people's 'real needs'.[5] NGO workers need to form close relationships with members of the local community if the 'givers of aid' are to identify and respond directly to the requirements of the 'receivers of aid'. Those involved in development work must be motivated by a desire to understand on a personal level those they are trying to help.

As mentioned in Chapter 1, in an attempt to understand what type of NGO is effective in forging the kind of positive relationship with target communities outlined above, the UK Department for International Development (DFID) turned its attention to FBOs. In March 2004 it commissioned a 'diagnostic study and workshop on DFID's engagement with faith groups and the role of faith groups in poverty reduction'.[6] The objective of the study was to ascertain to what extent FBOs could alleviate patterns of poverty and inequality; also, DFID wanted to find out what FBOs did differently from their secular counterparts. The initial report explored the history of various prominent FBOs from the world's main religions and concluded that faith was a vital motivational force behind their work. The report recommended further research to examine critically the effectiveness of these FBOs' work. In response to this recommendation, in March 2005 DFID commissioned a research consortium to generate detailed policy-related research on faith and development.[7]

What Exactly do FBOs Offer?

By commissioning both the diagnostic study and the research, DFID clearly believes that FBOs are doing something right in comparison with their secular counterparts. I shall now turn my attention to the question of what exactly FBOs offer. Taylor, in his book *Not Angels but Agencies*, asks: 'are religious FBOs merely Oxfam with Hymns?'[8] The suggestion that the work of FBOs may provide a model for a more consistent and fruitful approach to project planning and intervention requires further study and research. Tyndale suggests that faith groups:

> are more firmly rooted or have better networks in poor communities than the non-religious ones and that religious leaders are trusted more than any others. Faith-based organizations are thus seen as essential agents both for influencing the opinions and attitudes of their followers and for carrying out development work at the grass roots.[9]

I share Tyndale's high regard for the work of FBOs, though with some reservations. Although my experience of working with an intermediary FBO in rural Rajasthan (WFR)[10] left me rather critical of the way it operated, there was a level of commitment among its members, a mixture of Anglicans and Catholics, which I feel sure was sustained by their faith. Although its social development projects regularly encounter barriers and other problems, the WFR has maintained a presence in the same part of Rajasthan for more than 30 years, though, as I show in Chapter 6, it has changed its local partnerships. Long-term commitment, which Pottier believes is vital for sustaining positive development practices, is present in this FBO. And, from the members' conversations and actions, it was clear that they wanted to form relationships with the rural poor of Rajasthan.

Both Harcourt and Tyndale[11] believe that spirituality provides FBO members with a vital source of commitment and motivation. The dedication of WFR officers is visible in the religious language and symbolism they use to project their collective vision for the people of Rajasthan. In fact, their religious beliefs gave them the incentive to remain in the Rajasthani villagers' lives. However, my view departs from that of Tyndale and Harcourt who hold that faith ensures a person-to-person relationship with the poor. I believe that while faith may sustain an enduring link between people and places, it does not automatically result in meaningful dialogue. In my case study I in fact noted a lack of fruitful interaction between the FBO and the people it sought to help, which prevented effective interventions being maintained. In an examination of the role of religion in the work of FBOs, Clarke[12] describes how the teachings of the faith are subsidiary to broader humanitarian principles. While faith is important in mobilizing staff and supporters and can be used to convert or convince others of the need to take a particular course of action, it can also act in an exclusive way by forming the sole platform for engagement with a chosen group of recipients. It comes through strongly in all the work reviewed so far in this chapter and in the previous one that faith acts first and foremost as a source of motivation for the FBO's members.

Tracing the Roots of Christian Compassion

The desire to help the villagers of Rajasthan is rooted in the Christian notion of compassion. In my case study – as in most Christian FBOs – this motivation is described in terms of compassion. The Christian notion of compassion comes from the Greek verb *splagchnizesthai*,[13] which, according to Turner, appears in biblical Greek and resonates in new Christian and Jewish literature. Liddell and Scott[14] translate the verb to mean an internal bodily feeling experienced in the heart, lungs and liver. The metaphor 'to have compassion for' is described as being seated in the heart. Compassion is clearly a powerful emotion that has the capacity to influence behaviour.

Compassion is closely associated with both the notion of Christian duty and spirituality. This link between feeling compassion and the sense of duty that results from that emotion explains the dedication and long-term commitment of the staff of the FBO I observed. Symbolic expressions of the Christian notion of compassion through images of Christ helping the poor and dying embed a sense of duty into believers. In addition, the close relationship that Jesus is shown to have had with the poor encourages his followers to seek the same connection with those they wish to help.[15] The focus placed on the relationship with the poor explains why many FBOs remain present year after year. In other words, once a relationship is formed it is hard to leave those who are in need.

The desire to help the weak and needy is more entrenched and long-standing in those who articulate and experience compassion through religion. I am not saying that the members of a secular NGO lack compassion, but merely that the motivation felt is not expressed through such an elaborate symbolic narrative that stresses the forging of bonds between those who have and those who are without. It is therefore easier for a secular NGO worker to accept the existence of the insurmountable difficulties that prevent successful outcomes and leave a community to move onto the next.

The biblical roots of compassion can be traced to the establishment of an early Christian community founded on mutual love and the desire to help one another. In John's Letters it reads: 'The children of God and the children of the devil are revealed in this way, all who do not do what is right are not from God, nor are those who do not love their brothers and sisters.'[16] McGinn describes how the Christian concept of the spirit is present in all of us and is thought to compensate for the loss of Christ.[17] The spirit provides Christians with spiritual love and compassion; this was the gift bestowed upon Christ's followers. 'The resurrection of Jesus was the proof that he was this eschatological messiah, and for this reason the resurrection was associated with the giving of the spirit first to the disciples and then also to "all flesh" in the event of Pentecost.'[18] Paul taught that all members of the Christian community were bearers of the spirit, which exists to strengthen and comfort Christians until Christ's second coming. Paul stresses the unity and equality of God's gift of love (through the spirit) in that all members have the same quality and are obliged to work with others to maintain and strengthen the community.[19]

These examples clearly highlight the centrality of the desire to help others in Christianity. For example, Christian Aid, another Christian FBO, stresses how God's concern for the poor is a fundamental part of the biblical message. The following quote taken from Hebrews 13 (12) is posted on its website to highlight the importance of the Christian faith in the work they do. 'Do not neglect to show hospitality to strangers for by doing that some have entertained angels without knowing it.'[20] Clearly, Christian Aid feels that the action of helping the poor will be rewarded by God.

A Critical Perspective on Compassion

My case study shows that compassion by itself cannot bring good results. In fact, projects fuelled solely by compassion have limited impact. Compassion operates through symbolic projections of an objectified image of suffering. To be expressed it must be directed towards an object of pity and, in the context of the developing world, an image of an underdeveloped 'Other' has emerged. This symbolic construction of the 'Other' blocks the potential for direct dialogue with target groups and communities. The relationship is one sided in that the compassionate people are attempting to communicate with a fictitious image created solely for the purpose of helping them to fulfil their religious obligation.

WFR failed to assess its work critically enough in that it assumed that since its actions were motivated by compassion they would automatically bring good results and benefit the less fortunate. This assumption stems from the Christian origin of the term compassion, which is linked to the gift of the spirit and the obligation to follow the example set by Christ. Biblical accounts describing the life of Jesus suggest that everything he did brought good results. There was certainly no need for him to stand back and assess the effectiveness of his interventions.

Problems with gift giving

Although WFR stresses the desire to give to the needy, what it actually gives by way of aid is no different from what secular NGOs give. Stirrat and Henkel state that the act of giving in development is ethically problematic: 'here the act of receiving is hedged with conditionality at best, while at worst the gift may become a form, a patronage and a means of control.'[21] Aid is a vehicle through which the giver can attain dominance over the Other. Stirrat and Henkel go on to state that missionary organizations are in fact worse than secular NGOs. Although all aid agencies – FBOs and NGOs – require the receivers of their aid to conform to certain predetermined conditions, traditional missionary organizations require the Other to convert to a particular form of Christianity.[22] FBOs and secular NGOs insist on the Other conforming to their orthodoxies, which are embedded in participatory techniques designed to aid the transformation of the Other to the state of liberated person; the process of conversion to the will of the Other remains in both cases.

Stirrat and Henkel claim that the transformation of the Other can happen in a development context because the gift of aid is pure in that it does not require anything material in return.[23] This places the receivers of the gift in a position of indebtedness and they become pliable to the will of the Other. This process of giving is not concerned with what the receiver actually wants. As these scholars point out, there is a contradiction between an NGO agenda that wants people to realize that the West has got it right and the desires of local people for material goods. While local people have no desire to be anyone other than themselves, it is realistic to assume that they wish to improve their material standard of living and may be willing to comply with the will of the Other to achieve it. Parry sees the link between the free gift and salvation as purely a preoccupation of Western NGOs,[24] but believes that the gift could be reciprocal if givers would let go of their desire to transform the Other and raise the potential for their own growth through dialogue with others. An organization's faith sometimes hinders this reciprocal dialogue. Having a religion implies certainty that the path of that religion is the right one; people who are convinced that their faith holds all the answers to human existence are less likely to be open to other ways of living and being. The giving of aid therefore is likely to follow the pattern Stirrat and Henkel described in which receiving aid is tied to an expectation that the recipient will conform to the (religious) expectations of the giver. This exploration of aid as a form of gift giving is continued in the next chapter.

Background information to case study

I shall now analyse these arguments further through a specific case study of WFR. This FBO was founded in 1987 as a donor and then intermediary[25] to raise money to help the victims of the horrific drought in Rajasthan that year. WFR was primarily concerned with providing relief in the form of water, food and fodder. Gradually, it began to embark on longer-term social development projects, prioritizing health care and education. WFR operates through various partner organizations, all of which belong to the Gandhian movement, so it has a commitment to Gandhian ideology and principles. It predominantly raises money in the UK through a network of churches (all denominations). Most members of its board are practising Catholics or Anglicans.[26]

The homogenized image of the Rajasthani villager

My experience of this FBO, particularly the time I spent visiting the projects it funds in Rajasthan in January 2001, raised certain concerns for me. I came to the conclusion that its representatives had constructed an Other out of Rajasthani villagers who was needy, destitute and the focus of their compassion. I believe that their overwhelming pity for the Other blocked any chance of clear-minded, detailed discussions into the causes and implications of disempowerment. Images of starving, dying Rajasthani villagers stirred the representatives to return home to raise more money. While I am not dismissing these responses, and believe them to be rooted in real concern, I question the effectiveness of a dialogue in which the imagined sufferings of an Other, positioned as such by those with money and therefore power (donors), form the focus for action.

When a singular Other is constructed, the complexities of the needs that are present in a community are rendered invisible. One image comes to represent the whole; the community becomes a homogenous unit with a shared identity (weak and needy). Differences between individuals are ignored and subsequent projects are based on misrepresentations of what those affected actually desire. My primary criticism is that WFR roots its objectives in a permanent picture of a suffering Other and the face it gives this Other appears prominently in all its literature.

The image is of a young, low-caste woman who seems to have walked miles in search of water. She stands alone in the middle of a parched desert, with her face veiled because purdah is observed in much of rural Rajasthan. To WFR the veiled face is symbolic of her oppression and her young age suggests weakness and vulnerability. However, quite a lot of research exists that dispels this myth of

Rajasthani women as weak and passive. Gold and Raheja, Harlan, Joshi, and Sax all argue that Rajasthani women are in fact the strongest members of these communities because they are responsible for keeping the family going.[27] If they give up, their families go hungry. Certainly, the most forceful and defiant individuals I met during my fieldwork in rural Rajasthan were women. The image of suffering that WFR projects contradicts the ethnographic data of anthropologists who had spent years living among women in rural communities in north India. The following statement appeared on a WFR poster during a fund-raising campaign:

> a little girl, watching as her mother struggles to carry heavy pots of water home many miles from the well every day, even if she is ill, seeing her eat only what is left over after the men of the family have eaten, struggling with tiredness and stress from anaemia and from bearing and looking after many children. She knows that the confinement of the house and the endless chores she helps with now will be her lot in the future. If she or her mother is ill there are no women doctors who can treat her in the remote village in which she lives. She has been conditioned since babyhood that she must not complain or answer back even if abused. She has little hope of ever learning to read or write.

I am not for a moment suggesting that life as a Rajasthani woman is without suffering, but this image is inaccurate. It distorts our understanding of the social reality. The woman was asked to stand and pose for the picture. She was not alone but walking with her friends. We know from ethnographic field research[28] that the youngest daughter-in-law of a house is responsible for collecting water and groups of young women make the daily trips together, thus taking advantage of the opportunity to spend time with other women of a similar age and social status. WFR, however, has manipulated the facts to construct an image of a vulnerable, desperate woman as representative of an 'underdeveloped' person from rural Rajasthan.

As this Other, the Rajasthani villager never reaches a post-suffering state (the same picture has been used for years). Her image is used to promote WFR and motivate others to help. All the money is directed towards a drought-ridden desert village frozen in time. While I appreciate the need for an image to raise funds and increase support, this one objectifies Rajasthani villagers as pitiful beings, which counteracts the purpose of constructing a meaningful dialogue between the giver and receiver of aid.

The impact of faith on the work of WFR

WFR does not proclaim an intention to convert Rajasthani villagers to Christianity, but it does at times invite them to join in the prayers (usually for rain). WFR representatives clearly see the god to whom the prayers are directed as Christian. In these instances, prayer is used as the mechanism through which 'outsiders' convey what they feel the community's development priorities should be. Prayer is thought to unite WFR with the community it seeks to help. In reality, however, it fails to do this, not least because the people among whom WFR works are Hindu and Hindu worship takes a very different form. It is inappropriate to attempt to unite two such dissimilar religions through the Christian concept of prayer. The Hindu word for worship is *bhakti*, which translates as devotional worship. Hindus, unlike Christians, do not pray to a single god in a linear manner. Instead, their worship is heterogeneous and involves honouring various aspects of the eternal soul *Brahman*.[29]

I recall one occasion particularly vividly when I travelled with about ten members of WFR to a village deep in the Thar Desert in the district of Jodhpur. On our arrival, the WFR officers asked some local workers to gather the local community together. They then asked everyone to join them in worship to express their concern about the worsening drought. After a WFR representative announced that 'we pray to a God we can all relate to', all the members of the FBO present put their hands together in Christian prayer and the villagers followed suit (in rural Rajasthan placing your hands together is a greeting). Since the Rajasthani villagers' response to the event was a mixture of curiosity and quite some hilarity, they were hardly passively complying with the WFR's wishes. I cannot recall the exact words but the prayer in essence was asking God for rain.

After the prayer had been recited, the representative leading it turned and asked the translator if he could ask the community to recite a prayer for peace, which begins *Om shanti, shanti, shanti*. This prayer is commonly recited by Gandhi devotees, for it reinforces Gandhi's concept of *ahimsa* or non-violence. It struck me as odd that the FBO representatives did not ask if they could take part in a performance of *puja*, which is the traditional form of Hindu worship. Instead, they directed the villagers towards a response that omitted to mention Rama (the most widely worshipped deity in the region) or any other Hindu image.

At the time I saw it as a staged attempt at interfaith dialogue. The FBO representatives rendered their dialogue safe by erecting a boundary between their faith and any other worldview that seemed uncomfortably incompatible with theirs. The Christian Other who controlled the aid relationship felt threatened by Hinduism's hetero-geneous concept of a deity/god. I found this refusal to engage with the real religious lives of Rajasthani people strange given that these communities' religious beliefs and rituals reveal a lot about their concerns and hopes for the future.[30] It seemed odd that an FBO that stressed its human connection with the local people should ignore such a valuable source of information and insight. The prayer used in these village gatherings was a one-sided dialogue, the only benefit of which was to make WFR members feel that they were following in Christ's footsteps. Prayer in this context gives the WFR represen-tatives the illusion that they have made a deep connection with the poor and needy. I believe the following passage from a WFR newsletter written by the director supports this view:

> Wherever we go we are struck by the overwhelming hos-pitality and the knowledge that they will share their last cup of water with a guest. So we avoid the situation of sharing their last grain of corn but we share their overwhelming joy when they get water. We share their prayers of thanks and we share in their celebration of what water means to them. We admire

their courage and resilience and laugh with the young boys and girls who are eager to learn. We are touched deeply by the heroism of our partners who have given up everything in their service to the poorest of the poor.

This passage is filled with Christian symbolism. First, the image of the 'cup' resonates with the cup Christ and his loyal disciples shared at his last supper. Drinking from a shared cup is seen in Christianity as emphasizing the unity and equality in God's Kingdom between all who drink from it. The words 'share their prayers', describe Christian worship. In his mind, to whom are these villagers praying? In this passage girls are depicted as learning to read and write, whereas in the previous passage that option was not available to them. There are only five months between these newsletters; things cannot have improved that much in that time. I argue that these messages serve to blur our access to the real situation. It is impossible to grasp the full complexity of poverty when the facts are distorted by emotive language driven by an image of a pitiful Other and a desire to see all united in Christ.

Example of a development project

By analysing the limitations of a specific WFR-funded project, I highlight how faith can blind WFR workers to the social realities of poverty and suffering. In 1995, WFR launched a project designed to break the cycle of prostitution for a group of 30 daughters of prostitutes. In the area surrounding a partner's headquarters there are three colonies of prostitutes, all located only a few metres from the busy highway. This route is heavily used by truck drivers transporting goods through Rajasthan, Gujarat and down to Mumbai; and it is they who are the prostitutes' primary clients.

Prostitutes are untouchables. Their occupation and status as unmarried women places them outside the traditional caste structure and they are labelled impure. The local community regards them with quiet disgust, though their presence is tolerated without hostility. The prostitutes remain unmarried for life, though they may take partners whose role could be compared with that of a pimp in that they organize the woman's clients and take a (large) slice of their earnings. These partners often live with the women and remain unmarried. It is accepted that any daughters the women bear will later (usually from the age of 12) join their mothers in prostitution. Although health workers visit the women and encourage them to use contraception as protection against STDs, few use them on the grounds that their clients do not like them. Instances of HIV/Aids have not been monitored but are thought to be high.

WFR, with a Gandhian partner organization, believed that these prostitutes were the most vulnerable group in the area and so decided to set up a project to help them. The project was designed to break the cycle into which children born to prostitutes found them-selves. WFR, perceiving these women as so desperately poor that they could not afford to educate, feed or dress their children prop-erly, implemented a project to raise expectations and life possibilities for a group of children born into these colonies. It was decided that the children had to be taken out of their environment and placed in a stable home where their daily needs would be met. However, it was stressed that the mothers must be involved in this process and they were asked to take responsibility for clothing the children, which included washing their garments.

A home was constructed for the children within the already exist-ing headquarters of the Gandhian organization. It consisted of two large rooms for use as a boys' and girls' dormitory, one bathroom and a kitchen. An additional room was added to house the headmaster (a retired schoolteacher whose role was to supervise the children's education). The children attended the local school and so mixed with other children from the area. Two local women were employed to cook and wash up after them. The children live in the home for the duration of the school term and return to their mothers for the holidays, but receive regular visits from their mothers throughout the school term. The children were selected on the grounds of their mother's willingness to cooperate with the programme and their commitment to seeing their children freed from prostitution. Priority was given to girls because they were perceived to be most at risk. The children came to the home between the ages of five and eight.

The project lasted for approximately eight years. When I first visited it in 1995 the children's home was being constructed. On my return in 2001 the children looked clean and healthy, but the sex ratio had swung dramatically in favour of boys – twenty boys to only ten girls. I heard horrific accounts of girls being kidnapped by pimps and taken to prostitute circles in Mumbai. Their greatest success story is 14-year old Devi, who is the oldest child in the home and who has recently become engaged. Although she is still young, this marked a success for the project because it meant that she would not become a prostitute. Marriage would raise her life expectations and improve her prospects.

I do not know what happened to the other children because no long-term plans had been drawn up and the project folded shortly after I left. Since it looked as if they would have to return home, it is difficult to measure what the children gained from the project in real terms. The project was founded on a series of misassumptions, which contributed to its lack of long-term success. For a start, prostitutes are not the poorest members of the rural community. In fact, they were among the few groups that could afford to pay for water when the village well dried up. They were in a position to pay at least something towards their children's education, but naturally jumped at the offer of free education when it was presented. Initially, they had to agree to send their daughters, but as I mentioned they gradually replaced them with their sons. I argue that the FBO had a simplistic overall picture of what leads a person into prostitution. Saeed's[31] research on prostitutes in South Asia suggests that control over their finances and freedom from marriage were the two aspects of the profession that attracted the women the most. In other words, destitution and exploitation were not the only factors that motivated or forced a woman into prostitution. The women also had to agree to try and seek alternative employment. WFR tried to give them sewing lessons, but they were not gifted seamstresses and could not compete in a market already saturated with well-made clothes and textiles.

Although WFR attempted to consult the women directly, it firmly believed that they were exploited, oppressed and grindingly poor. While social injustice, violence and poor health did afflict their lives, they were also active agents in shaping their futures according to what they saw as the most fruitful course of action. Educating their boys seemed the best strategy for achieving economic security and perhaps raising their social status a little. Their daughters would always find it hard to marry because of their association with such an impure profession. If their boys became educated they at least might be able to find employment away from their mother's profession.

Separation of intention and action

To sum up, while I concur that compassion can benefit development work because of the long-term commitment and high levels of motivation it brings, it is necessary to address the dangers inherent in conflating it with action. Actions that come from compassion are invariably assumed to be good and so therefore rarely attract criticism. It is difficult to condemn people who claim to act because of their deeply felt love for others. However, criticisms must be made, not least because some FBOs may well, as in this case, be directing their actions towards an imagined other. The imaginary person then becomes the focus for their empathy and blocks the potential for real face-to-face dialogue. Yet, such critical questions provoke defensive reactions. They can be thrown back with the retort, is love no longer good? The answer of course is that compassion is good but that it must be combined with a willingness to reflect on the impact of action and a real desire to get to know those towards whom the aid is directed.

Conclusion

Despite my criticisms, I believe that WFR's work has great potential as a vehicle for long-term poverty alleviation. The determination of its members to remain in the communities in which they work is a vital component in development practice. To bring results, however, compassion must be coupled with an ability to look critically at the impact of development interventions. One must separate motives (rooted in compassion) from the impact of the FBO's actions on others.[32] Weaving religious narratives into the image of poverty that WFR projects renders it rigid. The picture of a lonely, destitute

Rajasthani woman was objectified as the static figure towards which WFR could express its love and concern and this blinded the organization to the complexities of poverty. FBOs may find critical assessments of their practices challenging. Questioning the benefits of the organization's actions may entail questioning the worth of compassion itself, which, in turn, may challenge the validity of the religion from which these emotions arise. If the members of the FBO were to realize that the image of poverty towards which so many prayers are directed was in fact fictitious, they could take it as a challenge to their faith, which in turn could cause internal questioning of the legitimacy of that religious tradition. The potential loss of faith that such an upheaval may cause could be seen as an unacceptable risk for those whose religion defines their existence. However, if the risk is taken the results could be immense and a successful partnership made possible between actors in development.

Chapter 6

Competing Visions of Development: The Story of a Faith-based Partnership

I SHALL now tell the story of the 20-year partnership between 'Village Service Rajasthan' (VSR) and 'Water for Rajasthan' (WFR), the intermediary discussed in the previous two chapters. To recap, the former is a community-level organization whose members support Gandhi's ideals and philosophy and try to live life as he did, and the latter is a UK-based Christian (Catholic and Anglican) donor organization.[1]

Through examining the relationship between these organizations I intend to demonstrate how, when 'faith' intersects with development, it often reinforces a largely Western neoliberal and feminist vision of how the world should be. In other words, 'faith' can be used as a marketing device to sell a feminist neoliberal vision of development. A shared belief in Gandhian principles underlies the relationship between the two development agencies. In effect, their belief is what motivates people involved in the UK agency to devote their time and money to the poor and suffering people of Rajasthan. The UK members of this organization conflate faith and charity and view 'giving' as a way of acting out their religion. In the previous chapter I argued that to 'give' or 'act charitably' requires a 'recipient' and I showed how the recipients of these charitable gifts exist as an imagined 'Other'.

The assumed needs of Rajasthani villagers are not negotiated through face-to-face contact between equal development partners but predetermined to fit the organization's neoliberal vision of development. The predetermined nature of the UK organization's approach to gift giving stands in stark contrast to the locally responsive and immediate style of the VSR. This difference in practice gradually chipped away at the foundations of their partnership and partly accounts for its demise. As Mauss's[2] work shows, any exchange of gifts implies reciprocity, which places the recipient in a position of indebtedness if he or she cannot repay the gesture. In Chapter 5 I reviewed the work of Stirrat and Hinkel[3] who argue that some Christian missionary organizations offer aid not only for the material benefit of the recipients but also for their spiritual salvation. The UK donor agency expects local people to reciprocate by collectively pursuing feminist neoliberal ideals rather than through religious conversion. Quarles van Ufford and Schoffeleers[4] describe the almost evangelical projection of a neoliberal vision as requiring a very similar process of conversion found in some religious organizations.

The individuals who make up the organizations I studied have a wide range of motives and views and, though I acknowledge this and try to convey some sense of each organization's fluidity, my main purpose lies elsewhere. I have pieced the story together from ethnographic observations I made while working with these organizations intermittently over a period of ten years. Because I want to compare and contrast each organization's dominant vision of development and track how it evolved, I deliberately present their relationship as largely homogenous and do not highlight the tensions within each organization. Since I am the storyteller I acknowledge that this tale is my interpretation of why the partnership lasted so long and why its demise was inevitable.

In exploring these organizations' identities and practices I draw on the same four terms employed earlier – faith, religion, feminist theology and neoliberalism. As mentioned at the start of this book, 'faith' is used to denote the experiential, spiritual dimension of people's personal religious lives. 'Religion' is used more broadly to describe a set of ideas and practices linked to an authoritative source, which could be a god, teacher or spiritual leader. 'Theology' is used to describe how faith and religion produce a distinct worldview; it relates to ideas about how the world should be and what 'transformation' is needed to achieve that vision. Feminist theology promotes gender equality and the challenges the oppressive structures that limit the material and spiritual potential of women. 'Neoliberalism' is 'a theory of political economic practices that human wellbeing can best be advanced by liberating individual entrepreneurial freedoms and skills.'[5] I show how faith, religion and feminist theology come together in pursuit of a neoliberal vision of development that ironically is founded on notions of a 'rational', 'secular' Self.

Both organizations have a strong theological sense of what the world should be like and what role they must play in shaping it. The UK group is feminist, with strong 'women's groups' within it. A set of deeply-held religious values and beliefs underlie the identity of each organization. These values and beliefs give each member a sense of purpose and fulfilment in life and include ideas about development or transforming the lives of others. Faith for each individual acts as a strong motivational force to ensure a lasting commitment to others in the organization and to the people whose lives they seek to change. The philosophical and theological discourse to which their faith connects helped them translate a vision of development into practice. Sharing Gandhi's ideas about social equality cemented the partners' commitment to see his principles enacted through development. However, their different theological outlooks gradually began to endanger the unity of cooperation between them.

I start this chapter with background information on the inception of the partnership. After seeing how the initial money was raised and distributed through the partnership from WFR to VSR and then to local people in rural Rajasthan, we see how tensions seeped into the relationship when funding was sought from larger donor bodies such as the UK Department for International Development (DFID). I then look more closely at differences and similarities in the visions of development that WFR and VSR pursue. WFR's Christian feminist theological view is compatible with a neoliberal approach to development; the Gandhian principles each organization upholds translate into practice differently, yet represent a link between them. WFR's different approach is incompatible with DFID's professionalization requirements. Finally, in the third section, I look at the breakdown of the partnership and show how the professionalization of WFR moves it more firmly towards a neoliberal, feminist vision of development.

Background/History of the Partnership

As noted, in 1987, during a period of acute drought in Rajasthan, a community-level Gandhian organization, 'Village Service Rajasthan' (VSR), and a small UK faith-based donor organization, 'Water For Rajasthan' (WFR), began a partnership[6] that would last for 20 years. On the inception of this partnership the directors of both organizations travelled to local villages to talk with the inhabitants about what they most needed and, unsurprisingly, water emerged as the top development priority. The WFR team returned home to start raising funds through its network of church congregations. At the start, WFR's role was to facilitate the flow of money from individual donors to VSR.

Religious fund raising

At first, funds were raised through individual contributions or church-based events that WFR hosted, and most donations came from 'people of faith'. WFR members persuaded churchgoers to accept the image of poverty and hopelessness they were in effect selling and the organization used important events in the Christian calendar as marketing opportunities to focus people's minds on the plight of the unfortunate people of rural Rajasthan. For example, the harvest festival, a time of fruitful bounty, was when churchgoers were asked to reflect on the plight of those who had so little. WFR's October 2008 newsletter contained the following quotation from the Bible: 'so now bring the first of the ground that you, O Lord have given me';[7] passages alongside the quote described the parched earth of rural Rajasthan and stories about water shortages leading to failed crops, dying cattle and suffering people. The message is direct; please give what you can, reflect on your own good fortune and acknowledge your responsibility to help others whose harvest is less than plentiful.

Faith is not only used to motivate people to give; it is also used to help market a particular vision of a 'good' and 'appropriate' future for

Rajasthani women. Words such as 'empower', 'hope' and 'equality', which few could deny are worthy values, were written alongside the photographs displayed to project this vision. This suggests that members of the congregation are not only meant to provide the poor with material support but they are also meant to pass on a set of values, both marketed as 'gifts' the organization wishes to bestow and embedding a concept of reciprocity into the process of aid. Since these values are not material they can only be realized if local people submit to their vision. Although missionary work and religious conversion in the traditional sense are not part of this organization's agenda, it nonetheless expects in return for its funds a conversion to the values and beliefs of feminist neoliberalism.

Apart from carefully chosen biblical passages, newsletters often contain prayers designed to generate empathy with the poor of Rajasthan. In one prayer, adherents were asked to conjure up an image of the poorest person they have encountered either during a visit to Rajasthan or in the photographs members have brought back, and to ask themselves during prayer whether 'their actions help or hinder that person's plight'. The emotive nature of this organization's fund-raising style is not unique. All agencies ask their members to imagine the lives of less fortune people as a way of highlighting the importance for us all to do what we can to alleviate suffering. In fact, numerous handbooks exist to help guide NGOs in their secular fund-raising activities.[8] However, WFR uses faith as a tool with which to raise money, sell development and ensure that people continue to give. Faith is not just used to generate emotional responses that move people to give, but it is also employed as a way of forging a connection between adherents in the UK and villagers in Rajasthan. The closer potential donors feel to Rajasthani villagers the more they are moved to give. In other words, the more intimate the physical face-to-face relationship between the donor and the poor Rajasthani villager, the stronger the desire to help. The organization hosted curry nights as a way of offering people the chance to sample an aspect of Indian culture. The food was served amid numerous display boards on which photographs showing the colourful beauty of the region were displayed alongside those that drummed home the devastating effects of drought and poverty.

Members returning from their annual tours were regularly asked to share their impressions of Rajasthan at meetings and in newsletters. These usually consisted of reports of personal encounters with Rajasthanis and photographs of members unveiling plaques dedicating projects to donors. The various members of the original donor's family tend to visit such plaques year after year, thus retaining visible links with the community for which they have raised money; the moments of quiet reflection help people process their feelings and connect to a part of the world they may never have seen. Faith employed in this manner is a useful tool for raising money and securing the long-term commitment of individual donors. I stress that I am not suggesting there is anything wrong or unique about these methods. I am merely seeking to identify how faith can help the business of raising money and selling a specific vision of development, which is a central aspect of WFR's work. WFR's role is to 'sell' Western development, not to work through new ways of doing development. At an early stage in the relationship, VSR and WFR worked side by side, with WFR conceding to VSR's superior knowledge and experience to decide spending priorities.

Money flows and tensions over spending priorities

Once raised, money was sent directly to VSR, which then went about the operational task of creating various water sustainability projects. Engineer members of WFR gave technical guidance and support, and the projects were largely successful in improving water harvesting methods and seeing villagers more easily through the drought period. Spurred by its success, WFR decided to apply for a grant from the UK Department for International Development (DFID). It wanted to replicate its triumph in a second region of Rajasthan where it was setting up partnerships with two other Gandhian community organizations. It chose to work only with Gandhian organizations at the grass-roots level because of the shared vision and work ethos that united them. The grant application was successful and the money was to be spent on a combination of water harvesting, sanitation and small business schemes. The development vision began to expand;

more money meant they could think 'bigger', not just in terms of regional coverage but also in terms of the diversity of projects they funded.

The UK organization was keen to do something to improve what it saw as a depressing life for the women of Rajasthan. VSR also began to think beyond water projects to developing other schemes. The VSR director's priority was a hospital, which he believed should be built near a busy highway running through Rajasthan on which many accidents occurred, usually because of trucks overturning. According to the director, local people often came to him with their fears about their children being run down and killed. Many local people, he claimed, wanted him to do something to reduce the fatality rate. The director approached WFR with a request to channel money into the hospital project, but WFR refused on the grounds that the hospital did not support its objective of improving gender equality. In other words, it did not respond to its conception of the needs of the 'poorest of the poor'. The director of VSR sought and secured state funding and built the hospital. The hospital is still running and has achieved wide acclaim for having made a significant contribution towards reducing road fatality rates in the area.

The Feminist Theological Vision of Development

I wanted to understand why the organization was so committed to its gendered vision. In conversations I learnt that many WFR members viewed the deprivation that women in this area of India suffered from a Western feminist and theological perspective. This perspective produced a distorted vision based on what the group felt existed rather than establishing what really existed through face-to-face conversations with actual Rajasthani women. This feminist perspective, backed by theology, enabled them to offer the 'gift' of Western freedom, which they hoped would be warmly received and reciprocated through seeing Rajasthani villagers transformed into liberated Western women. The dominant group of feminists in this organization frequently talked about the women they had met, but rather than document the specific conversations they had with them they described what they viewed as their depressing lives of drudgery.

This lack of face-to-face dialogue resulted in the production of an imagined 'Other' in the form of a representative Rajasthani woman. The nature of this woman's existence and her potential as a self-conscious actor in her own right were neither discussed nor acknowledged. Instead, the focus was placed on the oppressive, bleak circumstances of her life and the need for the UK agency to offer her the chance to be transformed.[9]

I return now to the story of this intermediary cum donor partnership between the WFR and VSR. The first disagreement between the two organizations arose from a clash over funding objectives, which I believe occurred partly because each organization's faith impacted differently on how members perceived and experienced the local communities in which they worked. As stated above, the core UK members were strongly influenced by feminist theology rooted in a white liberal discourse. In fact, they would discuss their theological and feminist beliefs at gender group meetings while also considering which projects to fund in Rajasthan. Before I go further I need to unravel some of the theological ideas discussed at these meetings.

Some early feminist theologians who were influential during the second wave of feminism, like Daly, Hampson, Loades and Schüssler Fiorenza,[10] have argued that religion, specifically Christianity, is responsible for promoting gender roles that leave women with few options other than those prescribed by marriage and motherhood. Mary Daly extended her criticism of religion by arguing that it has shaped repressive and brutal cultural practices across the globe. In *Beyond God the Father: Towards a Philosophy of Women's Liberation*, she describes how patriarchal religious values result in cultural practices such as foot binding in China and suttee (widow immolation) in India. Daly's work, and that of many early feminist theologians, has been criticized for its ethnocentric and essentialist tone. Kwok[11] has been particularly outspoken in stating that Western feminist theologians set out to rescue women from other poorer countries. She directly states: 'save brown women from brown men.' This mission to liberate other women from their repressive traditions brings feminist theologians into the field of development and clearly influences the views of many in WFR. The lens through which some feminist theologians view women of the developing world is both patronizing and problematic.[12] The theology of feminists from developing countries has had to acknowledge the dual layers of repression with which they live – patriarchy and ethnocentrism.

A heavy emphasis on documenting the repressive and negative aspects of Rajasthani women's lives has characterized WFR newsletters from the start. In keeping with Kwok's criticism of Western feminist theologians, the members clearly hold men and religion responsible for women's inequality in Rajasthan. According to this logic, a Rajasthani woman must abandon her religion and seek independence from her husband if she is to live freely. Yet, many religious women in the Western feminist movement, even those members of WFR who are particularly vocal on gender issues, remain both married and Christian. Rather than abandon both, they have renegotiated and reinterpreted the repressive aspects of their lives.[13]

I observed little effort being made to understand the importance of religion in the lives of many Rajasthani women. As Kwok points out, many women in the developing world express a desire to adhere to their traditions because it gives them a sense of identity, dignity and pride. Similar arguments have been made with regard to Hindu women in Rajasthan.[14] It is probable that many Rajasthani women, like members of WFR, reflect on and reinterpret aspects of their religious tradition. When I told a senior member of the organization about my observations of women performing a ritual to Sita, the ideal woman in Hinduism who is depicted as submissive to her husband's authority (described in greater detail in Chapter 8), her response was 'they must find another role model'. I return to this discussion later when I question why so many WFR members see Hinduism as problematic for women. Many members of their gender group saw both the Virgin Mary and Mary Magdalene as symbols of courage and defiance, even though the Virgin Mary had performed a domestic and subservient role as the mother of Jesus. Yet, the same sympathetic interpretation was never used to understand similar role models in Hinduism, such as Sita.

From their particular theological and neoliberal standpoint, the WFR members could only see Rajasthani women in one way.[15] Their feminist biblical depiction of Mary Magdalene, whose actions and devotion to Jesus some members of the group believed had been misjudged, had entrenched a neoliberal stress on gender equality in their common psyche. They therefore equated the tireless labourings of these women with the brutality of religiously-endorsed patriarchy. In other words, they compared women's exclusion from certain areas of mainstream Rajasthani society with the experiences of Mary Magdalene, who was marginalized because of her devotion to Jesus.

An analysis of the organization's newsletters over a period of ten years revealed one narrative told through the lives of all Rajasthani women. It always begins in the same way by describing the burden the female gender carries from birth. Sometimes the stories focus on young girls taking responsibility for their brothers at the expense of their own education. Others focus on young veiled women having to continue with their domestic duties at home after a full day of working in the field. The connection made between Rajasthani women and the injustice Mary Magdalene suffered created a homogenous image of a woman repressed by patriarchy. Combine this one-sided image with a neoliberal emphasis on economic efficiency and there is but one solution – income generation.

WFR members questioned neither the accuracy of their view of Rajasthani women nor the wisdom of the economic solutions they proposed. Their emotional tie with the region and sense of closeness to the 'woman' whose life they sought to transform merely deepened their sense of assurance. I have no wish to question the 'good' intentions or compassion behind these sentiments, but think that it is necessary to draw attention to the ways in which faith intersects with feminist theology and neoliberal principles to create fictitious notions of other women's lives and the changes needed to liberate them.

While many women are poor, gender and development (GAD) scholars now recognize that focusing too narrowly on economic disadvantage can detract attention from improving human rights. Given its economic vision of gender equality and inveterate feminist theological perspective, however, WFR remained convinced that it was following the right path to transformation, which Eyben described as 'women must work for aid, rather than aid work for women.'[16] In other words, the emphasis was on getting women into paid employment. Even in the most recent newsletter, WFR members wrote positively about the number of women now benefiting from employment and said how many women were able to save money and therefore build economic independence through a cooperative savings scheme. WFR encourages its new partners to favour women as employees.

On one occasion, when I travelled with a group from WFR to visit a desilting, irrigation project, representatives excitedly took photographs of women working on the project. These would later be used to show donors that their money had brought positive changes to the lives of poor Rajasthani women by providing them with employment. Projects that focus on employment will not remove the wider, deeper inequalities that detrimentally affect women's lives. As Cornwall and her co-editors state, the view that they will remove such inequalities is based on the assumption that:

> If only women had greater access to and [more] control over money, they would exercise autonomy in ways that would free them from the shackles of subordination to men, achieving with this the freedom to make their own choices, which many development actors regard as the fundamental ingredients of empowerment.[17]

Had the WFR members taken a closer look at the photographs, or even taken a step back from the situation, they may have got a clearer sense of the heavy burden that these women already carry. Many of the women worked with young children strapped to their backs. This horrified some representatives, but did not seem to dampen their joy at seeing the women employed. The plethora of well-documented research on over-burdened women seems to have done nothing to change the WFR's outlook. Since the emancipation of Rajasthani women involves educating girls in preparation for better-paid employment, the WFR funded a village school, which a group of its members and I visited. Although the WFR members were thrilled to see so many girls seated at the front of the classroom grasping their slates, I was unconvinced and when I returned a few days later, this time with some VSR members, very few girls were in attendance. The VSR members told me that the parents knew that WFR was visiting so made sure that their daughters attended that day. The community wanted the school to exist, but prioritized the education of boys over girls. Clearly, many parents had not been sold the feminist neoliberal message that the intermediary agency promoted.

The Gandhian vision of development

In the examples I have so far given, the faith of its members drove WFR into launching a marketing campaign founded on a narrow image of what was needed, but had a different impact on the work of VSR. The latter adopted a more humanistic approach derived from Gandhi's respect for all religions and spiritual communion with the environment. As I showed in my summary of Kumar's work in Chapter 4,[18] Gandhian organizations stress the importance of village service, or *gram seva*.

Gandhi's ashrams (communal living spaces) expanded the concept of the public sphere beyond the discursive exchanges of educated men. Ashrams were created to show how people from different social backgrounds could choose a new way of life, the central feature of which was an undifferentiated divide between the public and private spheres. Gandhi wanted to reach as wide a constituency as possible; he wanted to bring the private sphere into the open to challenge the inequalities enacted there. VSR incorporated this notion of the 'personal as the political' as a central core of its concept of and approach to development. Its focus on trying to rectify and equalize gender relations between husband and wife took the director right to the heart of the private domestic sphere. Furthermore, he frequently encouraged women he knew were suffering from domestic violence to share their experiences with other women so that together they could look for possible solutions. For a woman to share her experiences of domestic violence means acknowledging and revealing to others the intimate details of her suffering. Although the spaces in which this was done were confidential and secure within the VSR domain, they still represented 'public' settings. Pursuing this approach was not going to achieve dramatic or instant results, but VSR was committed to it because it supported the idea that individuals initiated the pace of change.

In Gandhi's ashrams there was just one kitchen and the inhabitants dined in single rows, washed their own plates and cutlery and took it in turns to clean the communal pots. Rudolph and Hoeber Rudolph describe life in an ashram as political theatre: 'creating a new and distinctive form of the public sphere. It was marked by the visible practice of simple living, the performance of physical labour and polluting tasks, making and wearing *khadi* [homespun cloth], doing [for] yourself, living with and learning from comrades of diverse backgrounds.'[19] Asceticism and discipline were the central tenets of Gandhi's *swaraj* (the pursuit of self-sufficiency and communal non-hierarchical living). VSR has incorporated many of these features of simple living into its work, including sitting in rows facing each other at meal times, which gives members a chance to discuss their feelings about their work. The core members work long hours, wear *khadi* bought from a local Gandhian cooperative, are sensitive about not using more than they need, particularly water, and rarely take time off apart from festival days.

Parekh believes that Gandhism remains influential in building development-oriented social movements because Gandhi was 'the first person in history to lift the love ethic of Jesus above mere interaction between individuals to a powerful and effective social force on a large scale'.[20] WFR's enthusiastic acceptance of Gandhi's ideals is because Christians, as Parekh explains, see Gandhi as living in the same way as Jesus lived. *Satyagraha*, another core value at the heart of Gandhi's approach incorporating non-violence, resistance, civil disobedience and dialogue between individuals across divides, encourages individuals to imagine living in other people's shoes to achieve what Gandhi calls 'situational truth'.

VSR and WFR had different views on what constituted the barriers to women's advancement. VSR focused on reversing the inequalities between husband and wife that allow men to see violence as a legitimate way of 'controlling' their wives. The localized face-to-face approach meant that the organization felt it had built a reliable picture of women's lives and concerns. Violence emerged time and time again and the organization resorted to all sorts of measures in its attempts to reverse the pattern of gender relations that specifically supported domestic violence. The research undertaken at the Institute of Development Studies in Jaipur, which I discuss further in Chapter 9, addresses the concern to tackle domestic violence. Mathur,[21] for example, records such high levels of systematic abuse of women as to suggest that it has become the norm. The director of VSR would frequently ask husbands to stop beating their wives and, in his efforts to show them how they were supposed to behave towards their wives, he would tell them stories about Hindu couples that evoked religious imagery. For example, he would often tell the stories of Rama and Sita or Krishna and Radhi, which stress the need for husbands to protect and look after their wives. Sharad Joshi (leader of the Lakshmi Mukti campaign in Maharashtra) has also used this approach in his campaigns to get fathers to hand over land to their daughters as inheritance and break the dependence women experience in marriage through practices like the dowry.[22] VSR would promote its vision of gender equality by reminding local people of Gandhi's teachings. Its approach was more direct than that of WFR in that it openly admitted that it wanted to change the ways men and women related to each other in the domestic sphere of their lives.

Similarities and differences in approaches

The direct face-to-face approach was not, however, any more effective in changing gender relations in rural Rajasthan than the efficiency model WFR used. In fact, some scholars argue that patriarchal religious images may even serve to legitimize marital violence in Rajasthan.[23] Resurrecting these same images to demonstrate appropriate male behaviour may well deepen feelings of male dominance. There are, for example, many different versions of the Rama and Sita story and some of these, which the VSR director failed to mention, depict Rama being violent towards Sita.[24]

On closer analysis it becomes apparent that because 'faith' and 'theology' impacted differently on development in each organization, their respective approaches to women's development also differed. WFR adopted a neoliberal efficiency model whereby women sought independence from their problem – namely their husbands – by taking on paid employment. VSR, on the other hand, tried to respond directly to the concerns that the women shared with them on a day-to-day basis. The WFR's 'faith' component serves to embed in its members an image of women as poor and in need of help, while VSR calls on religion to communicate with abusive husbands. In each case, as the experiential aspect, religion and faith act as strong vehicles through which visions of development are constructed and acted upon and then marketed to Rajasthani communities.

The subtly different ways in which faith and religion intersect with development affect how each organization seeks to achieve Gandhi's notion of situational truth. Faith, expressed through prayer and meditation, gives WFR an internal mechanism for communicating with and, ostensibly, getting closer to local people. Although its members feel that this emotional bond increases their empathy with others' problems, I am unsure quite how situational the bond really is given that the connections are made with a fictitious rather than a real person. WFR is attracted to the idea of striving for 'situational truth' because it likes to imagine what it must be like to live in poverty.

Gandhi emphasized the importance of 'feeling' in gaining knowl-edge. 'The heart must work together with the mind if deliberate processes are to produce shared truth.'[25] Believers like the idea of relating to the poor emotionally and spiritually because it allows them to express and apply their theology practically. Both VSR and WFR acknowledge the centrality of their emotions in the work they do. VSR members incorporate meditative spaces into their daily lives and WFR members share these spaces when they visit. The quiet moments of reflection they generate ensure that faith influences the discussions they then have about their development goals and priorities. Because VSR approaches situational truth differently, namely by forming personal relationships with local people, the quiet moments that the two organizations share provide WFR members with the real stories that local people have told during the course of

145

their daily activities, which the organization can then embellish with religious images and use to disseminate its moral ideas about how women should be treated.

The Professionalization of WFR and the Emergence of an Intermediary Organization

As the UK-based WFR grew in confidence, it more consciously began to form an idea of how 'proper' development should be done. It became influenced by its funding relationship with DFID, which resulted in the emergence of a model of development that reflected the latter's bureaucratic, secular, scientifically-oriented style. Systems of accountability, monitoring and evaluation began to appear on the agendas of WFR board meetings. This shift in focus and practice also signifies WFR's new identity as an 'official' intermediary. I use the word 'official' because in a sense WFR always acted to facilitate the direction of funds from donors to VSR. However, securing funding from a large donor such as DFID meant it needed to do more than produce photographs to prove it had directed funds efficiently. The WFR membership did not see this more official intermediary positioning as constraining, but it undoubtedly led to the demise of the partnership. VSR felt pressured by and alienated from the development process of accountability and, when it failed to produce regular accounts, frustrations built up in the UK. Gradually, the UK agency ploughed more and more of its money into supporting community organizations elsewhere in Rajasthan. These other organizations were more responsive to the administrative tasks required to partner the UK agency.

Diminishing shared vision and the allure of neoliberalism

At the start a shared vision was easy. The UK donor felt comfortable with VSR's Gandhian philosophy and perspective; the message of embracing all beings regardless of their religion or caste resonated well with the UK agency's largely Christian membership. Gandhi became the link that bound the organizations together. Gandhi drew on many biblical teachings and one WFR member remarked that the Sermon on the Mount, which stresses the unity of all human beings regardless of their background or position, had inspired and influenced Gandhi's work. Gandhi's teachings on untouchability and social equality are well known. WFR members believed that Gandhi, whom they equated with Jesus in terms of suffering and pious devotion, had taken Christ as a role model. WFR newsletters used poetic, religious-sounding narratives to describe the similarities in the lives of the two men. Some members of WFR may well have been getting to know Jesus through Gandhi, which would perhaps explain the visits to Gandhi's ashram in Ahmedabad and constant references to the simplicity of their respective lives and to both men being persecuted for upholding their principles.

Had VSR had an overtly Hindu identity, the same depth of relationship may not have been possible. The Christian worldview that drives the UK agency's activities rests safely within Gandhi's humanistic teachings. While the UK agency disregarded the existence of Hinduism in the local communities, the local Gandhian organizations used local Hindu religious buildings and sites as spaces in which to meet local people. They consulted local Hindu priests about development priorities and viewed them as sources of strength in motivating the organization's leadership to push on with its work.

The main reason the UK agency failed to engage with Hinduism was, as I have already touched on, because it blamed religion for women's disempowerment and for the caste system. This was apparent in many conversations I had with members about how they understood women's social inequality. Many members noted the presence of Hindu goddesses and figures in villagers' homes. Popular feminine images in Hinduism include Sita (devoted, loyal wife to ideal man Rama), Lakshmi (consort to Vishnu, goddess of wealth, beauty and happiness) and Paravati (consort to Siva, 'daughter of the mountains' connected with fertility and motherhood). Some WFR members thought that these images embedded women's subordination in the social and cultural fabric of Rajasthan. Kinsley[26] describes how symbolically these images project notions of wifehood, motherhood, beauty and compliance with a domestic role. WFR members linked this symbolism to social reality. They felt the images endorsed a gender ideology that secured a patriarchal system of social relations within which women fared less well even than poor low-caste men.[27]

Gandhi's emphasis on getting close to local people and traditions resonated with the UK agency, which believed that its annual trips to 'the villages' would serve that purpose. WFR, in keeping with its Gandhian principles, would respond to local needs as they emerged and the director would encourage local people to share their problems with him. He would fund projects initiated informally at meetings and collectives because he had learnt from experience that projects instigated from outside often failed to win support, as the following example of a project designed to improve the anti-drought provision in a village demonstrates. The village pond was desilted and saplings were planted around it to increase the amount of water it would retain. Although the villagers initially supported the project and even helped to plant the saplings, within six months they were allowing their goats to eat the saplings on the grounds that the project had failed. They therefore utilized the only aspect of the project they felt had any benefit – namely the saplings, which became fodder for their goats. The villagers felt that the time required for the project to succeed was unacceptably long. In other words, they needed quick solutions to immediate problems, which a longer period of dialogue prior to the project's inception may well have revealed. Lack of fodder is an urgent problem especially at times of drought. WFR engineers working on the project felt frustrated at the villagers' response. Clearly, the engineers' scientifically oriented model clashed with the local, immediate needs of the community.

The latter's informal day-to day style made accountability difficult and revealed why VSR could not produce regular or detailed accounts. Its director found it emotionally impossible to turn people away who came to his home asking for help. He often gave money to individuals, village elders or tribal leaders for their communities and people would approach him for help in keeping water supplies going in the shorter term, usually by purchasing water tankers from privately run companies. This meant that the designated projects had insufficient funds ploughed into them to progress at the pace WFR wanted to see. In fact, in a private conversation with me, he complained despairingly about the WFR board insisting on knowing how money was spent on specific projects.

The VSR director felt that WFR failed to appreciate the urgency of the problems in rural Rajasthan and unrealistically concentrated on creating projects that would only bear fruit in the medium or long term. VSR expressed concern that WFR was not responding to 'needs' but operating according to how it thought life should be led in the rural communities its members visited. VSR members often felt trapped between the demands of local people seeking help to overcome immediate crises in their lives and the demands of WFR to meet its long-term objectives. The web of power relations that existed between the constituents of the aid chain complicated matters further. WFR had the money needed to effect change, but needed VSR's support, reputation and local contacts to enact its vision. VSR had some power to decide who should receive the money but emotionally felt powerless to resist the demands of local people.

Mosse, who describes how policy is 'cooperated from below',[28] urges researchers to recognize that, despite the rigidity and dominance of Western policy frameworks, local people have power to ensure the success of development practice. Olivier de Sardan[29] argues that anthropologists have a significant contribution to make because they analyse the spaces in which the different development actors come together. This, as my case study of VSR confirms, produces a more accurate, albeit more complex, picture of development. Nevertheless, funding remains the most powerful factor in the aid chain. Without it, locally responsive approaches are limited, but access to it depends on how well an organization can fulfil the neoliberal criteria for effective development.

The neoliberal vision of development

Scholars such as George, Harvey, and Peet[30] argue that the hegemony of neoliberalism as a mode of discourse is such that NGOs struggle to produce any real alternatives; they are locked into a global aid chain structured around neoliberal values. According to Harvey, 'it has pervasive effects on ways of thought to the point where it has [become] incorporated into the common sense way many of us interpret, live in, and understand the world."[31] All human actions have been brought into the domain of the market; in other words, neoliberalism holds the view that only economic efficiency and productivity can assure the quality of human existence. As stated previously, neoliberalism seeps into and exists harmoniously alongside other visions of development through the universality of its core values, namely 'human dignity' and 'individual freedoms'. These values are also central to Gandhism and Christian feminist theology.

Despite their shared approach to faith, the emergence of dissimilar ideas about how to 'do' development created irreconcilable differences between the partners. Given that a similar language of transformation underpins feminist theology and neoliberal economics, the allure of the neoliberal model of development had something to do with the breakdown in the partnership. WFR co-opted the neoliberal idea that an economically productive populace was a happy populace. Happiness for Rajasthani women involves their empowerment, which can only happen once they are financially independent.

Funding from DFID brought the clipboard, a further visible marker of a shift in WFR's approach. The clipboard-style evaluative model disconnected WFR members from the 'situational truth' they hoped to experience. This became clear to me during a trip to a village where toilets had been installed in each homestead. A large donor who wanted to see sanitation improved funded the project. Building toilets where there were none seemed like a logical and obvious way of transforming hygiene and bringing positive changes to general standards of health. Most of the homesteads were made of traditional solidified cow dung and mud cakes. The added extension of the toilet room was made of brick. The villagers were visibly proud of this new addition to their homes.

As we inspected the toilets it became clear to me that they were not being used. They were too clean for an area suffering severe water shortages. Furthermore, each toilet had a small vase of flowers in it intended to honour the Western visitors. Corners of some of the rooms were used as storage for food grain. Some toilets had rolled up sleeping mats in them suggesting that family members slept in the room. I was confident that not one of the rooms was actually used as a toilet. At the end of the visit the evaluation sheets contained lines of ticks indicating that toilets were there and sanitation had thus been improved. Although local people welcomed the room and it contributed to raising standards of living, the link between the toilet and improved health standards was exaggerated. Had the objective of the visit been other than to fill out a form, perhaps WFR members could have engaged in discussion about the benefit the rooms had brought to the villagers' lives. The group may then have gone away with a quite different idea of what kind of development the villagers most wanted to see.

As already stated, WFR favoured a direct, responsive approach to giving when asked, which brought it to different conclusions about how its money should be spent. However, its more quietly expressed vision of how to approach development became lost amid the deafening blare of the transformative agenda that linked toilets to health. Better health would produce a more productive workforce that would become more active in the economy and thereby raise family incomes and improve living standards.[32] This link is persuasive, but the approach to achieving it is authoritative, for it excludes local experiences and alternative views of development. What this example shows is that, despite WFR's conversion to a neoliberal efficiency model, local people embraced the toilet project by manipulating the outcome to reflect an important goal – an extra bedroom and more storage space. VSR seemed to acknowledge the will and agency of local people and sought to respond to the demands people made rather than seek to dominate and impose a different vision of development. Equally, VSR failed drastically to transform local people's lives because its scarce funds could not stretch to long-term projects.

Conclusion

To sum up, WFR has formed new relationships with other Gandhian organizations working in the same state and these seem to be enduring better than the original partnership. This is partly due to the 'professionalization' of the operational structures and reporting mechanisms these organizations use. In searching for new partners, WFR looked for organizations able to conform to, or at least buy into, aspects of its development vision. The new vision is a blend of feminist theology and Gandhian philosophy underpinned by a neoliberal economic model.

As WFR members acquired more knowledge about India and Gandhi they increased in confidence and became clearer about what concepts they wanted to market to their donors back home. Gandhi's approach to life offered a secure lens through which to make sense of social relations in India, while also offering a way of converting faith into action. Gandhian ideals posed no threat to their faith, feminist theology or secular model of neoliberal efficiency towards which their main donor directed them. Though not intending to pass judgement on the effectiveness of any of the visions examined, I questioned what opportunities exist for real alternatives to emerge if they do not embrace neoliberalism in some way.

I highlighted how 'visions' of development are not only marketed but also force recipients of aid to look at their lives in a new way. In effect, a sort of conversion is expected of them in return for the material assistance they receive, which resonates with the expectations of many early Christian missionaries and contemporary evangelical organizations.[33] VSR was indigenously rooted in the local community; its members had family connections with and emotional ties to the land and people around them. Hence, their more intimate insight into people's problems, which was evident from their focus on domestic violence and reluctance to turn people away when they came asking for help, usually money. This vision, driven by a Gandhian-inspired spirituality, was both supportive and responsive; it won the organization the trust of local people.

However, its refusal to conform to the professionalized way of working that WFR adopted meant that it lost significant amounts of funding. This reduced the amount of help it could offer local people. Remaining committed to its vision produced some long-term change. The hospital has been heralded a success and has brought a greater level of emergency health provision to the area. It was built because local people lobbied for it. Similarly, the strength of local leverage over the development agenda can be seen in the sanitation project. Although most local families had no intention of using the toilets for the purpose for which they were built, they clearly appreciated the additional space they provided. Thus, in this chapter we have seen how three visions existed in a web, with some parts of the web working in unison while others resisted being pulled into a more hegemonic and global system of 'doing' development.

Chapter 7

Gender, Gandhi and Community Organizations

W E shall now explore the different ways in which gender and Gandhi's philosophy have been interpreted and used to shape distinctive approaches in three community organizations. The comparison centres on the work of the two organizations already encountered in Chapters 4, 5 and 6, namely Village Service Rajasthan (VSR) and Village Development Project Jodhpur (VDPJ). Now, to enable a more extensive assessment of the similarities and differences between each organization, an additional case study is introduced – the Gandhian Memorial Society (GMS) in Pune. In looking at differences in how the organizations structurally approach their work, two features stand out, 'leadership' and 'women's empowerment'. These categories change as each organization undergoes the process of translating Gandhi's style of leadership into the contexts in which it works and each organization interprets Gandhi's ideas on the role of women in different ways. The comparison between the project management styles of 'Village Service Rajasthan' and 'Village Development Project Jodhpur' is analysed more closely in Chapter 10 through consideration of how they approach their health-care programmes. The focus in this chapter is on how each organization structures its day-to-day operations and the impact that Gandhi's ideas about gender have had in shaping their approach.

From the comparisons presented in this chapter, we see that no assumptions can be made about an organization's nature or operation, even if it belongs to the same movement as another organization and is founded on the same teachings and philosophy. My ethnographic research reveals distinctive, albeit slight, differences in how each thinks about and responds to gender. The importance of religion both as a focus to unify participants and as a source of motivation is a strand that runs through all three organizations. The material in this chapter, which I collected over a period of approximately ten years, is derived from observations of the day-to-day running of these bodies and from informal and formal conversations. The people with whom I spoke included each organization's leaders, employees, trustees and members of its donor agencies, as well as the so-called beneficiaries of its work. As with all the ethnographic material presented in this volume, I have used pseudonyms.

The chapter is divided into three sections. In the first I draw out the key differences between VSR and VDPJ. In the second I present data on the third case study, the Gandhian Memorial Society (GMS) in Pune. I consider the roots of GMS's distinct approach, which Gandhi's teachings on gender influenced, and then look at how each organization has interpreted Gandhi's philosophy on women differently. In the last section I consider in greater detail Gandhi's teachings on religion, gender and development and ask why his philosophy has has been so important in shaping the perspectives not just of the Gandhian movement in India, of which my case studies are a part, but also of the activists working on women's rights. Why is it that, despite his underlying acceptance of patriarchy, Gandhi remains such an inspirational figure for prominent activists like Madhu Kishwar?

The Different Approaches of Two Community Organizations

The director of Village Service Rajasthan (VSR) tries to emulate Gandhi's ethos and solitary life. This translates into a rather linear management structure, which, though guided by local needs and views, places responsibility for delivering services on the shoulders of the director. The director's daughter-in-law and unmarried daughter oversee his domestic welfare.

A husband and wife share equal responsibility in leading the second organization, VDPJ. They spoke to me about the importance of a non-hierarchical operational structure and of how they model their working day on Gandhi's notion of communal living. The chores and activities are divided equally between everyone and I

believe that this emphasis on equality in all aspects of the organization's work spreads outwards to the relationships they make with
the local people they invite into the organization's grounds for
training and support. These occasions always include a social
gathering at which the team serves food to highlight that no one is
too good to serve others. On closer look, however, it became
apparent that gender did indeed play a part in the division of labour,
for the wife assumed responsibility for her husband's domestic
welfare. Although decision making appeared to be shared, home-
based (as opposed to ashram-based) domestic tasks were not. This is
not a criticism but reveals the distinct way in which they have
interpreted Gandhi's model. Gandhi, as I go on to discuss, held that
gender divisions in household chores should be respected, with
women as the primary carers and homemakers. His vision therefore
did not involve a shift in patriarchal gender relations and this can be
seen in the approach of both VSR and VDPJ. Both organizations
stress the central Gandhian teaching advocating respect for all
human beings as equally valuable.

The third organization, the Gandhian Memorial Society (GMS)
based in Pune, Maharashtra, is run by a woman called Sunjata. It
focuses on women's empowerment and educational projects. In
recounting the organization's work and ethos I also recount aspects
of Sunjata's life story, retold here with her permission and full
consent. I do so because her approach differs from that of the first
two organizations and raises interesting questions about the positive
impact of female leadership on achieving empowerment for women. I
do not suggest that GMS is more successful in its work with women
than VSR or VDPJ, but its sole focus on women is unusual (according
to Sunjata) for a Gandhian organization. I also believe that its success
can at least in part be attributed to the influence and impact of
Sunjata's leadership as a woman and a role model.

Translating Values into Practice

The Gandhian Memorial Society, Pune
GMS is housed in what is now called the Aga Khan Palace in Pune,

which has become a national monument of India's freedom movement. Following the launch of the Quit India Movement in 1942, the British colonial government interned Gandhi, his wife Kasturba and his secretary, Mahadevbhai Desai in the palace from 5 August 1942 to 6 May 1944. Kasturba and Mahadevbhai both died during their internment and their *samadhi*s are located in the grounds. Not surprisingly, the palace has become a national and international place of pilgrimage. After his wife's death, Gandhi requested that the palace be developed into a place of emancipation for women. On the centenary of Gandhi's birth in 1969, HH Prince Karim Agakhan donated the building to the nation as a mark of respect for Gandhi and his philosophy. On 15 August 1972 a Gandhian museum was inaugurated and, in 1980, the Gandhi Smarak Nidhi transferred the museum's management, the *samadhi*s and the palace campus to the Gandhi National Memorial Society in New Delhi (the Gandhian movement's main headquarters in India).

The primary goal of the society is to offer vocational training and education to enable rural women to seek employment or set up their own small businesses, or, as Sunjata put it, 'to empower women through training and education'. In 1988 the GMS set up the first women's training centre in India, which was called Kasturba Mahila Khadi Gramodyog Vidyalaya. Initially it only taught weaving, but it now offers a choice of 23 trades to 1500 women a year.

Sunjata sees education as a tool through which women can learn: 'I am an independent human being. I can think; I can decide; I can lead my life.' She describes the process of empowerment in terms of being an 'awakening and a knowledge of rights'. She talked enthusiastically about her successes and keeps detailed records of the progress of all the women who participate in her training programmes. She believes that her success rate, measured by the number of women who are now financially independent, is around 70 per cent. She attributes this success to the follow-up system she implements that offers women ongoing support. She also believes that motivation is a crucial part of training and that without it women will not be pushed to effect changes in their lives.

I asked her from where she derived her motivation and she replied

'God'. She begins each day by reading a random passage from the Gita and performing *puja*. If a residential course is running, she performs the ritual with her female participants. She deliberately built ritual spaces into the training because the majority of students are religious and she felt that it was essential that the organization should recognize and acknowledge the importance of religion in their lives. This helped to build trust between all parties involved in the programmes and was a way of expressing mutual respect. In accordance with Gandhi's stress on a humanist or interfaith approach to religion, these rituals were non-denominational, though Sunjata, like many Gandhian activists, is a Hindu.

Later in the book, in Chapter 10, I examine how both VSR and VDPJ integrate rituals into their health programmes to help build more effective communication between participants and trainers. The women on Sunjata's courses begin their day with prayer at 5.30 a.m. and they pray again at 9 a.m. before the training for the day officially starts. Both participants and trainers attend these sessions. According to Sunjata, these are times when participants and trainers can share their reflections, express empathy towards each other and allow problems to surface and be discussed.

Sunjata lives with her family in a house located within the Aga Khan Palace complex. After graduating with a Masters' degree in business and commerce she decided to dedicate her life to welfare work. She claimed that reading Gandhi's teachings had profoundly affected her approach to life and that her father had supported her decision. She is a passionate advocate of Gandhi's philosophy and sees him as supporting women's equality and empowerment through the concept of *Shree Shakti*, or women's power and inner strength. She incorporates Gandhi's teachings into the empowerment programmes she offers rural women because she strongly believes that his message of social equality and respect for everybody offers motivation and a clear vision towards which to aim. She hopes that the women who complete her courses will go on to be financially successful, but to remember the social welfare needs of others and give back what they can.

Translating Gandhi's philosophy into practice

Gandhian philosophy remains popular with women's organizations and with activists who draw on it to plan non-violent yet forceful campaigns for women's rights.[1] Gandhi has, however, been criticized for not going far enough, for failing to advocate the need to restructure social relations to remove both gender and caste hierarchy.[2] Instead, he wanted to improve the status quo and see India strengthened as a free, independent and self-sufficient country.

The work of GMS is firmly rooted in Gandhi's notion of empowered womanhood. Gandhi stressed that women had a vital role to play in carving and sustaining an equal society. He talked about the concept of *sarvodaya* as an awakening of everybody, including women, to their potential as human beings. Gandhi stated:

> My contribution to the great problem of women's role in society lies in my presenting the acceptance of truth and *ahimsa* in every walk of life, whether for individuals or nations. I have hugged the hope that in this woman will be the unquestioned leader and having thus found her place in human evolution will shed her inferiority complex.[3]

Saxena holds that Gandhi encouraged women's participation through *satyagraha* and *ahimsa*, which demasculinize the political arena by removing violence and challenging male dominance of leadership positions. Gandhi stated: 'the women of India tore down the purdah and came forward to work for the nation.'[4] Activist scholars such as Kishwar[5] argue that Gandhi was a pioneer for women's rights because he increased their participation in public life. Gandhi emphasized that the achievement and conceptualization of political and social change should be a joint responsibility shared by men and women. Kishwar is forthright in her view that Gandhi did more than most to promote the potential of women and to motivate a female presence in political life.

Gandhi's teachings on women contain contradictions, especially over the issue of leadership given that he laid so much emphasis on their reproductive role as mothers and 'keepers of the hearth'.[6]

Unlike Kishwar, Saxena argues that Gandhi had a patriarchal gendered view of social relations, saw politics as a male domain and thought that women should keep out of public life. She believes that Gandhi held that men and women needed to support each other in fulfilling their roles but advised against crossing into the other's territory. This view of gender is apparent in the leadership structures of my first case study, VSR, in which the director focuses on his public role and leaves domestic matters to his daughter and daughter-in-law. In my second case study, VDPJ, the husband and wife team share responsibility for coordinating the organization but, as I mentioned, their tasks are often gendered. Patel[7] believes that Gandhi's views on gender relations shifted over time and that in later life he advocated a partnership between husband and wife, as we see in the example of VDPJ. That Gandhi articulated a notion of female leadership at all, however, blurs any clear articulation of his gender ideology, but the specific construct of leadership he envisaged for women built on what he felt to be their natural female qualities. He felt that female leaders should act as role models to other women, thereby encouraging them to take up the cause of the Indian nation. Women in his eyes were naturally 'long-suffering, selfless and self-effacing'[8] and this made them strong role models for strengthening the Indian nation.

Sunjata understands her position in terms of being a role model and is clearly politicized in the way she speaks about women's rights. She firmly believes that she represents a financially independent woman. Although she is married she assumes responsibility for GMS and her husband is not present in the day-to-day operations. Sunjata believes this is important because it helps her convey a message to participants about the capacity of women to take control of their lives without the need to defer to their husbands.

It is hard to draw conclusions about what impact different leadership structures have on the visions of development each organization pursues. The first two organizations, VSR and VDPJ, do not focus exclusively on empowering women but instead aim to develop sustainable livelihoods for the communities in which they work and GMS only works to improve the status and position of women. From my conversations with the leaders of each organization, it is clear that Gandhi's teachings influenced how they approached their work ideologically and practically. My research also shows that each leader interprets and translates Gandhi's core beliefs slightly differently.

Gandhi on Gender, Religion and Development

To unravel what is distinct about Gandhi's approach to gender, religion and development, it might be helpful to compare the case studies examined in Chapter 3 of the Ramakrishna, Guru Mata Amritanandamayi and Sadhu Vaswani missions. Although there were differences in their approaches to gender, similarities were evident in the way in which the Hindu concept of *seva* provided a focus for charitable actions, which in turn formed part of the individual devotee's spiritual journey. While Gandhi embraced the concept of *seva*, he did not specifically link it to spirituality or to the notion of a spiritual journey. Gandhi, however, articulated his social and political ideology through a concept of God. For Gandhi, God represented 'truth'; and understanding this truth involved living life according to a specific code of conduct. The word *satya,* meaning 'truth', is derived from *sat,* which means 'being'. Gandhi described how nothing exists outside truth and so *sat* is the most common name for God 'and where there is truth, there is also knowledge which is true. ... Devotion to this truth is the sole justification for our existence. All our activities should be centred in Truth.'[9]

The pursuit of truth was for Gandhi an expression of *bhakti* or devotion to God. 'There should be Truth in thought, Truth in speech and Truth in action.'[10] For Gandhi a guiding principle directing this pursuit of truth in everyday life is *ahimsa*. 'The principle of *ahimsa* is hurt by every evil thought, by undue haste, by lying, by hatred, by wishing ill to anybody. It is also violated by our holding onto what the world needs.'[11] *Ahimsa* means universal love but this cannot be fulfilled without utter selflessness, which in turn is not possible if devotion is given to just one person. Gandhi advocated *brahmacharya* or chastity even between married couples to ensure that energies are focused on the needs of others. Gandhi was not anti-family but is clear that an individual's responsibilities extend beyond the comfort of his or her immediate family. Closely connected is the concept of *yajna*, which means an act directed to the welfare of others, done without desiring any return for it whether temporal or spiritual in nature. Gandhi stated: 'This body therefore has been given us, only in order that we may serve all Creation with it.'[12] However, renunciation did not mean abandoning family life. *Swadeshi* stands for the final emancipation of the soul from its earthly bondage. 'A votary of *Swadeshi* therefore, in his striving to identify himself with the entire creation seeks to be emancipated from the bondage of the physical body.'[13] For Gandhi religion was a source of motivation, space and time for reflection and this is very much the way the Gandhian organizations I have studied use religion.

A thread running through the ideologies of the Ramakrishna, Guru Mata Amritanandamayi and Sadhu Vaswani missions, as well as present in Gandhi's philosophy, is a clear distinction between the gender roles of men and women. Women's capacity to bear children conflates with a concept of mothering, which in turn prescribes a woman's role as closely attached to nurturing and rearing children. Although Amma does not talk extensively about gender roles, she highlights the natural inner qualities that women possess because of their biology and links these to an innate capacity to show love and act with compassion to everybody. Amma, however, believes that these mothering qualities can transcend gender and that men should seek to experience the urge to nurture and love others just as a mother loves her child. Gandhi's biological determinism underpins Sadhu Vaswani and Vivekananda's views on gender roles separating and delineating the spheres in which men and women should focus their energies and attention. Despite the almost anti-feminist tone of some Gandhian philosophy, Gandhi's writings continue to shape and motivate the work of activists working to empower Indian women.

Gandhi and feminism

Activists like Kishwar have struggled with the term feminism. They find its Western origins problematic and instead seek inspiration in the Indian-rooted ideas of Gandhi. Many people still find Gandhi's philosophy relevant because he sought to shape a society that would allow each person to express his or her identify free from the political and cultural impositions of others. In her article 'Horror of Isms: Why I Do Not Call Myself a Feminist',[14] Kishwar resists pressure from inside and outside India to call herself a feminist. She refuses to call *Manushi* a feminist publication because she claims she wants to include all oppressed people in her work, men as well as women; she opts instead for 'a journal about women and society'. Kishwar compares Western feminism with the doctrine of a 'liberated woman', arguing that 'in societies like India we accept differences and diversity as a way of life and take it for granted that different groups and communities are likely to have their own cultural preferences and ways of life.'[15] My analysis of an intermediary FBO in Chapters 4, 5 and 6 highlights this assumption held by some feminist development practitioners outside India that they 'know' the right vision of transformation for Indian women. Kishwar's vision draws on Gandhi's philosophy. She states:

> I would like to see a world in which the means for a dignified life are available to all human beings equally, where the polity and economy are decentralized so that people have greater control over their lives, where the diversity within and among groups and individuals is respected and where tolerance and equality of rights and responsibilities is fostered at all levels.[16]

Although Kishwar strongly opposes feminist ideologies, others in India use the term 'feminist' to describe themselves. Sunjata is adamant that she is a feminist and that feminist ideals combine with Gandhian concepts to drive her work. Jain and Singh,[17] who are critical of Kishwar, state that many activists in India hesitate before using the word feminist because it has become associated with a form of militancy that undermines the values and moral codes of the Indian tradition. I argue that a feminist approach helps to shape a distinct vision of development that focuses on women's empowerment. Although what constitutes empowerment may shift for different women, if gender equality is to be achieved the critical unpacking of core philosophies must continue. As I argue in Chapters 8 and 9, patriarchal values still determine social relations across the globe and these values are in turn sustained through the continued acceptance of teachings that advocate gender divisions. Although Gandhi and many other religious, secular and humanist teachers remain powerfully relevant, it is important to analyse their impact on sustaining a patriarchal ideology that stops many women achieving prominence in professions or even autonomy in their everyday lives.

Conclusion

In this chapter I compared and contrasted three case studies of community development organizations, all of which form part of the Gandhian network in India. Through the use of ethnographic data I showed how each organization interprets Gandhi's vision of development slightly differently. I did not evaluate the relative effectiveness of each organization, but sought rather to show that no assumptions can be made about the approach and priorities of an organization, even when it professes to belong to the same movement and seems to be based on similar values and beliefs. I also analysed Gandhi's philosophy on women and pointed to the contradictions inherent in his teachings. Despite these contradictions, in which Gandhi stressed human dignity and equality yet retained a patriarchal vision, he remains popular and influential, guiding the work of many activists in India and across the globe. I argued that while the significance of his teachings on human rights and freedom must be preserved, it is also important to continue the feminist project of deconstructing the patriarchal foundations of social relations cross-culturally. It is only when the sources of patriarchal beliefs about how men and women should live their lives have been eradicated that gender equality can really be achieved.

PART III

Religion as a Feminist Resource

I N this part I combine the approaches of religious studies, gender and anthropology to show how religion can both benefit and disadvantage women. I draw attention to the need to challenge the patriarchal aspects of religion and highlight how this is being done, often by religious women who reject the parts of their tradition they find oppressive and life limiting. Women who oppose or seek to restructure their religion often draw on those aspects of it that they find positive and inspiring. Emma Tomalin[1] introduced the notion of 'religious feminism' to describe how religious women utilize aspects of their tradition to challenge and change its oppressive parts. Religion can be both part of the problem and offer solutions. Outsiders, especially feminists, tap into and use religious spaces when negotiating change and transformation in women's lives.

While development actors have differing perceptions of what 'poor' women need, the processes they design to raise consciousness and empower the women towards whom the development projects are targeted often have the opposite effect. With insufficient physical communication between donors, intermediaries and local women, the latter feel marginalized and their voices fall silent. Religions, or more specifically religious spaces, offer one way of overcoming the communication barriers between religious women on the one hand and secular or religious feminist outsiders on the other. In the chapters that follow we shall see how eager the promoters of secular feminist discourses, whether Indian or Western, are to blame religion in general and Hinduism in particular for the oppression of women. I argue that a more balanced perspective is needed that endorses the value many women place on religion as a vehicle for self-expression and realization. This perspective should by no means ignore the disastrous impact religion has had in shaping the social and cultural environment of so many women across the globe.

Chapter 8

Physical Religious Spaces in the Lives of Rajasthani Village Women

H OW do physical religious spaces and the faith of individuals contribute to effective development practice? As described at the start of this book, faith is a distinct aspect of religion that denotes a personal and spiritual relationship with a divine being. The focus here is on Hindu and Christian notions of the 'divine' and 'sacred'. As mentioned in Chapter 3, Hindus worship the divine, the unified world soul or *Brahman*, through a multitude of gods and goddesses, each representing one aspect of the central God head.[1] Christians worship God directly as the source of truth and wisdom about all things. In both traditions the term 'sacred' denotes the character and nature of religious spaces. Sacred spaces are defined by their association with the divine. In other words, the divine spirit is thought to occupy sacred spaces, thus allowing adherents to communicate to and through it. As in previous chapters, the emphasis continues to be on the operation of faith as a guiding, motivational force in people's lives.

The term 'religion' is used more broadly to characterize sacred spaces within which people may express their faith in the divine, explore beliefs and values and receive teachings. In communities where religion forms an important part of daily life, a focus on the views and feelings expressed within religious spaces can help development practitioners understand why people act as they do and offer them a way through the often contradictory beliefs and attitudes people display. It can help them unravel some of the complexity of development and understand why change may or may not be desired in a particular area and by a specific group. For example, it can clarify why a woman remains in an abusive relationship, or why someone does not want to take scientific medical advice but turns instead to a traditional healer.

Religious spaces in this context refer literally to the physical spaces in which rituals take place. Individuals and groups create religious spaces in which to express their faith in the divine and to conduct a dialogue with the sacred images. The communication that occurs may follow the same pattern each day or may be spontaneously created from the believer's need to work through a problem or give thanks for a joyous experience. Religious spaces can be formal – a temple, church or mosque – or informal, private places in which an individual feels safe and secure. An individual or group may occupy private religious spaces. The private nature of these spaces means that the occupants share the same need to express a specific experience and/or work through a shared problem. Religious spaces serve a multitude of functions within a given community. They are fundamental in the formulation of moral and spiritual beliefs, which in turn produce embedded social relations that can affect people's lives positively or negatively.[2] As argued in Chapters 2 and 3, religious groups can manipulate and use religious spaces to project a worldview that might be destructive.[3] Some religious spaces serve to create open and honest dialogues between the members of an FBO, the FBO and its donor, and the FBO and local people. Finally, looking into and studying the religious spaces of local people can give development practitioners a better understanding of the concerns and priorities of others.

In this chapter I return to VSR, the intermediary/donor faith-based organization examined in Part II, to show how it uses religious spaces in three ways. First, it incorporates reflective, meditative space into its daily routine, which helps it sustain a long-term relationship with its donor and gives individual members the opportunity to think critically about the value of their actions. The open discussion that follows brings members closer together. Second, VSR deliberately steps into religious spaces that hold importance for the communities in which it works. For example, in a deliberate attempt to acknowledge the importance of religion in the lives of those with whom they hope to work, VSR members will worship in a village temple yet perform *puja* in a family's home. Once a desire to connect with people has been communicated some sections of a community (usually male elders) feel comfortable openly discussing the kind of development they would like to see. Third, VSR uses religious spaces to access the experiences and concerns of people, like younger women, who are excluded from public meetings. For example, it created a secure physical environment within which three Rajasthani women felt safe enough to perform a ritual together honouring the strength and courage of Sita, the ideal woman in Hinduism. All three women had been subjected to domestic violence and Sita too is purported to have suffered at the hands of a violent husband.[4] The ritual space the women created became important in enabling them to reflect on their experiences personally and to share their stories with others. Each woman gradually worked through her own strategy and was supported by VSR in achieving her desired outcome.

There are three main sections to this chapter. The first contains a review of work on how to improve communication between practitioners and local people, which includes a critical evaluation of participatory and human development approaches to development.

In the second section we see how VSR uses religious spaces to foster effective communication between its membership, donors and community leaders. Members of both organizations connect through a shared faith that acts to secure their commitment to working together.

In the third section we see how, by creating a secure environment, the VSR encouraged three women to explore their experiences of domestic violence though ritual. Development practitioners have difficulty reaching young women and discussing personal traumas like domestic violence is particularly problematic. The ethnographic material I present shows how private ritual can create a safe neutral environment in which young women can communicate openly and work through their traumatic personal experiences.

Religion, Communication and Participation

Cooke and Kothari, Crewe and Harrison, Gardner and Lewis, Hobart, Mosse, and Pottier[5] claim that, despite the adoption of participatory approaches to development, communication between NGOs and local communities remains poor. Local knowledge is ignored and assumptions are made about what people need. Laws,[6] writing on participatory research, responds practically and sensitively to these critiques by devising techniques that reflect the diversity of views and experiences present in any one location. Development practitioners need to use appropriate techniques to encourage different groups in any given community to voice their own development needs. She is clear that the success of participation depends on the relationship between the practitioner and community members. She remains adamant that participatory approaches are crucial to development, but that practitioners must adapt them to ensure they aid effective communication with all sections of a community.

Laws's resumé of participatory methods resonates with the capability and human development approaches of scholars such as Nussbaum.[7] Nussbaum is committed to developing a universal, holistic approach to human development that appreciates the diversity of human capabilities while supporting the individual through the process of instigating his or her own transformation. Laws stresses that participatory techniques are inadequate for accessing quieter, more privately-expressed views. I suggest that those working with the capability and human development approach to development must also face this problem, yet scholars working within the human development approach are less direct than Laws about recognizing how difficult it is to communicate with marginalized groups. The need to find a common frame of reference is central to the effectiveness of the capability approach. Nussbaum looks at how a concept of universalism can encompass diversity. Yet, unless the full diversity of experiences is heard, how is this possible? Participatory methodologies depart from human development approaches in their preoccupation with constructing techniques to enhance communication across development divides. While these discourses share similar conceptual ground, I focus my contribution more squarely on participatory scholars because I feel they have been largely blind to the potential of religion as a resource in their quest.

In seeking to support an equal expansion of human capability, development practitioners must be able to understand exactly what limits human potential. This entails forming close personal relationships with marginalized groups. The views that dominant groups endorse are more easily heard. Concerns about some issues, such as drought and food security, are more readily discussed because the community feels their effects collectively. Issues perceived as private matters, such as domestic violence, are not discussed in public forums. Even attempts to work with groups of young women in more informal settings have brought only limited results in terms of encouraging them to talk about their experiences of violence. Neither Laws nor Nussbaum has a solution to how these more sensitive topics may be accessed. Laws expressed the hope that a critical awareness that some groups remain marginal in many dialogues will push practitioners to think creatively about how to reach different sections of a community.

It is in hearing and communicating with marginal groups that a focus on religion can help. The most intimate and personal relationship for individuals with a faith is likely to be with their concept of the divine. Within the spaces created to worship, individuals may feel relaxed and safe enough to communicate experiences they cannot express in other contexts. Nussbaum recognizes the vital importance of religion as a resource in the development of human capability and accuses feminists and gender practitioners of seeing religion solely as a barrier to human development. Nussbaum points to the internal spiritual dimension of religion as a transformative path that adherents see as an integral part of their wider development as human beings. The translation of religion into rigid patriarchal practices may repress women and must be challenged if one is to support their development. At the same time, religion as a source of personal identity and motivation must be recognized as linked to the enhancement of individual capabilities. However, reaching and incorporating the personal aspects of religion into a participatory and/or human development and capability methodology needs to be thought through practically. I argue that if the subdisciplines of the anthropology of development and the anthropology of religion were to be brought together they could provide the methodological tools with which to access religious spaces and then use the insight for the purpose of development.

Work within the subdiscipline of the anthropology of development has gone some way towards improving our understanding of local knowledge. It has also problematized the process of identifying who is in need and of critically analysing the strategies for responding to that need. Anthropology has been used to evaluate projects so that lessons can be learnt and better practice built.[8]

As stated in Chapter 2, religion has been studied at a local level in the subdiscipline of anthropology of religion.[9] Anthropologists like Aigbe, Akinnasi, Angro, Barber, Bennett, Gold, Gottlieb, Hirschkind, James, Knauft, Lambek, Rappaport, Sanders and Swantz[10] emphasize the importance of religion as a source of the beliefs and values that structure everyday life. Very little of the literature, however, attempts to combine the anthropological perspectives on religion and development, yet these two subdisciples have something to contribute to participatory development practice.

When viewed as a series of physical spaces, each fulfilling an important function in the believer's life, religion emerges as a powerful source of insight into the lives of others. This is not least because faith, expressed within religious spaces, is a source of motivation that shapes actions. This insight could lead the outsider to a fuller understanding of the problems facing individuals and communities. Critical examination of how religious spaces are constructed and used within a community could also point to instances when religion marginalizes some into repressive gendered roles.[11] Accusations of witchcraft and the violence used to enforce them is one example of a religious, cultural and social mechanism used to control women.[12]

As reviewed in Chapter 2, the anthropology of religion literature shows that religion encompasses more than just faith in a god. People turn to religious spaces over and over again to work through problems and seek answers. Anthropological studies on healing, witchcraft and spirit possession emphasize the use of private spaces for the expression of personal trauma and problem solving.[13]

A micro focus on religious spaces could add to the insights that development practitioners who employ a participatory or capability approach gather. The anthropology of religion critically challenges the homogenization of religion by highlighting how religion brings both positive and negative affects to the lives of others. Long-term anthropological work, such as that of Gold and Raheja,[14] shows how women use religious spaces not only to conform to orthodox expectations, but also, in private moments, to challenge and often mock the values and beliefs they think repress them. This sort of long-term research complements the often short-term emphasis of participatory work. The considerable length of time many anthropologists devote to their research enables them to build closer relationships with sections of the community.

Gold and Raheja, as well as von Mitzlaff,[15] show how close relationships with informants help researchers identify the complex, contradictory perspectives through which individuals view the world. The relevance of this insight for development practitioners is the honesty of the views expressed within some religious spaces. For example, Erndl,[16] who studied the possession rituals of the Hindu mother goddess Mataji, argues that religious spaces offer women opportunities to express frustrations and work through their responses to problems. The term *Mataji* also refers to a woman recognized for having a close relationship with the divine goddess. The role of a *Mataji* is described as empowering, often giving the woman the chance to pursue a socially accepted life outside marriage. The close relationship the *Mataji* has with the divine goddess is thought to be more important than a life dedicated to a husband and children.

Erndl identifies social spaces before and after the *Mataji*'s ritual possession when women from different age groups, castes and social positions sit and chat. In situations where there are few occasions for social interaction, Erndl believes that these rituals provide important opportunities for female contact, for it is during such moments of sharing and social intimacy that they often find solutions to the challenges they face. She cites the example of a woman who was helped by the time she spent with other women in these preritual spaces to decide on a course of action to confront her husband's violent behaviour. These spaces are endorsed by men who are happy for their wives to participate in *Mataji* rituals because they believe they are performed for their benefit. Erndl also mentions that such spaces are missed by NGOs, yet hold a wealth of insights into women's lives. She sees the social spaces created by rituals as cracks in the patriarchal system. These cracks offer NGOs the opportunity to appreciate the experiences and agency of those women whose lives they hope to affect, but they could also enable better, more effective communication between development partners.

Having reviewed the contemporary literature on participation that stresses the importance of listening and responding to the needs of others, it is apparent that merging the separate contributions made by the subdisciplines of the anthropology of development and the anthropology of religion could make a further contribution to the participatory goal of 'listening to others'. The evidence has so far focused on what insights can be gained from an ethnographic focus on religious spaces. I now present an example of how VSR used religious spaces to build dialogue between its members, donor and the community leaders whose permission is required to launch a development project. Religious spaces successfully contribute to positive dialogues because those who occupy them share a faith that builds a relationship of trust between them. By taking an anthropological perspective I am able to highlight the practical contribution that 'faith', expressed within religious spaces, can make to development.

Religious Spaces and Fruitful Dialogue

In Chapters 5, 6 and 7 I detailed how the Gandhian organizations I studied (VSR, VDPJ and GMS), incorporated religious spaces into the start and end of each day. I now draw again on the case example of VSR which, at the time of my fieldwork had been working in the same area for 20 years and had strong links to the national Gandhian movement. As we saw in Chapter 6, VSR is situated in a hamlet 150 kilometres from Jaipur, was founded in the early 1980s and supports a range of water harvesting, irrigation and social welfare projects.

In Chapter 7 I looked more closely at the Gandhian philosophy underpinning the work of VSR and the other organizations with which I have spent time. All, including VSR, stressed the importance of living according to Gandhi's core ideal of *gram seva* – village service. Service is the driving force behind the actions of those who work for Gandhian organizations. Gandhi drew on many religions and in a sense went beyond affiliation to a specific tradition to a humanistic, interfaith position.[17]

As I explained in Chapter 4, I categorize VSR and other Gandhian organizations as faith-based because faith motivates their members' actions. In my conversations with individual members of VSR it was clear that many of them regarded themselves as Hindu. Since most of the workforce came from the surrounding villages it is hardly surprising that they should bring their religious values and beliefs with them into the organization. The management of VSR felt that meditative spaces within which the whole team could sit together provided cohesion and strong bonds. Within these spaces Hindu prayers were shared and *puja* performed. *Puja* is a form of Hindu worship in which chosen deities are honoured. Following the more formal, structured actions of performing *puja* and reciting prayers, each member would be encouraged to share his or her thoughts and concerns.[18] Interactions within this space were often very open and frank. The management felt that the religious nature of the space contributed to a feeling of safety, which made those occupying it feel able to speak.

When the UK faith-based donor 'Water for Rajasthan' (WFR) visited VSR each year, its members would join the religious spaces. Then, at the close of each day the members of both organizations would sit together in silence, reflecting on the day's events. Individuals from WFR would recite a Christian prayer, to which the Gandhian representatives usually responded with a Hindu prayer for peace, *Om Shanti*. I observed these sessions and felt that, as the trip progressed, the two groups became closer to one another. The warmth and empathy expressed in this space cemented a respectful acknowledgement of each other's faith. This respect then translated into effective dialogue, which resulted in shared development goals and objectives. Members of the WFR seemed to listen carefully to the experiences and local knowledge of those working for the VSR.

I stayed on after WFR returned home to observe how VSR members interacted with the Hindu communities in which they worked. Although their work often engendered hostility, VSR tried to counter this through the use of religious spaces and VSR members would spend time in local temples performing *puja* and mixing with local people as they came to worship. VSR leaders felt that if they showed communities that they respected the religious dimension of their lives, they would win trust and support for the initiatives they hoped to introduce. Primarily, it was the male elders whose support, in the first instance, VSR targeted. The social and political power dynamics were such that permission had to be sought from the male elders. In addition, meetings were often held between senior members of VSR and local religious leaders in the hope that their trust would be gained. VSR hoped that religious leaders would endorse their work and persuade the wider community of their good intentions.

We have seen how faith becomes a useful focus for communication when it motivates each party to act. Faith can be experienced emotionally and encompasses a drive to reach out to others. I shall now explore in more depth how, by seeking to understand the faith of others, deeper insights into their lives can be gained. We shall see how religious spaces, if created in a safe environment, provide a creative platform from which to work through strategies and overcome problems. NGOs and FBOs could follow the example below and encourage marginalized groups to use ritual processes to express personal, sensitive experiences. This approach could help overcome the difficulties that Sophie Laws identifies in getting excluded groups to share their concerns.

Ritual Spaces as Sources of Insight into Domestic Violence

Development practitioners have difficulty hearing the voices of young Hindu women in rural Rajasthan and communicating with them. An ethnographic focus on ritual provides us with the means to analyse social constructions of personhood and to understand the self-perceptions and identities of Hindu women. The Rajasthani women I observed performing religious rituals live in villages approximately 150 kilometres from Jaipur. The villages from which they come are populated mainly by upper-caste Rajput and lower-caste Kumhar (potters) families.

I initially visited this region of Rajasthan between June and August 1995. To conduct research, I spent five months living with Rajasthani village women both in their homes and in the centre from which the Gandhian FBO operated. This gave me the opportunity to observe their daily routines and, in particular, to see the part that rituals played in them. I gathered most of the data during the time I spent with three women – Poonam, Devi and Parvati. My ethnographic data on the lives of these three women were first published in a book I wrote called *Challenging the NGOs: Women, Religion and Western Dialogues in India.* I summarize their stories again here to show how useful religion is as an approach to understanding the lives of Hindu women. In my original research, all three women clearly understood the nature and purpose of my research and I feel confident they were happy for me to use their life stories, despite the deeply personal experiences they recounted. I have naturally disguised the identity of each woman in order to respect and protect her privacy. Poonam and Devi are Rajput, whereas Parvati is a Kumhar; all three live within an hour's drive from the town where they worked for VSR.

Poonam's story
Poonam (32 years old) is one of four daughters born to a poor Rajput family that lost its money through a bad investment and a father who squandered it recklessly. Her father had no money to offer as a dowry for his daughters. When Poonam was 18, her father handed her to a man 30 years her senior. She married and had a son, but her husband drank and beat her regularly. Gradually, desperation set in and Poonam ran away with her child. She had to leave during the night taking only the clothes she was wearing. When she left she headed for VSR headquarters, 40 kilometres away. She had heard it was run by a caring man who would not turn her away. She arrived on the

179

doorstep of Deepak's house in the early hours of the morning (she had managed to hitch a lift once she reached the road). VSR provided her with the means to live alone without her husband. Poonam now lives in a small town not far from the VSR base where she works as a nursery nurse. She has not remarried and cares for her son alone. Her natal family visits from time to time to help her with childcare (no financial help is given). Poonam experiences some hostility from her local community. She is the only single mother in her town (apart from women who have been widowed). On my first visit I stayed with her for about two months. I stayed with her again when I returned in February 2001.

Parvati's story

Parvati is a 30-year-old married Kumhar woman and the mother of two children, a boy (aged ten) and a girl (aged eight). She lives in a hamlet on the outskirts of town in a two-roomed mud house along with her husband, who is an alcoholic and regularly beats her after a drinking binge, her widowed mother-in-law and her children. Parvati worked as a cook and cleaner at VSR headquarters. While I was there, she cooked for and looked after the district nurse, who was resident at the headquarters. She also cooked for 30 women training to be village health workers when they stayed at the headquarters (July 1995). On my return in February 2001 she had a new job cooking for the children at a home based in the headquarters.

Devi's story

Devi is a Rajput woman by birth although she married a South Indian man and has spent her married life in Tamil Nadu. She is 35 years' old and has a 15-year-old son. Devi escaped a violent marriage. She struggled for years to remain with her husband because she did not want to bring shame on her family, but after 17 years of abuse she could take no more and left with her son. She decided to return to her family in Rajasthan where she felt she would be safe. On arriving she was told that VSR was looking for a cook. She took the post and was provided with accommodation and food for both herself and her son. Her son enrolled at the local high school.

◆ ◆ ◆

All three women performed *puja* twice daily at shrines in their homes or, in Devi's case, at the shrine she constructed for herself in her room in the VSR headquarters. *Puja* can take place at home, in a temple or at a community public shrine. Hindus often choose to worship in their homes, and are likely to choose gods and goddesses that address their concerns. Regional traditions also play a part in determining which particular deities are worshipped. The fact that women perform *puja* in the home reinforces their traditional roles as wives and mothers.[19] The traditional dictates of this role require them to make the focal point of the ritual the wellbeing of their family, which centres them in the domestic sphere. *Puja* therefore becomes an integral part of their daily activities, and they hope that through its performance twice daily they will protect their family. Poonam and Devi still performed *puja* even though they no longer live with their husbands. They did so (they claimed) because they are still mothers. Despite their circumstances, they still perform *puja* to emphasize the importance of their children's security and wellbeing.

The daily routine and pattern of *puja* follows a structure not unlike the one the anthropologist Fuller[20] recorded. However, I believe that the ritual Poonam, Devi and Parvati performed late each morning displayed personal reflections of their individual self-perceptions and, as such, it was unique to them. Once the bulk of the day's chores were completed, at around 10.30 a.m., each woman took a break. Whereas *puja* is an accepted part of a woman's daily routine, known and encouraged by male family members, the Sita ritual was performed by the women privately; while Parvati's husband may have known it existed, he did not have knowledge of its content and its significance in allowing her to voice her feelings towards his abuse. The personal nature of the feelings expressed through the ritual highlights the women's freedom to construct and perform rituals. I argue that they had chosen to construct this ritual because it fulfilled a need to enforce or express a particular aspect of their identity.

What is the significance of Sita?

What is particularly interesting is that many feminists scorn Sita for projecting a repressive image of women.[21] Sita appears in the Hindu epic, the *Ramayana*, with her husband Rama. Rama is banished to live in a forest by his father the king, acting on the instructions of Rama's stepmother who does not want Rama, but her son, to succeed as king. Sita is presented as the loyal and devoted wife who follows her husband into exile. One day Ravana, an evil demon, kidnaps Sita and takes her to his palace in Sri Lanka from where Hanuman, the monkey god, rescues her. Rama doubts her fidelity and makes her walk through fire to prove her innocence, which she does. The story goes on to see Rama become king and heralded as the ideal leader and man. Sita is commended for her role as the perfect, loyal wife.

One can see from this narrative why feminists might view Sita as a less than suitable role model, but she is popular with women and men in India and various debates have been waged as to why.[22] Many worshippers believe that Sita showed courage and defiance in the face of such harsh treatment.[23] Many view Rama's insistence that Sita endure the physical pain of the fire test as evidence of his wish to punish her violently. This interpretation of Rama as a perpetuator of violence towards his wife means that Sita's story resonated with the experiences of Poonam, Parvati and Devi.

The woman (or women if this ritual is performed collectively) removes a ring from her finger. She then kisses the ring and touches her forehead with it. She chants the story of Sita's kidnapping by Ravana and her rescue by Hanuman and his army of monkeys. Each time the name Sita is mentioned she kisses the ring and touches her forehead and heart. The ritual ends with the glorification of Sita. The woman praises Sita for her courage in exile and in the hands of the evil demon, and asks for inspiration to be like her. That Rajasthani women can glorify Sita in a ritual they construct for themselves and perform privately suggests that, to Poonam, Parvati and Devi, Sita was not a repressed figure. Instead, they saw something in her image that reflected their own interests, and ultimately found her a source of strength. The ritual reveals a process of internalization, which occurs through its production and performance. It is an embodiment of the personal experiences of each woman. As such, the ritual represents a space in which each woman is able to articulate her story confidentially. That she chose to use her spare time to perform this ritual reveals her agency and creativity. It also affirms her need to express the trauma she experienced. The performance of this ritual opens up an internal, private space, which allows a woman to voice her innermost concerns and anxieties. This process of voicing traumatic experiences with others who understand and empathize has a therapeutic function. This particular representation of Sita means that she is able to conduct a dialogue with a divine, sacred image whose story reflects her own. She injects Sita's image with the qualities she needs to cope with her own experiences, primarily courage and stoicism.

To Poonam, Parvati and Devi, Sita was and is a powerful symbol of courage and strength. They need to incorporate these important values and qualities into their lives to overcome the harsh realities of life as Rajasthani women. The symbols women attribute to Sita allow them to make sense of their past or 'collective history of suffering'.[24]

It is not just the symbols attached to Sita that are important, but also the physical enactment of the ritual itself. When they were together, Poonam, Devi and Parvati would sometimes choose to share the performance of this ritual. There were other women at the centre, but it was they who felt a connection because of their shared experience of violence and so, in performing the ritual together they offered support to one another; this was clear because Devi never performed the ritual before meeting Poonam and Parvati. The generation of such bonds is a vital part of protecting women's self-esteem in the face of indigenous injustice. The ritual represents a creative and embodied process that both enables women to cope with abuse and, as is clear from this example, inspires responses to that abuse.

I often wondered why Parvati remained in her violent marriage when she did not have to, for Deepak repeatedly asked her to leave her husband and offered her a secure home at the centre. Parvati refused, saying, 'why should I be the one to leave? I haven't done anything wrong.' She felt that her husband should leave because he was the one who had shamed their family. In fact, she was so defiant that she displayed her bruises each time her husband took his drunken rage out on her. Although Hindu women in this part of

Rajasthan practise purdah, Parvati chose not to veil her face, thus allowing those she passed to see her bruises. Parvati's pain was evident, yet she refused to leave, not because she felt she must remain a loyal faithful wife (she does not want to live with her husband any more) or because she was a passive victim (the vocalization of her pain was a clear indication of that), but because she clearly believed she had done no wrong and wanted her community to realize that. Running away would place the focus on her; the members of her community were likely to accuse her of abandoning her husband and his brutal crimes would be covered. Displaying her pain publicly was a way of protesting against the injustice in the hope that the community would support rather than stigmatize her. Performing the ritual affirmed the values she needed to endure her struggle. In addition, the affirmation she got from Poonam and Devi enabled her to cope with the violence.

Devi seemed torn between the two strategies adopted by Poonam (leaving a violent husband) and Parvati (staying in an attempt to shame her husband). Two months after I left, I learnt that she had returned to her husband in South India. Whatever her reason, I know it is not because she is weak or unable to stand on her own, so perhaps she was adopting a third strategy. She has shown her husband that she can leave and cope on her own, that she does not need him. She will be able to hold over him the constant threat of leaving him again and can remind him of her strength to stand up to him.

The ritual created a space within which the women could explore their experiences and consciously or unconsciously consider strategies to challenge the constraints they endured. Possessing different perspectives on their experiences did not hinder the solidarity the women expressed through performing this ritual as a group. What was important was the respect the women showed each other through the preservation of a space within which each had the freedom to articulate her unique and personal responses to violence. In this sense ritual does not just function to build identity but is also about the construction and maintenance of boundaries within which individuals are safe to reveal their innermost feelings.[25]

VSR played a crucial role in this ritual process. It provided physical shelter and employment for each woman. Within the safety of the headquarters the women could meet, connect and share their deeply personal experiences of violence. VSR was embedded and respected in the local community. By employing the women VSR was able to send a message to the community that the women deserved to be supported rather than stigmatized. This highlights how development interventions need not directly challenge social inequality, but can, as in this example, involve the creation of secure physical spaces that can then be used by individuals and groups to respond to injustices in their own terms.

Conclusion

We have seen how a focus on religious spaces can provide development practitioners with useful insights into the lives of others. Through participating in rituals and other forms of religious worship, development practitioners can show that they respect and recognize a community's religion as an important dimension in its life. It shows a willingness and desire to get to know groups within a community and to listen to their needs and concerns. I have demonstrated these arguments through a case study of VSR working in rural Rajasthan. VSR utilized meditative spaces for internal reflection urging members to think about the value of their actions. Members of this organization actively sought to join local people in temple worship and the performance of *puja* in people's private homes and at village shrines.

My ethnographic case study showed that participating in religious spaces helps to forge bonds between those who occupy them. This was seen in the close relationship between WFR and VSR when they came together in a religious space at the end of each day for individual reflection and group discussion. A visible closeness between the members of these two organizations was apparent, which secured the commitment of each individual to the organization. Finally, three women who performed a ritual together became connected within this religious space because they helped each other come to terms with their experiences of violence.

The examples of religious spaces given in this chapter highlight the power of 'faith' as a vehicle for open and honest dialogue. I

185

reviewed the work of Laws, who stresses the vital importance of close trusting relationships in development, and of Nussbaum, who asserts that religion must be included in a concept of human development because of its transformative quality and importance to people's inner lives. I then stated that neither participatory nor human development capability approaches can confidently reach and understand the experiences of marginalized groups. Nussbaum acknowledges the importance of religion for personal development and expression but fails to demonstrate how it may be used practically in grass-roots development. Ethnographic research shows that for people with a strong faith, personal experiences are likely to be expressed within religious spaces where the adherent feels safe communicating with divine and sacred images or concepts.

By using an ethnographic methodology a more complex insight into the formation and expression of views can be understood. Also, the creative and dynamic qualities of rituals and other religious spaces can be appreciated as vehicles in reaching development solutions. This approach holds huge potential for the capability approach of Nussabuam, who wrestles with the negative aspects of religious practices on gender relations. In my case studies it is within religious female spaces that women negotiate their own responses to violence, drawing on religion to drive actions and to build greater human capabilities. The development practitioner can not only learn about the lives of others through listening to the dialogues that take place within religious spaces, but, as in the example given in this chapter, could actively incorporate such spaces into a wider participatory and human development strategy aimed at empowering people to use their own capabilities to work through solutions.

Chapter 9

Positioning Religion in Research and Activism to End Domestic Violence in Rajasthan

THE focus of this chapter is on domestic violence, which, as we saw in the previous chapter, is present in the daily lives of many Rajasthani women. At the beginning of this book I mentioned the feminist motivation behind my work and my wish to record women's concerns and responses. I want to understand why some Hindu women draw on their religion to challenge and/or cope with domestic violence whereas others see it as partially responsible for its perpetuation in Rajasthan. My work on domestic violence incorporates the views of secular activists as well as Hindu women. Both groups acknowledge that religion plays a part in endorsing a patriarchal gendered ideology that normalizes male control over women and sanctions the use of violence against them. Many Hindu women see aspects of their religion as creative spaces for self-reflection and social networking. Some activists see religion solely as a problem and do not acknowledge that some Hindu women view it as both positive and negative. I consider what anti-domestic violence campaigners might gain by incorporating 'women only' ritual spaces into their wider strategies of communicating with and working alongside Hindu women.

My research on domestic violence spans six years and during this time I spoke with activists based in Jaipur who campaign specifically on domestic violence. I also reviewed research published by the gender research group at the Institute of Development Studies, Jaipur (IDSJ), and spent time listening to and observing the ritual activities of Hindu women, many of whom are regular victims of domestic violence.[1]

The women's movement in India has successfully launched coordinated campaigns against gender violence from grass-roots to state and national levels. Campaigns were mounted in Rajasthan over the suttee (widow burning) of Roop Kanwar on 4 September 1987 and the gang rape of the *Sathin* (local community worker) Bhanweri Devi on 22 September 1992. Bhanweri Devi was part of the Rajasthan Women's Development Programme, which the state government launched in August 1984. These horrific cases of violence against women mobilized national and transnational feminist groups, which succeeded in heightening awareness of the pervasiveness of violence against women in Rajasthan and across the globe.[2] In Rajasthan activists have been effective in demonstrating against the violence that accompanies practices such as female infanticide, child marriage, suttee and dowry.[3] Violence associated with socio-cultural practices or other public demonstrations of brutality against women should be separated from the distinctly domestic form of violence that occurs away from the public gaze. Although the same patriarchal ideology condones all these forms of violence, domestic violence remains the most difficult to campaign against precisely because it is invisible to the public and therefore impenetrable.[4] I concentrate on domestic violence, so do not discuss other forms of cruelty to women. I understand domestic violence to mean physical, sexual, mental or emotional abuse of a woman at the hands of a member of her family.

How can religion help activists challenge domestic violence? Given that domestic violence is considered a very private matter, women find it is hard to challenge their abusers in public, yet they recognize its injustice and regularly think about how best to respond to it. To reflect on her plight a woman understandably needs seclusion and privacy and, for a religious woman, this opportunity is best presented in her ritual life. Although the activists I have met acknowledge and respect the agency of the women with whom they work, they find it extremely difficult to change the pattern of domestic violence that is endemic in the society. The periods set aside for ritual practices provide a suitably intimate environment in which activists could talk to the women about their options and support them in whatever decisions they choose.

This chapter is divided into four sections. In the first I examine the links between religion, culture and domestic violence as understood in the interviews I conducted and in the relevant literature, including working papers from the IDSJ. In the second I look more closely at how religion is used in analyses of domestic violence. In the third I show how rituals offer many practising Hindu women a comfortable and safe environment in which to reflect, either alone or with others. In the fourth I consider what practical benefits a focus on religion might bring to the work of activists. In particular, I suggest that activists use some religious spaces to aid their communication with women whose lives are affected by domestic violence.

The Link Between Religion, Culture and Domestic Violence

Over a period of six years I got to know 12 feminist activists in Jaipur who are dedicated to combatting domestic violence. I spent time in a short-stay home for women who leave violent relationships and observed the work of various other rural organizations where I met a number of Hindu women who turned to religion for support in coping with violent relatives, usually husbands. Many of the feminist activists working in Jaipur have links with the Rajasthan University Women's Association (RUWA). RUWA was founded in 1975 to provide a forum for women in higher education, to support female scholars and to campaign for less privileged women. It has about 500 members who carry out a range of activities designed to improve women's lives and promote human rights.

Their close network ensures that the activists are able to join forces at times to collaborate on particular issues and one of these has been domestic violence. I interviewed a founding member of RUWA who was then directing a collective of approximately ten human-rights organizations, which together decided to divert some of their resources towards mounting defiant and coordinated action against domestic violence, which continues to obstruct women's empowerment. The state-funded Rajasthan Women's Development Programme (WDP) identified domestic violence as a significant impediment to the success of initiatives to increase the visibility of women in decision-making forums.[5] In other words, the women were refusing to participate in the programme because they were worried about how their husbands might react.

The programme has now virtually collapsed. While significant gains were made, mainly through the efforts of the women's movement in Rajasthan and various new initiatives like the educational programme for women 'Mahila Samakhaya', the WDP's failure to change gender relations in the state is, according to IDSJ researchers, due partly to the violent backlash such initiatives provoke. According to IDSJ working papers, husbands and other relatives are deeply suspicious of projects that specifically focus on women.[6] Srinivasan and Bedi[7] have collected and analysed extensive empirical data from South India that reveal that outside intervention can in fact increase levels of domestic violence. Following the demise of the WDP in Rajasthan towards the end of the 1990s women's organizations in the state began to step up their campaigning to eradicate violence against women and specifically domestic violence.

At the time of my last research trip in October–November 2007, the most up-to-date information on services and third-sector organizations for victims of domestic violence was a UNIFEM-funded resource directory called *Support Services to Counter Violence against Women*.[8] The directory lists 23 NGOs working in Jaipur, but reports that, despite this and a specific state policy on women drawn up in 2000, very little progress has been made towards eradicating domestic violence. This lack of progress is not for want of will and determination on the part of the feminist activists and many Hindu women with whom I spoke, or for want of creative initiatives. The stubborn persistence of domestic violence partly reflects the extent to which it is seen as a private matter, so silently accepted as a normal part of everyday life, which is frustrating for those who are trying to help. The activists and researchers believe that domestic violence is endemic in the state because so many cultural and religious practices (including purdah, dowry and child marriage) impose tight controls on women's lives.

Purdah physically limits a woman's mobility outside the domestic sphere and requires her to veil to reflect feminine modesty.[9] The dowry, in which the bride's family make marriage payments to the groom's family, reduces women to economic commodities and leaves them vulnerable to violence if the in-laws or husband feel that insufficient money was raised.[10] Child marriage, which is particularly prevalent in poor families because it avoids the need to raise a high dowry, results in girls having even less control over their destiny than in adult marriages.[11]

The activists I interviewed reluctantly admit that programmes to reverse perceptions of domestic violence as normal face an uphill struggle. Following the introduction in 2005 of the Protection of Women from Domestic Violence Act (PWDVA), Rajasthan recorded a high number of filed domestic violence cases. According to a 2008 UNIFEM monitoring and evaluation report conducted by Lawyers Collective, the number of recorded cases in Rajasthan since the legislation was introduced stands at 7435 with only Andhra Pradesh, Uttar Pradesh and West Bengal recording higher numbers. These statistics paint a bleak picture of domestic violence in Rajasthan. Although this high number of reported cases can be explained in part by the effectiveness of activism in the state, my informants felt that it was also reflective of the especially deep-rooted and endemic problem domestic violence represents to Rajasthani women.

On being asked what she thought was the best approach, the director of the collective of organizations fighting domestic violence said that her organization promoted the idea of 'responsiveness'. She claimed that 'there is no point in forcing a woman to act before she is ready; furthermore, each woman must decide upon her own course of action.'[12] The organization states that there is more than one way to achieve a life without violence and that each woman must discover what path is the right one for her. Emphasis is placed on the importance of one-to-one counselling to help women think through their options. This body funds counsellors who work in both the two 'women only' police stations in Jaipur, which were set up primarily to encourage women to report cases of violence against them.

Midway through our conversation she broke to answer a call, which she openly took in front of me and I heard her say, 'but she must act, as her life is in danger.' Later she admitted to feeling intensively frustrated when women failed to act when their lives were obviously in danger and help could be offered. Although she understood their reluctance, which was most often based on fear of having to leave children behind, she was genuinely concerned for their lives and this made it hard for her to resist the urge to push them. Campaigning on such an emotive and urgent issue places the people who work in this area of women's rights in a very difficult position. The delicate line between being responsive and pushing women to act emphasizes the importance of open communication between activists and those they want to rescue from a life of violence.

These activists often have to take a leap of faith into the unknown and rituals could offer them useful sites for dialogue with their clients. Unfortunately, by blurring the distinction between religion and culture, many of these activists, as well as quite a few scholars, see religion solely in terms of its function to entrench patriarchal values in the society, so they fail to recognize its importance for many Hindu women. Overcoming this blind spot could help reinforce the responsive style of work that most activists aim to practise in Jaipur and improve their communication with the women. As things stand, the activists believe that domestic violence exists because girls are socialized into accepting patriarchy, which means that they also accept the attendant constraints on their life opportunities and the authority of men to make decisions. Scholars often emphasize the role of religion and/or culture in reinforcing and validating this socialization process.

The UNIFEM directory of NGOs working on domestic violence in Jaipur suggests that women internalize female role models (like Sita):

> The awareness of a gender identity begins with deliberate training on how to be a good woman. The image of a good woman who is obedient, sacrificing and religious still has a

firm hold on the imaginations of women in the state. By observing fasts, festivals like Teej, Ganagaur, Karrachauth, and das mata, young girls are oriented into the patriarchal set-up by creating a value and deswabuly [sic] of husbands and their long lives.[13]

What the passage is essentially describing, though not explicitly stating, is how religion helps to create and sustain the wider social environment in which Hindu girls grow up. In Bowie's[14] description of the relationship between religion and culture, it is religion – as the source of authority and the purveyor of divine truth about the world – that prescribes how people should live and behave. Religion sanctions and legitimizes cultural practices through messages conveyed in religious texts, the teachings of leaders and specific codes of conduct. This clearly integrates the link between religion and culture, so explains the tendency to conflate the two.

Some academics, notably Narayan, are critical of Western scholars who use culture and/or religion to explain the existence of domestic violence in Indian women's lives. Narayan calls this phenomenon 'death by culture',[15] arguing that the same analysis is not used to explain why violence exists in the daily lives of women in the USA. Narayan is right to raise this inconsistency and to point to the essentialist and exotic nature of some Western feminist discourse. I believe that the women victims of domestic violence and activists alike can benefit from the insights derived from both religion and culture. Scholars of gender and religion have long argued that religion should always be included in discussions about violence, irrespective of how secular or religious the society. King[16] has written extensively on how religion and culture work together to keep misogyny alive throughout the world.[17] I do not wish to give the impression that religion alone can explain domestic violence, but rather that it is something that those who work closely with women at the grass-roots level tend to highlight.

Parliwala[18] and Basu[19] caution against conflating the different forms of violence and giving singular, linear explanations for their existence. Instead, scholars must carefully balance the analysis and acknowledge the existence of a web of interlocking factors that will change in shape according to the type of violence and the location and context in which it occurs. The activists I interviewed by no means promote religion above other aspects of the social, political and economic fabric of Rajasthan, but they do, however, point to various religious traditions, ceremonies and cultural practices that promote women's inferiority and submissive role as wives and mothers, which leaves them vulnerable and exposed to domestic violence. Some informants felt that women needed to reject religion altogether to be empowered, but careful attention to the relationship between religion and culture reveals that not every aspect of religion and culture are problematic. Instead of dismissing religion and/or culture wholesale, it is more helpful to isolate as problematic those aspects that legitimize the cultural and social norms that deny women basic human freedoms and result in domestic violence.

How is Religion Used in the Analysis of Domestic Violence?

I have shown above that in some material and in conversations with activists religion and culture are not always clearly delineated. Another reason for this conflation is that Hinduism is difficult to define. It is widely acknowledged, particularly among scholars of Indian religions,[20] that Hinduism is a label that early colonists imposed artificially on a diverse assortment of religious beliefs and practices. Given the wide array of religious and cultural traditions in existence in India today, it would be virtually impossible to group them into a single category without being accused of over simplification. However, since I seek to establish in what ways religion might help activists address domestic violence, I shall select those aspects of Hinduism I consider most relevant to our discussion of domestic violence in Rajasthan. For this purpose, I distinguish between religion as a belief system and religion as communion with the divine. The belief system, mostly acquired from texts and/or oral traditions, is disseminated by an elite group of religious leaders who are usually men and of the high Brahmin caste. The experiential dimension consists of adherents entering into a relationship with aspects of the divine (*Brahman*) through a process termed *darsan*.[21]

The rituals they perform involve repeating patterns of behaviour before an image symbolically conceptualizing the sacred eternal truth, which is regarded as a source of knowledge or inspiration.[22]

The pantheon of Hindu gods and goddesses stretches into an array of local deities that possess the identities and qualities that reflect the historic experiences and needs of their community.[23] A female adherent can experience her religion more freely through the daily performance of *puja* (the ritual to honour gods as welcome visitors) in private, informal moments at home, away from the direct gaze of her husband, religious leaders or other dominant figures. Many Hindu women carry out these rituals informally and without male instruction or observation.[24]

The IDSJ publishes working papers on domestic violence through its gender research group. Collectively, this material provides readers with an analytical framework through which to view the link between patriarchy, culture, religion and domestic violence. Activists working in the state use the papers to help understand the problems and develop practical strategies. Some papers adopt a negative view of religion and interpret the patriarchal symbols reflected in religious rituals as endorsing male dominance and violence. Joshi and Hooja produced a paper on *vrats*, the rituals women perform for the well-being of their families and which they believe form a vital part of women's socialization, and on *kathas*, narrations of stories dealing with the prosperity and longevity of husbands in which wives are depicted as devoted, pious and self sacrificing. According to Joshi and Hooja, 'a study of the subject matter of the *kathas* clearly affirms patriarchy.'[25] *Kathas* highlight the exclusive focus on male wellbeing and women's role in ensuring divine protection of their families. Joshi and Hooja emphasize that this relationship with the divine is a source of pride for women and perhaps explains why religion remains an integral part of their lives.

Pearson's[26] research on women performing *vrats* in Benares, as well as my work on rituals among a group of Rajasthani women,[27] reveals that the women enjoy the sense of control they have over the ritual spaces in which they express their internal and reflexive feelings. Pearson's informants describe how the rituals disclose how much power they can wield over their husbands, brothers and sons. Being responsible for protecting the wellbeing of their male relatives carries with it the power to decide whether or not they wish to perform that role. Women describe the embodied experience of performing *vrats* as empowering and liberating. I noted similar responses from the rural women who came together because of their shared experiences of domestic violence. Performing rituals is seen as an important way of working through bad experiences and seeking the strength to fight back. Furthermore, as I show later in an account of my visit to a short-stay home in Jaipur, the pattern of performing rituals daily can provide an emotional anchor in a life that has been disrupted or even uprooted. For a religious woman who has left a violent relationship, recreating her *puja* shrine and trips to a temple can help in the painful process of adjusting to a new way of life.

Mathur, a key figure in the research group, believes that women are being abused because the female body is looked upon as a symbol and site of community identity. 'The woman's body is continuously made to fit and mould to societal expectations with a severe denial of rights, her bodily integrity constantly violated.'[28] Activists blame this relationship of submission and dominance, which shapes gender relations, for the high number of cases of domestic violence. Violence is endorsed as a legitimate mechanism for husbands to use to ensure that their wives stay loyal and dutiful. Mathur[29] describes how sentiments expressed on a daily basis claim that a man is entitled to hit his wife if she is disobedient, legitimize and engrain the violence. For example, it is not unusual to hear phrases such as 'husbands will beat', 'husband has the right to beat his wife', 'because the man is the breadwinner, beating is also a man's right'.[30]

Religion and culture collude to help embed these sentiments into the behaviour and attitudes of men and women. Confusingly, both men and women express these sentiments, suggesting that women are complicit in maintaining the social and cultural conditions that render them vulnerable to violence. This has led to the development of programmes designed to encourage women to challenge the normalization of violence and turn their backs on the traditions that help endorse it. Activism concentrates on supporting women in understanding that violence used against them is wrong and must be challenged, an approach that Mathur and the gender research group at the IDSJ recommend. Mathur highlights that practitioners in Rajasthan focus on helping women create a positive sense of self, which they need if they are to become active against violence.[31] She outlines areas for action, the last of which reads: 'Programme interventions such as Mahila Samakhaya need to be supported and replicated as forums for the expression of women's self-identity and behaviour as defined by women themselves.'[32]

Mahila Samakhaya, a woman's educational and empowerment programme operating throughout India,[33] offers women-only spaces to encourage participants to discuss their problems. It clearly supports women as active, empowered agents, yet seems to assume that they can only communicate openly in spaces that NGOs create. From her remarks that 'poor non-literate women given the space and support can reflect, articulate and challenge injustice'[34] and 'catalysing change would necessitate a change in self-image leading to a change in social image',[35] Mathur seems to think that women need self-help groups to spark off change in their lives, but for some women this transformation starts in the ritual spaces within which they reflect personally or with others on the impact of domestic violence on their lives and look for ways to eradicate it.

Basu, who has conducted extensive research among women from all caste and class backgrounds in Delhi,[36] describes how women tread an ambiguous line between accepting and resisting violence. They are reluctant to abandon their traditional gender roles for fear that destabilizing 'normal' family life will increase rather than decrease their vulnerability. Basu believes that women still go along with patriarchal dowry practices because they affirm their cultural identity. She claims that because her informants perceive themselves as belonging to a 'collective Indian culture' and use the plural 'we' when talking about Indian tradition, they automatically see themselves as part of that patriarchal structure. The process of self-identification is, however, more complex than that, for many Indian women recognize that the system subjugates them yet they remain with men who have internalized the values of a highly misogynistic tradition. While all Basu's female informants recognized that their tradition subjected them to grave injustices, they would speak of their subjugation in spaces in which they felt safe, which is where female religious rituals come into the picture.

Rituals as Reflective Social Spaces

Rituals in general can be understood as embodied processes of personal expression.[37] However, shifts in meaning and the embodied experience of performing the ritual may happen even if the actions remain the same. Onlookers may observe similar patterns in ritual and assume that the values and concerns remain the same, but rituals are not static and adapt in response to time, place and the adherent's needs. In the previous chapter I mentioned the importance of ritual activities as coping mechanisms in everyday life. The spiritual dimension of ritual opens up an internal space because it centres on the adherent's sense of embodiment. Rituals are reflective spaces in which adherents can think about their experiences. Within ritual spaces the individual wrestles with his or her own subject-in-process. An internal dialogue occurs between the individual and the divine image they have chosen to worship. Out of this relationship the subject is constantly recreated in opposition to what they see in the divine image. For example, women who worship Sita, portrayed in some narratives as the ideal woman in Hinduism and in others as a woman wronged and harshly treated by her husband Rama, may reflect on her story and compare it with their own. A female adherent may draw out aspects of Sita's character that she sees in herself or would like to project because she thinks it may help her cope better with her life.[38] This personal, internal aspect of ritual is highly creative, gradual and accumulative, thus allowing the adherent to respond to the challenges of everyday life.

Harlan,[39] who also works in Rajasthan, talks about how the physical relocation of ritual to new and different surroundings gives women a chance to explore ideas and express experiences they are unable to do through the solitary act of *puja* in their own homes. When women come together to perform rituals at religiously significant times, they share their perceptions of the process and articulate embodied experiences of the divine. Harlan states that as a result of hearing the perceptions of others an individual will question and perhaps change his or her own self-perceptions and worldviews. As the adherent changes so too does her relationship with the deities she worships.[40] According to Harlan, new ideas may be explored within the reflective space of *puja*.

During a visit to a short-stay home for women fleeing violent situations, I observed two women create and worship at a *puja* shrine. They were Devi, aged 18, who had married at 12 and whose in-laws and husband beat her almost daily for no given reason, and Susila, who was in her thirties and had finally left her husband who abused her regularly after drinking. Both women had to travel a long distance to reach the short-stay home, which they had heard about by word of mouth, and they both performed *puja* at shrines they had created for themselves. I asked them why they did so in this setting and they described how it gave them a structure and sense of home. It also helped them think about the children they had left behind. A further reason, though neither woman mentioned it, may have been that the process of creating a shrine together enabled them to build a valuable bond of friendship with one another.

An adherent's experience of a ritual is determined not by the physical actions but by the environment in which it is performed. In other words, adherents bring to the ritual space their ever changing perspectives on the world. Since the physical actions of *puja* and *vrats* are focused on male family members, their performance constantly evokes the woman's relationships with them. If violence characterizes her marriage the embodied, emotional dimension of her ritual will explore this experience and perhaps allow her to contemplate alternative gender relationships. Similarly, the rituals performed after a woman leaves a violent relationship will be used to help her recreate a sense of home and work through the loss she might feel at leaving people, particularly children, behind.

As my research shows, as well as that of Harlan, women's rituals also function as social spaces. Women interact both before and after the ritual performances to share their experiences and ideas. Joshi and Hooja record that women claim to be in 'control' of their performance and are not forced to do it. In other words, if women actively choose to perform rituals that on the face of it appear to support patriarchal ideals, they must also be getting something positive from them. The spaces within which *vrats* take place are women-only spaces. As informal spaces they fulfil an important function as social networks.

The practical benefits of religion

Activists could usefully incorporate already existing women-only ritual spaces into their efforts to communicate and build trusting relationships with women subjected to domestic violence. By stepping into and participating in religious activities, activists can display empathy and understanding towards some of the women with whom they wish to work. Before rituals can form part of existing strategies, ethical concerns need to be confronted. An outsider can only step into the private spaces of others when invited. The outsider will then only be a witness not a facilitator who wishes to provoke change. As a witness, the outsider observes and listens, closely examining the complex array of apparent contradictions that form each woman's subjectivity. Any attempts to alter the nature of the space or to steer conversations in a particular direction would be an intrusion and potentially damage the occupant's positive experience of the space. However, an activist's participation in these spaces not only indicates the women's acceptance of her as a person to be trusted, but the space also provides a ready-made forum in which to discuss domestic violence. The use of these spaces may therefore be worth the ethical risk.

Informal spaces, whether religious or purely social, reveal women articulating discomfort towards aspects of their lives and acting to remove and/or alter factors standing in the way of their happiness. Meyers[41] claims that when a woman appears not to act on or even voice discomfort at what outsiders view as oppressive, it may be because no real alternatives exist, rather than a lack of awareness or false consciousness. A second kind of fear, fear of the alternatives, may prevent Rajasthani women taking action against, or loudly exclaiming, the injustices they suffer.[42] All the activists with whom I spoke admitted that life becomes tough when a woman leaves her husband. She may be unable to bring her children with her and, even when a new home is found for her, members of the community may view her as a failed woman. Social stigma and economic insecurity may make a single woman's life painfully difficult.

Abusive husbands are issued with court orders to pay maintenance, but often refuse to do so, thus adding to a woman's financial insecurities. People prefer the security of a known evil over the risk of what might succeed it. In addition to the lack of real practical alternatives, the shift in identity from a married woman back to a single woman involves a leap of faith. The woman must trust those urging her towards this redefinition of her status. Organizations in Jaipur have made significant progress in campaigning for the creation of safe, secure environments in which women can report abuse. For example, counsellors based at the two female-run police stations mentioned earlier offer emotional and practical help to women trying to come to terms with the abuse they have suffered. This approach is felt to be effective, but, as with any under-funded initiative, it has limitations. From a conversation with the director of the collective, it was clear that women who report abuse have insufficient time with a counsellor and many have to return home before their family notices their absence. Also, they have to travel great distances from rural locations outside Jaipur. This means there is little time to foster a trusting relationship between the counsellor and woman, which is essential if a drastic change in circumstance is to be effected.

Informal spaces can offer the activist or researcher a useful venue in which to enter a meaningful dialogue with women in need of support. Rather than waiting for the women to come forward of their own volition and officially report the abuse, activists and researchers could seek out the moments when women are naturally prone to discuss such matters. In other words, the activists could come to these pre-existing spaces to listen to and witness the processes through which each woman works out her solution to domestic violence. The presence of activists might encourage women to think more creatively about their alternatives and reassure them that support is available should they choose to make a drastic change in their life. This use of informal spaces could build on the success of Mahila Samakhaya's work in creating safe havens in which women can discuss violence openly. Two approaches could work in parallel – the use of already existing informal spaces in which outsiders can slowly build sensitive trusting relationships with the women and the deliberate creation of spaces for the explicit purpose of discussing how to end domestic violence.

Conclusion

In summary, culture and religion collude and combine with other social, political and economic factors to limit women's opportunities to express discontent, thereby perpetuating the patriarchal status quo that sanctions domestic violence. This is something that activists, Hindu women and scholars all recognize. Many religious spaces are occupied solely by women and used on a daily basis and, as such, are experienced as safe, secure moments in the lives of the female adherents. Through her relationship with divine images a woman is free to express her innermost thoughts and feelings. Also, before and after worship the women tend to gather and share the thoughts they had expressed during worship. If such spaces were given greater visibility, activists could use them to reach out to the women they are trying to help. To return to my central argument, though religion is a force that contributes towards sustaining patriarchy, it also forms an important part of many women's lives in that it accords them dignity and purpose. Activists and researchers may find religion a useful and potentially constructive tool through which to strengthen the dialogues they have with women suffering domestic violence.

Chapter 10

Puja as an Approach to Health Care

I N bringing together the discussion in the previous chapters on the relative usefulness of religion, I now present a practical example of how some community organizations use religion strategically as part of their approach to women's development. It has been demonstrated that religion is helpful practically and theoretically in three main ways. First, through observing female-only religious rituals an outsider can gain insight into a woman's self-perceptions and worldview. Second, through participating in women's religious spaces an outsider can communicate more closely with groups of women about their lives and the things they may want to change. Third, religion plays an important part in perpetuating patriarchal cultures, which explains why gender inequalities remain so deeply entrenched.

I now build on these arguments by focusing on how religion forms an important dimension in the approaches of the Gandhian organizations 'Village Service Rajasthan' (VSR) and 'Village Development Project Jodhpur' (VDPJ), the case studies drawn on in Part II and Chapter 8 of this part. We shall see how differently religion shaped the management styles of the projects these organizations designed to train Rajasthani women to become community health workers. While both projects stressed a wish to implement a participatory approach to the work, each interpreted this very differently in practice. The second of these projects was more adamant in its insistence on the need for close relationships and open dialogue between all parties involved, so challenged any barriers or hierarchies that arose between participants. The first project, by contrast, maintained a hierarchical structure in both its organization and in the relationships with the trainee health workers.

I believe that the second project was more successful because its leaders had more insight into the participants' lives and that they gained their insight partly through participating in the performance of *puja*. In fact, even the most senior member of the NGO both took part in the ritual and expressed solidarity with the trainees. While *puja* is the term given to a form of Hindu worship or ritual acknowledging the divine nature and power of the deities,[1] it more specifically refers to 'honouring guests'. In other words, adherents treat the chosen gods and goddesses as if they were honoured guests in their home.

In both organizations, the trainees performed *puja* daily, but only the second NGO recognized its significance in the women's lives and incorporated it into the training schedule. The NGO's respect for this religious activity in part explains the meaningful connections that emerged between all involved in the second project. Performing *puja* offered the NGO workers a practical vehicle through which they could visibly and emotionally communicate a desire to relate to the trainees.

It was evident, however, that an awareness of the social, cultural and religious aspects of people's lives are essential components of any successful development initiative.[2] If managers understand how the participants see the world then effective dialogue becomes possible; and effective dialogue, in turn, produces shared goals and a commitment to achieve them. The management of the second NGO performed *puja* to show empathy for the women. *Puja* also represented a secure space in which the women were encouraged to share the problems they encountered in their social and cultural lives. The NGO then responded by envisaging what potential difficulties the women might face in their duties as community health workers.

A comparison of these two projects shows a contrast between the spaces within which the trainees relaxed and socialized and the formal, structured training sessions. In both projects the performance of *puja* was central in creating shared informal spaces within which the trainees got to know each other and out of which vital support networks emerged. The second project's inclusion of these spaces helped to bridge the hierarchal divide between managers and participants and contributed to a closer, longer-lasting relationship (11 years). The first project, by contrast, operated an autocratic, top–down management style, demonstrated by the inappropriate use of formalized participatory techniques. This project folded three years after its inception, thus emphasizing the value of informal spaces in bridging divides between management and project participants.

Puja is essentially a dialogue between adherents and their chosen deity or deities, and it can be used to express concerns and anxieties about development initiatives. The reflective dimension of *puja*, which the second NGO recognized, helped to ensure the long-term success of the project.

I begin this chapter with a critical analysis of the autocratic approach of the first FBO (VSR) before moving on to examine the positive benefits of the more sensitive approach of the second NGO. Then, in the third section, I cover the social, cultural and religious functions of ritual and conclude that *puja* and other ritual spaces could form part of a dialogical management style.

The focus is not on the religious beliefs and values of the Gandhian organizations, but on the different styles of management they adopt despite their shared origins.

Village Service Rajasthan (VSR)

The key objective of this project was to train a group of 30 Rajasthani village women as community health workers. I first visited the NGO's headquarters in July and August 1995 and I was staying there when the project started. It was thought that by giving the village women a new role as health workers, the training would serve both to empower them and provide health care to the wider community. In line with contemporary development discourse, there was an emphasis on the need to increase community participation through the involvement of the women in the project's implementation. Despite this focus on participation, the project has now ended. My fieldwork trip (from November 2000 to June 2001) confirmed that there are no community health workers in employment.

The ages of the women selected to be health workers ranged from

20 to 60. All were literate and came from a mixture of tribal and caste backgrounds. Their individual statuses varied according to age and stage in life, but all were married with children. Some were also grandmothers. It was thought that the older women, with their higher status and ability to command respect, would be able to support the younger ones whom other community members (especially men) might regard with suspicion.

The training took place at the NGO's headquarters. Because most of the women lived some distance from the hamlet (on average a two-hour journey away), the course was residential. The women slept on rolled-out mattresses on the floor of a large room they shared. The course was broken into two seven-day sessions with a fortnight's break between them, when the women would return home. They followed the same timetable each day and, in an attempt to identify any spaces in which they reflected on their personal feelings about the programme, I recorded their daily routine:

6.00–7.30 a.m.
Get up and wash from troughs of cold water in the two washrooms adjacent to the sleeping room. Wash and hang up a set of clothes ready for the next day. Perform *puja* individually and in groups at the shrine they had created for themselves in the sleeping room.

7.30–8.30 a.m.
Have breakfast, which two local women cook. After breakfast doze or sit together singing songs. Many of the songs were devotional, narrating the Rama and Sita story.

8.30–9.00 a.m.
Congregate in the sleeping room, now cleared of sleeping mats. Sit on floor and drink tea. Say a prayer together and sing a devotional song praising Rama for bringing them together and expressing hope for the success of the project. A project worker and not the women initiate this meeting. A project facilitator lights joss sticks and hands them to one of the women who waves them around the room symbolically to purify the air ready for the day's work.

9.00–11.00 am.
A local doctor, community nurse or project coordinator leads first training session.

11.00–11.30 a.m.
Take tea.

11.30–1.00 p.m.
Health professional or project coordinator leads second training session.

1.00–2.00 p.m.
Lunch, then sleep, chat or go for a walk. Some visited the local temple.

2.00–4.00 p.m.
A health professional or project coordinator takes third and last training session of the day.

4.00–7.00 p.m.
Drink tea and sit around chatting. Collect and fold washing done in the morning. Some wander around the nearby area stopping to chat to people (mostly women).

7.00–8.00 p.m.
Dinner cooked by two local NGO employees. Then perform *puja* together. Sometimes a group of them would go to the village temple to perform *puja* and afterwards sit in the temple grounds talking.

8.00–10.00 p.m.
The project leader might come to speak with the women. He would meet them in his office where he would sit on a chair while they sat at his feet. He would ask them how they felt things were going and tell them how pleased he was with their progress. Sometimes he would ask them to sing for him and they would oblige with a traditional devotional song. These interactions were formal and after he had left the mood relaxed, the women would spend time talking, singing and dancing. They would unroll the sleeping mattresses and go to bed before 10 p.m.

The formal training

The external 'experts' who devised and delivered the training programme made no effort to become part of the support network that the women were developing: in fact, the health professional leading each session would sit above the women on a chair at the front of the room while the women sat on the floor. The trainers took the women through a variety of key primary health issues, including antenatal and postnatal care. There were two sessions on nutrition, childhood diseases and illnesses, and the physical development of babies. Others were on the diagnosis and treatment of conditions commonly suffered by children and adults, such as calcium deficiency, malaria and dehydration. The women were taught how to identify illnesses that may require antibiotics and other medications. They were shown how to administer drugs and told what information to give about them.

Most of the time was devoted to family planning. Posters were mounted around the room suggesting the ideal number of children to be two per couple.[3] Training was delivered on contraception. Videos, textbooks and talks with visual aids were all employed as teaching techniques. The style of delivery was top–down; the health professional claimed superior knowledge and made only one attempt to elicit the trainees' views. This entailed drawing maps of their bodies as a way of conveying how they viewed female biology. The health professional who led these sessions was a woman because the management had decided that the trainees were more likely to open up to another woman.[4]

After sketching her body on plain paper each trainee was asked to label it. She then had to come to the front of the group and describe her picture and talk through the labels. Further exercises were then done in which the women were asked to describe, by adding to their picture, how particular bodily processes worked, beginning with reproduction. They were asked specific questions, for example, why do you have periods? When did you start having periods? The questioning became quite intrusive. Questions were put to the women about how they might prevent themselves having more children. After each series of questions had been asked, the women had to come to the front and again show the rest of the group their picture and describe what they had drawn and why.

After the women had gone through their explanations, the health professional leading the session displayed a biomedical diagram of the female body. She talked at great length about the biomedical processes depicted in the diagram. This particular method of body mapping was used at numerous training sessions, mostly in relation to family planning and antenatal and postnatal care. All the exercises followed the same form. The women had to offer explanations on various issues using their pictures, after which the health professional would talk through the biomedical diagram.

At the start of the second seven-day course, after the two-week break, the women were tested verbally to see if they had retained what they had been taught on the initial training course. Towards the end of the course the emphasis became more practical and the women were given a bag containing literature and medicines to distribute. They were then taken to the villages they had been assigned to visit regularly for meetings with the village elders and project coordinator.

Each village health worker was assigned a different group of about three villages, depending on distance and size. All were within walking distance of their villages. The women were to hand out treatment as needed and take payment for medicine where possible. They were only to offer treatment for the illnesses they had been taught to diagnose. If they did not recognize a symptom they were told to refer the patient to the travelling medical team that visited each village once every two months. The medical team would make a special trip if the community health worker thought it necessary.

A nurse would visit each health worker once a month. She would replace any drugs and medicines given out and take the money the community health worker had taken. They would also pay them at this meeting. Each village health worker was expected to visit her assigned villages at least once a week; this would involve about two full days of work. They might be sent for more frequently if an emergency occurred, for example a difficult birth.

Problems

During the residential programme the women relaxed when alone. This change in atmosphere starkly highlighted the lack of communication between management and trainees. The project had structural, organizational problems that could have been identified from the start had the NGO shown more sensitive awareness of the social, cultural and religious aspects of the women's lives. Gender roles in rural Rajasthan limit female activities outside the household, yet the project expected the women to be away from home for lengthy periods. Many of the younger women had never before been away from home for that long. In addition, the majority of the women had childcare responsibilities, which the NGO expected them to put on hold for the duration of the course.

At first all the women managed to leave their children at home with other family members, which the system of joint family households made possible. The male members of a family remain in their natal home throughout their lives. On marriage a woman leaves her parents and moves to her husband's house, where she joins other wives who have married his brothers. As children are born so families grow, but they remain under one joint roof. Towards the end of the training programme this separation became an increasing strain both on the trainees (who claimed to miss their children) and on the family members left to shoulder the responsibility (other wives or the mother-in-law in the joint family). Gradually, husbands began arriving with offspring and leaving them with their mothers. Some husbands would try to persuade their wives to come home.

This problem should have been foreseen, for when they were alone the women would discuss their families and children. It was clear that most of them missed being at home and some of the younger ones, in particular, expressed concern about being apart from their young children. The private space created by the shrine offered a valuable outlet to express feelings about the project. Women were constantly seen performing *puja* at the shrine. When I asked why they were performing it so frequently, the response came, 'for my husband and children'. Although it is usual for women to perform *puja* for their families,[5] the frequency with which they did so indicated their increased need to worship. In addition, some of the women would visit the local temple daily, which they would not have much time for at home.

The rigid divide between women and health professionals did little to encourage honest and open communication. In addition, the training schedule consisted of sessions led by different people. Occasionally, one person would lead a few sessions, but on the whole the face at the front changed, so the women had little chance to develop a relationship with their trainers. When a session came to an end, the facilitator would get up and leave the room to socialize with the project managers who were based in a different room, leaving the women to chat among themselves. The women were left to try and make sense of the new information given to them, and they gradually came to realize just what sort of impact the role of community health worker would have on their lives. They discussed these concerns and anxieties among themselves.

The lack of communication meant that a series of assumptions were made about the women's lack of 'real' biomedical knowledge and simplistic perceptions of body and health issues. The body mapping exercise served to support this view. Research conducted by Gold and Raheja[6] reveals that Rajasthani women have a strong sense of their own physicality. The health professionals in this case study failed to respect the trainees' awareness and self-perception, which further divided the management from the participants.

Perhaps the project's greatest flaw was that it underestimated the time burden this additional role would place on the women.[7] All the women are mothers with time-consuming domestic responsibilities. To fulfil their role as community health workers and spend whole days visiting different villages, other family members would have to take on their usual responsibilities. Although this was possible at the start of the project, the strain on those left behind soon became too great. Gradually, more and more of the women returned to their domestic duties full time and gave up their extra responsibility as a community health worker.

By comparing this failed programme with a similar yet successful one, I identify what crucial factors were absent in the former project but existed in the latter. Specifically, from the outset the management of the second NGO identified the cultural and social difficulties the trainees faced. Furthermore, they acknowledged the importance of religion in the women's lives. This NGO encouraged the performance of *puja* as a way of ensuring that the women reflected on their difficulties and developed a support network to share their concerns.

Village Development Project Jodhpur (VDPJ)

VDPJ launched its project to train 40 village women as community health workers in 1996. Mrs Sharma is the organization's co-director and she, with the rest of her management team, selected the trainees. The women were invited to an initial training course at VDPJ's rural base. From the outset an attempt was made to understand and overcome any barriers to the women's commitment. Many came from great distances but were able to bring their children with them for the duration of the course (seven days). A crèche was set up in the centre grounds, which meant that the women could participate fully in the training sessions. VDPJ was able to include a wider range of women than the first project and the management campaigned hard in local communities to promote the status of a health worker. As a result, women from high-caste Rajput families came forward as prospective trainees. Traditionally, women from high-caste families observe purdah particularly strictly, which physically limits their public movements and certainly prohibits employment.[8] In rural Rajasthan both Hindu and Muslim women veil their faces and are restricted in what they can do outside the domestic sphere. The public invisibility of Rajput women is thought to reflect positively on family honour and is a sign of high status, but a community health worker is one public role that is seen as fitting for a Rajput woman. The high status attributed to it by the employees of VDPJ has helped.

All health workers were encouraged to save a proportion of their salary in a cooperative bank. Mrs Sharma claimed that it would not only give them more economic independence but would also provide a motivational incentive to ensure their commitment to the course.

The women got up at around 7.00 a.m. and were invited to morning meditation and group discussion. Breakfast was taken in the community kitchen and shared with other NGO workers. The daily sessions, many of which Mrs Sharma led, would begin at around 9.30 a.m. and took the form of a series of workshops. Sometimes the women watched videos about an aspect of health care and at other times they participated in more practical exercises like tying bandages and dispensing pills. Some sessions were held in a hospital in the centre's grounds where doctors or nurses would teach the participants about various procedures and instruct them on how to diagnose basic illnesses. Volunteer patients from the local village were recruited for role playing exercises and the trainees would be observed applying their knowledge and skills.

After the initial seven-day course the women returned to their villages. They took part in a series of four further seven-day training courses over a period of six months. By the end of that time they were able to begin practising as community health workers. This project succeeded for the following reasons. The health workers continue to return to the training centre for 'refresher courses' in which knowledge is reinforced and techniques practised. The women themselves decide on the content of these sessions in accordance with how they feel they are progressing. In addition, new information is conveyed in the hope that the women will develop as health practitioners and thus be able to offer more comprehensive health provision.

VDPJ workers visit the community health workers on a regular basis and make extra visits if the women request them. This may happen if a community reacts hostilely to a health worker's advice or treatment (for example family planning). If a patient is too seriously ill for her to treat, then medical backup is sent. VDPJ stresses that the health workers should not feel isolated, but see them as part of a wider structure that operates to reinforce and support their work.

The inclusion of puja

A significant aspect of this project's management approach was that efforts were made to build open and equitable dialogue between everyone involved. Space for informal interaction was created within the training programme. Time was set aside for the performance of *puja* and quiet reflection. The working day began and ended with a period of meditation, which everybody involved in the project attended. During this quiet time the women were encouraged to reflect on what they had learnt and voice any areas of confusion or matters of concern. Those present were then asked to share their feelings. Meditation and prayer were followed by less structured interaction. Songs and stories were often exchanged.

Facilitators tried to link themes back to issues discussed during the training, for example attitudes towards childrearing and health. Such exchanges helped foster a relaxed atmosphere that made the women feel part of a community that valued them as equals and respected the contribution they were to make. These spaces also functioned to forge trusting relationships. As noted in the first project, exchange between the women became more open as the training programme progressed. The performance of *puja* served to establish bonds and connections. The women were encouraged to create their own shrine in the main room where the bulk of the training took place. The shrine functioned in a similar way to that in the first project. It was where the trainee health visitors could exchange views about the project and share thoughts they were uncomfortable voicing in front of the whole project team. It also gave the management a chance to show the women that they acknowledged and respected *puja* as an important part of their lives. Mrs Sharma performed *puja* at the shrine on a daily basis.

As time went on, some women began to feel anxious about their ability to cope with the project and expressed their concerns during the collective meditative and social period. For example, during one period five women openly confessed to having an uncooperative family, or a husband or other family member who was violent; they worried that these domestic pressures would make it difficult for them to carry out their duties. When I asked one of them when she first felt able to talk about her problems, she said that she had confided in some of the other health workers and it was they, in turn, who had encouraged her to put the problem to the whole team. A chain of dialogues can be seen. *Puja* and meditative practices built and strengthened connections between those involved in the project, with the *puja* shrine in the training room acting as the first stage and giving the women the trust and confidence they needed to voice their fears to the whole team. Mrs Sharma believed that respecting spaces in which problems could be shared improved the productiveness of the health workers.

The methodology of this project clearly encouraged inclusivity, yet no formalized participation techniques were used. In this case the NGO built up a network of local workers who had the respect of the surrounding communities. Spaces were then created to develop friendships between all participants. The performance of *puja*, space for reflection and informal discussions all functioned to create a stable support network.

Why is puja so important?

In my records of the daily pattern the trainees adopted, space for *puja* and other religious activities, including quiet reflection and trips to the temple, emerged as key features of both programmes. The importance of *puja* in particular was evident in that both groups of trainees felt the need to create a shrine and the *puja* they performed followed the accepted pattern seen across India.[9] When they embarked on a new venture that took them away from their domestic lives, the shrine seemed to provide a link to their homes and familiar routine. I asked a number of trainees from both projects why they had created the shrine and they invariably said 'because we have one at home'. In both projects, while watching the women first create and then worship at the shrine, it struck me that the space created through the performance of *puja* had importance beyond the symbolic link to 'home' and to honoured deities. Friendships were formed during the shared act of negotiating the construction of a shrine and deciding which deities to place in it. The wider social interactions that sprung from the performance of *puja* enabled the women to challenge and explore the differences between them. The women in both projects came from a range of caste, tribal and age backgrounds but friendships were formed across these divides in both programmes, which is unusual in India.

As discussed in Chapters 8 and 9, rituals in general can be understood as embodied processes of personal expression.[10] They are not static but adapt and change in response to time, place and the needs of the adherent.[11] The women created a *puja* shrine together from whatever materials they could find. In both cases, the NGO management let the women take deities dotted around the headquarters. The shrine was not an exact replica of their own, but it was a product of their collective efforts. It partly reflected the need for the women to work effectively together. Team work was a central facet of both community health-care programmes.

The preparations, exchanges and conversations associated with the performance of the ritual also influenced each woman's experience of the training. In her work on *puja*, Harlan[12] talks about how the physical relocation of ritual to new and different surroundings offers women the chance to explore new experiences and ideas. In the context of these community health-care projects new ideas may be explored within the reflective space of *puja*. The social mix of the health workers' backgrounds would in and of itself have brought a number of different life experiences to the training sessions. Hearing and exploring the experiences of others would have provoked an internal change (to differing degrees) within each participant.

It was not possible for me to delve into the intimate relationships each woman had with the deities displayed in the shrine. As I observed the women worship individually and in groups I felt that they used this time to work through aspects of the project. This seemed likely since *puja* was woven into the formal training sessions, so the ideas discussed during the training would have been fresh in the women's minds as they worshipped. For example, the women may have used this space to make sense of the new biomedical ideas presented to them about their bodies. They may also have used the ritual to absorb the impact this new role as a community health worker would have on their lives and family. What my observations clearly revealed is the importance of *puja* as a means of friendship building. This friendship developed over the duration of the training. By the end a visible closeness between the women was apparent.

Conclusion

In this chapter I have presented two case studies of projects designed to train and initiate village women as community health workers. Both stressed the importance of participation, but took different approaches towards achieving it. The first NGO incorporated a participatory exercise into the training schedule. The women were asked to sketch a body map to represent how they felt female bodies worked. I contrasted the inappropriateness of this exercise and the women's lack of engagement in it with the exuberant and open interactions within the group at other points in the training. Social spaces were often focused on *puja*. The women worked together to create a *puja* shrine and accompanied each other to the local temple. The performance of *puja* linked the women to their homes and created a vital reflective space within which they could respond individually to the challenges the project presented.

The second NGO recognized the significance of these spaces and ensured that they were incorporated into the training programme, which led to relaxed and open relationship between the NGO members and the trainee health workers. A vital support network was created between the women, helped by the social and ritual time they spent together. Participation in the second case study could be seen through emphasis on communication and trust. Effective communication enabled the second NGO to anticipate certain needs, like childcare, without which the women may have been unable to participate as fully in the project as they did. The project also left the women feeling more empowered and independent. Clearly, the sensitive relational approach of this second case study represents the more successful management model. I conclude by urging both researchers and practitioners of development to think more creatively about how rituals (including *puja*) could be incorporated into a more dialogically focused approach.

Conclusion

I N this, the conclusion to the book, I stand back from each of the three parts to reflect on how they connect, what they can say as a whole about religion and its relationship to human development. In attempting to summarize the main contribution of this book I shall draw on the work of Jonathan Benthall, who in turn has utilized Bourdieu's concept of religion as a shifting field. Benthall[1] argues persuasively that religion has always been there and is unlikely ever to disappear as a dominant structural force in our lives. He believes that even processes that appear to be secular have strong ideological foundations, which followers support with such force that they could be branded spiritual, hence his use of the term 'secular spirituality'. These arguments are not unlike those of Quarles van Ufford and Schofferleers,[2] reviewed in Chapter 1, who believe that the prevailing development discourse of neoliberalism is presented and pursued with the strength of religious conviction. Benthall offers a possible explanation for the permanence of religion in our lives through the work of Bourdieu[3] who, like Weber,[4] argued that society cannot be analysed simply in terms of economic classes and ideologies. He developed the terms of *doxa* and *habitus* to denote a relationship between a subconscious and structured field of human experiences. Within the *doxa*, subconscious beliefs and concepts exist that through the *habitus* form ideas about how individuals should live and behave in the world. Religion plays a significant role in perpetuating symbols that rest in the subconscious but then later find expression in an array of articulated beliefs, practices and institutions.[5]

Religions possess a great capacity to evolve and adapt to an ever-changing world, perhaps because deep-rooted subconscious symbols, feelings and impulses support the belief systems on which they are based. It is impossible to prove why religion is so permanent, but something about its inherent spiritual and deeply personal dimensions, as my ethnographic research in Part III shows, fulfils a human need for reflective space. Simultaneously, other dimensions of religion help to foster impulses in some people that drive them to dominate and control the lives of others.

I have tried to depict religion as complex, constantly evolving and yet never losing its interconnective dynamic. To analyse its impact on people's lives and on shaping different concepts of development, it is necessary to break it down into analysable segments. Consequently, I have looked at spirituality and faith as well as at the institutional and organizational dimensions of religion and religious traditions. Although people can derive hugely positive benefits from religion, usually through its spiritual dimension enabling devotees to express personal thoughts and feelings without fear of societal repercussions, religion should be approached with wariness, especially when it intersects with conceptions of development. The gendered perspective I took in this analysis of the overlaps between religion and development enabled me to examine how far religion's patriarchal and authoritative foundations still present significant barriers to achieving social equality and justice, particularly for women. As I showed in Chapter 3, hierarchical religious organizations manipulate the language of rights by overlaying its terms with a spiritual stress on 'love and compassion', which masks other objectives or prevents critical analysis into the lack of structural change the organization actually achieves.

I have urged caution in accepting and embracing religious organizations as safe bets when it comes to delivering on goals of social equality. As my case studies in Chapter 3 highlighted, religious organizations often propound the concepts of compassion and love, which seem to fit neatly with visions of social equality. However, my critical analysis into these organizations drew out differences between them and the dominance of patriarchy in two, which certainly runs counter to feminist Indian and Western goals of female emancipation.

My focus on religion and gender revealed competing visions and concepts of development, and showed how inappropriate it often was to pursue Western ideas about how the world should be. My research also revealed that even when some members of a community support certain goals, others remain marginalized. Young women especially are often silenced by processes of consultation that fail to include them in dialogues. In Chapter 7 I highlighted that, despite the array of participatory approaches development professionals now deploy, this failure to communicate and reach out to the most marginalized groups continues. I have argued throughout but in Part III in particular that development practitioners must pay closer attention to the culturally and religiously shaped spaces within which different groups communicate. Failure to recognize the cultural and religious nature of many social interactions has resulted in the continued exclusion women from decision-making forums.

In short, Western development professionals and agencies still systematically ignore the religious-cultural dimension of people's lives. The reason for this is more likely to be lack of confidence in knowing how to tap into these spaces than ignorance or a failure to recognize that religion and culture are important in shaping how people see the world and ultimately regard 'development'. In other words, as outsiders, many development practitioners lack the skill or appropriate language to communicate effectively with different people about the importance of their spiritual lives and cultural practices. Recognizing the centrality of religion and culture in people's lives would give the practitioner a better insight into the lives of local people and what sort of future they envisage for their communities. Chapters 8, 9 and 10 contained practical examples on how one might bridge this communication gap.

These arguments need to be heard at this point because national and international funding agencies seem to have reached a consensus that religion and the organizations that come from them are good at development. The Department for International Development states that funding to FBOs will double in the years to come. This sharp increase in funding is because DFID believes that FBOs are best placed to deliver localized forms of development and already have the community infrastructure needed to achieve this. In its 2009 White Paper DFID stated that it would 'double [its] support to faith-based groups, [thus] recognizing the unique contribution they can make in both delivering development on the ground and connecting with communities here and abroad'.[6]

Through the close ethnographic case studies of various types of FBOs presented in Chapters 3, 4, 5 and 6, it is clear that having a local presence does not necessarily mean being better placed to respond to local needs or to produce the transformations large donors are after. Furthermore, religion is one of the worse culprits there are when it comes to producing gendered perspectives and structures that marginalize certain groups. I hope that the critical analysis employed in this book will highlight the need to develop a means of evaluating the impact of not just FBOs but also of religion more broadly on development initiatives. Funding FBOs because they recognize and often incorporate the local community's religious views is one strategy, but when either secular organizations or FBOs bring the insights of religion, gender studies and anthropology to bear on their approaches, they can, as we have seen, come up with a more perceptive, reflective and face-to-face approach to development.

Above all else, the terms religion and development must continuously be questioned and analysed against the backdrop of shifting global power allegiances and discourses. Local and global political relations shape these terms and the agendas they set. To understand the shifting sands of our time we must look towards forging interdisciplinary partnerships that utilize the different lenses that macro and micro studies have crafted. Academics should not be afraid of working within the spheres of religion that are not clearly visible to their sense of empiricism. Although the deeply personal experiential side of religion is hard to penetrate, it is here that individuals find the inspiration and strength to demand changes in their lives, as the testimonies and stories told in Part III highlight. Furthermore, personal religious spaces help create social platforms that bring people together to act in a common cause.

Notes

Introduction

1. U. King (ed.) *Religion and Gender* (Oxford: Wiley Blackwell, 1995); U. King and T. Beattie (eds) *Gender, Religion and Diversity: Cross Cultural Perspectives* (London: Continuum, 2004).
2. A. Escobar, *Encountering Development: The Making and Unmaking of the Third World* (New York: Prinkel, 1995) p. 24; D. Harvey, *A Brief History of Neoliberalism* (Oxford: Oxford University Press, 2005); J. Sachs, *The Development Dictionary: A Guide to Knowledge as Power* (London: Zed Books, 1992).
3. A. B. Jenkins and N. Alexander, 'Who Rules the World Bank', bank information center http://www.bicusa.org/EN/Article.3327.aspx, 2007; D. Kapur, 'Who Gets to Run the World? *Foreign Policy*, 2000, p. 121; D. Kapur, J. Lewis and R. Webb (eds) *The World Bank: Its First Half Century* (Washington: Brookings Institution Press, 1887); N. Woods, 'Making the IMF and World Bank more Accountable', *International Affairs*, 77 (1) 2001, pp. 83–100.
4. Jenkins and Alexander, 'Who Rules the World Bank'.
5. U. King, 'Religion and Gender', in Ursula King and Tina Beattie (eds) *Encyclopaedia of Religion* (New York: Macmillan, 2005).
6. J. Ferguson, 'Means and Ends of Development: The Uses of Neoliberalism', keynote conference paper, The Ends of Development: Market, Morality, Religion, Political Theory, VU University Amsterdam 19–20 June 2008.
7. G. Esteva, 'Development', in W. Sachs (ed.) *The Development Dictionary: A Guide to Knowledge as Power* (London: Zed Books, 1992); M. Hobart (ed.) *An Anthropological Critique of Development: The Growth of Ignorance* (New York: Oxford University Press, 1993).

Part I. Mainstreaming Religion and Gender in Development

1. Harvey, *A Brief History of Neoliberalism*, p. 5.

Chapter 1. Mainstreaming Religion and Gender in Development

1. V. Desai and R. Potter (eds) *The Companion to Development Studies* (London: Arnold Publications, 2002); M. Rahnema and V. Bawtree (eds) *The Post-development Reader* (London: Zed Books, 1997); S. B. Schech and J. Haggis, *Culture and Development: A Critical Introduction* (Oxford: Blackwell, 2002).
2. For example, see A. Ghatak, 'Faith, Work and Women in a Changing World: The Influence of Religion in the Lives of Beedi Rollers in West

Bengal', *Gender and Development*, 14 (3) 2006, pp. 375–83; E. Tomalin, 'Religion as a Rights-based Approach to Development', *Progress in Development Studies*, 6 (2) 2006, pp. 93–108; E. Tomalin, 'The Thai Bhikkhuni Movement and Women's Empowerment', *Gender and Development*, 14 (3) 2006, pp. 385–97.

3. C. K. Wilber and K. P. Jameson, 'Religious Values and Social Limits to Development', *World Development*, Elsevier, 8 (7–8) 1980, pp. 467–79.

4. F. von der Mehden, 'Religion and Development in Southeast Asia: A Comparative Study', *World Development*, 8 (7/11) 1980.

5. S. Qureshi, 'Islam and Development: The Zia Regime in Pakistan', *World Development*, 8 (7/11) 1980.

6. T. Ling, 'Buddhist Values and Development Problems: A Case Study of Sri Lanka', *World Development*, 8 (7/11) 1980.

7. J. Benthall, *Returning to Religion: Why a Secular Age is Haunted by Faith* (London: IB.Tauris, 2008).

8. R. Robertson, *Globalization: Social Theory and Global Culture* (London: Sage, 1992).

9. P. Beyer, *Religion and Globalization* (London: Sage, 1994).

10. D. Eade (ed.) *Development and Culture* (Oxford: Oxfam, 2002); E. Tomalin, 'Religion as a Rights-based Approach to Development', *Progress in Development Studies*, 6 (2) 2006, pp. 93–108; W. Tyndale (ed.) *Visions of Development: Faith-based Initiatives* (Aldershot: Ashgate, 2006); and K. A. Ver Beek, 'Spirituality: A Development Taboo', *Development in Practice*, 10 (1) 1 February 2000, pp. 31–43.

11. Eade, *Development and Culture*, p. ix.

12. Ibid.

13. V. Tucker, 'Introduction: A Cultural Perspective on Development', *European Journal of Development Research*, 8 (2) 1996, pp. 1–21.

14. Tyndale, *Visions of Development*.

15. www.rad.bham.ac.uk

16. C. Rakodi, 'Understanding the Role of Religions in Development: The Approach of the Religion and Development Research Programme', *Working Paper 9*, 2007 (www.rad.bham.ac.uk).

17. Ling, 'Buddhist Values and Development Problems'; von der Mehlen, 'Religion and Development in Southeast Asia'.

18. J. Haynes (ed.) *The Politics of Religion: A Survey* (London: Routledge, 2006); S. Thomas, *The Global Resurgence of Religion and the Transformation of International Relations* (New York: Palgrave Macmillan, 2005).

19. L. Reychler and T. Paffenholz (eds) *Peace Building: A Field Guide* (Boulder, CO: Lynne Reinner, 2000).

20. J. Haynes, *Religion and Development: Conflict or Cooperation?* (Basingstoke: Palgrave Macmillan, 2007); I. Linden, *A New Map of the World* (London: Darton, Longman & Todd, 2003).

21. S. Alkire and E. Newell, *What Can One Person Do? Faith to Heal a Broken World?* (London: Darton, Longman & Todd, 2005); S. Harper (ed.) *The Lab, the Temple and the Market: Reflections at the Intersection of Science, Religion and Development* (Bloomfield, CT: Kumarian Press,

2000); S. White and R. Tiongco, *Doing Theology and Development: Meeting the Challenge of Poverty* (St Andrews: St Andrews Press, 1997).
22. K. Marshall, 'Development and Religion: A Different Lens on Development Debates', *Peabody Journal of Education*, 76 (3–4) 1998, pp. 339–75; K. Marshall and L. Keough, *Mind, Heart and Soul in the Fight against Poverty* (Washington, DC: World Bank, 2004); G. Ter Haar and S. Ellis, 'The Role of Religion in Development: Towards a New Religion between the European Union and Africa', *The European Journal of Development Research*, 18 (3) 2006, pp. 351–67.
23. S. Alkire, 'Religion and Development', in D. A. Clark (ed.) *The Elgar Companion to Development Studies* (Cheltenham: Edward Elgar, 2006) pp. 502–10.
24. S. Deneulin and S. Bano, *Religion in Development: Rewriting the Secular Script* (London: Zed Books, 2009).
25. P. Quarles van Ufford and M. Schoffeleers (eds) *Religion and Development: Towards an Integrated Approach* (Amsterdam: Free University Press, 1998).
26. Ibid., p. 1.
27. See Chapters 4 and 6 in this volume.
28. S. Deneulin, 'Development as Freedom and the Costa Rican Human Development Story', *Oxford Development Studies*, 33 (3/4) 2006, pp. 493–510.
29. G. Clarke, 'Faith-based Organizations: An Overview', in G. Clarke and M. Jennings (eds) *Development, Civil Society and Faith-based Organizations: Bridging the Sacred and the Secular* (Basingstoke: Palgrave Macmillan, 2008).
30. R. Pearson and E. Tomalin, 'Intelligent design? A Gender Sensitive Interrogation of Religion and Development', in G. Clarke and M. Jennings (eds) *Development, Civil Society and Faith-based organizations: Bridging the Sacred and the Secular* (Basingstoke: Palgrave Macmillan, 2008).
31. Ibid., p. 47.
32. M. Molyneux and S. Razavi, *Beijing Plus Ten: An Ambivalent Record on Gender Justice* (Geneva: UNRISD, 2006) cited by Pearson and Tomalin, 'Intelligent Design?'
33. Tyndale, *Visions of Development.*
34. See Chapter 6.
35. Linden, *A New Map of the World.*
36. Alkire and Newell, *What Can One Person Do?*; Harper, *The Lab, the Temple and the Market*; W. Tyndale, 'Idealism and Practicality: The Role of Religion and Development', *Development*, 46 (4) 2003; Tyndale, *Visions of Development.*
37. Tyndale, *Visions of Development.*
38. White and Tiongco, *Doing Theology and Development.*
39. See Alkire, *Religion and Development*; Deneulin, 'Development as Freedom'; Linden, *A New Map of the World.*

40. A. Sen, *Development as Freedom* (New Delhi: Oxford University Press, 2004).
41. R. King, *Orientalism and Religion: Postcolonial Theory, India and the Mystic East* (London: Routledge, 1999).
42. U. Kothari (ed.) *A Radical History of Development Studies: Individuals, Institutions and Ideologies* (London: Zed Books, 2005).
43. C. de Rivero, *The Myth of Development: The Non Viable Economies of the 21st Century* (London: Zed Books, 2001).
44. G. Clarke, 'Faith Matters: Faith-based Organisations, Civil Society and International Development', *Journal of International Development*, 18 (6) 2006, pp. 835–48.
45. K. Gardner and D. Lewis, *Anthropology, Development and the Postmodern Challenge* (London: Pluto Press, 1996).
46. R. Peet, *Geography of Power: The Makings of Global Economic Power* (London: Zed Books, 2007).
47. See E. Crewe and E. Harrison, *Whose Development? An Ethnography of Aid* (London: Zed Books, 1998); Gardener and Lewis, *Anthropology, Development and the Postmodern Challenge*; J. Pottier (ed.) *Practising Development: Social Science Perspectives* (London: Routledge, 1993); J. Pottier, A. Bicker and P. Stilloe (eds) *Negotiating Local Knowledge: Power and Identity in Development* (London: Pluto Press, 2003).
48. B. Cooke and U. Kothari (eds) *Participation: The New Tyranny?* (London: Zed Books, 2001); Kothari, *A Radical History of Development Studies*.
49. T. Bradley, *Challenging the NGOs: Women, Religion and Western Dialogues in India* (London: Tauris Academic Studies, 2006); Gardener and Lewis, *Anthropology, Development and the Postmodern Challenge*; S. Laws, *Research for Development: A Practical Guide* (London: Sage and Save the Children, 2003).
50. M. Angro, *The Culture of the Sacred: Exploring the Anthropology of Religion* (Prospect Heights: Waveland Press, 2004); F. Bowie, *The Anthropology of Religion: An Introduction* (Oxford: Blackwell, 2000); S. Glaizer, *Selective Readings in the Anthropology of Religion: Theoretical and Methodological Essays* (Westport CT: Praeger, 2003); D. Hicks (ed.) *Ritual and Belief: Readings in the Anthropology of Religion* (Boston: McGraw Hill, 2002); M. Lambek (ed.) *A Reader in the Anthropology of Religion* (Oxford: Blackwell, 2002).
51. Hobart, *An Anthropological Critique of Development*; A. Kumar Giri, *Conversations and Transformations: Toward a New Ethics of Self and Society* (Maryland: Lexington Books, 2002); P. Quarles van Ufford and A. Kumar Giri (eds) *A Moral Critique of Development: In Search of Global Answers* (New York: Routledge, 2003).
52. Crewe and Harrison, *Whose Development?*; T. Hefferan, *Twinning Faith and Development: Catholic Parish Partnering in the US and Haiti* (Bloomfield: Kumarian Press, 2007).
53. Pearson and Tomalin, 'Intelligent Design?', p. 51.

54. Tomalin, 'The Thai Bhikkhuni Movement and Women's Empowerment'.
55. A. Rew, 'Samen op Weg? Travelling Together? Religious Reform and Female Empowerment in Northern Orissa', in O. Salemink, A. van Harskamp and A. Kumar Giri (eds) *The Development of Religion/The Religion of Development* (Delft: Eburon, 2004).
56. Bradley, *Challenging the NGOs*.
57. L. J. Peach, 'Human Rights, Religion and (Sexual) Slavery', *Annual of the Society of Christian Ethics*, 20, 2000, pp. 65–87.
58. Tomalin, 'The Thai Bhikkhuni Movement and Women's Empowerment', p. 385.

Chapter 2. Understanding Global Development through Religion and Gender

1. Beyer, Religion and Globalization.
2. P. Beyer and C. Beaman, *Religion, Globalization and Culture* (Leiden: Brill, 2007); D. Hopkins, L. Lorentzen and E. Mendieta, *Religions/ Globalizations: Theories and Cases* (Durham, NC: Duke University Press, 2002); M. Tehranian and J. B. Lum, *Globalization and Identity: Cultural Diversity, Religion and Citizenship* (Piscatawy, NJ: Transaction Publications, 2006).
3. Hopkins et al., *Religions/ Globalizations*.
4. S. Coleman, *The Globalisation of Charismatic Christianity* (Cambridge: Cambridge University Press, 2000); M. Warburg, A. Hvithamar and A. Wasmind, *Baha'i and Globalisation* (Aarhus: Aarhus University Press, 2005).
5. C. Elliott (ed.) *Global Empowerment of Women: Responses to Globalization and Politicized Religions* (London: Routledge, 2007).
6. Bowie, *The Anthropology of Religion*.
7. J. Pratt, *Class, Nation, Identity: The Anthropology of Political Movements* (London: Pluto Press, 2003).
8. S. Alvarez, E. Dagnino and A. Escobar (eds) *Cultures of Politics/Politics of Cultures: Re-visioning Latin American Social Movements* (Boulder, CO: Westview Press, 1998); M. Leach and I. Scoones, 'Mobilising Citizens: Social Movements and the Politics of Knowledge', *IDS Working Paper Series*, 2007, Brighton: Institute of Development Studies; D. Meyer and S. Staggenborg, 'Movements, Countermovements and the Structure of Political Opportunity', *Amercian Journal of Sociology*, 101 (6) May 1996, pp. 1628–60.
9. J. Burdick, *Looking for God in Brazil: The Progressive Catholic Church in Urban Brazil's Religious Arena* (Berkeley: University of California Press, 1991); K. Norget, 'Progressive Theology and Popular Religiosity in Oaxaca', in C Smith and J. Prokoopy (eds) *Latin America in Motion* (New York: Routledge, 1999); A. Sen, *Shiv Sena Women: Violence and Communalism in a Bombay Slum* (London: C. Hurst & Company, 2007).
10. J. Benthall, 'The Middle East', *Anthropology Today*, 7 (2) 1991, pp. 11–15.

11. M. Edelman and A. Haugerud (eds) *The Anthropology of Development and Globalization: From Classical Political Economy to Contemporary Neoliberalism* (Oxford: Blackwell, 2005).
12. J. Haynes, *Religion in Third World Politics* (Buckingham: Open University Press, 1993); J. Haynes, *Religion in Global Politics* (Harlow: Longman, 1998); J. Haynes (ed.) *Religion, Globalization and Political Culture in the Third World* (Basingstoke: Macmillan, 1999); Haynes, *The Politics of Religion.*
13. www.wfdd.org.uk
14. J. Howell and J. Pearce, *Civil Society and Development: A Critical Exploration* (Boulder, CO: Lynne Rienner Publishers, 2002).
15. J. Fox, 'Religion as an Overlooked Element of International Relations', *International Studies Review*, 3 (3) 2001, pp. 53–73.
16. Thomas, *The Global Resurgence of Religion*, p. 23.
17. M. Juergensmeyer, 'Religion in the New Global Order', 'Religion in the New Global Order', 2005, http:www.maxwell.syr.edu/Moynihan/programs/sac/paper_20pdfs/marks_20paper.
18. Bowie, *Anthropology of Religion.*
19. J. L. Brain, 'Witchcraft and Development', *African Affairs*, 81 (324) 1982, pp. 371–84; M. Gessler, 'Traditional Healers in Tanzania: The Treatment of Malaria with Plant Remedies', *Journal of Ethnopharmacology*, 48, (3) 3 November 1995, pp. 131–44; V. Kamat, *Negotiating Illness and Misfortune in Post Socialist Tanzania: An Ethnographic Study in Temeke District Dar es Salaam*, Ph.D., Emory University, Department of Anthropology, University Microfilms International, 2004; L. Kendall, *Shamans, Housewives and Other Restless Spirits: Women in Ritual Life* (Honolulu: University of Hawaii Press, 1985); F. Kramer, *The Red Fez: Art and Spirit Possession in Africa* (London: Verso, 1993).
20. T. J. Csordas, *The Sacred Self: A Cultural Phenomenology of Charismatic Healing* (Berkeley: University of California Press, 1994); S. Feiderman, 'Struggles for Control: The Roots of Health and Healing in Modern Africa', *African Studies Review*, 28 (2/3) 1985; M. Lambek. *Knowledge and Practice in Mayotte: Local Discourses of Islam, Sorcery and Spirit Possession* (Toronto: University of Toronto Press, 1993); L. Legerwerf, *Witchcraft, Sorcery and Spirit Possession: Pastoral Responses in Africa* (Gweru: Mambo Press, 1987); A. Masquelier, 'Lightning, Death and the Avenging Spirits: Bori Values in a Muslim World', *Journal of Religion in Africa*, 24 (1) 1994, pp. 2–51; O.B. Rekdal, 'Cross-cultural Healing in East African Ethnography', *Medical Anthropology Quarterly*, 13 (4) 1999, pp. 458–82.
21. P. Geschiere and F. Cyprian, 'Domesticating Personal Violence: Witchcraft, Courts and Confessions in Cameroon', *Africa*, 64 (3) 1994, pp. 323–41; J. Janzen, *Discourses of Healing in Central and Southern Africa* (Berkeley: University of California Press, 1992); A. Manji, *Magic, Faith and Healing: Mysteries of Africa* (Pittsburgh: Sterling House, 2003); M. Marwick (ed.) *Witchcraft and Sorcery* (Harmondsworth: Penguin, 1982); R. Pool, *Dialogue and the Interpretation of Illness:*

Conversations in a Cameroon Village (Oxford: Berg, 1994); Rekdal, 'Cross-cultural Healing'; M-L. Swantz, *Blood, Milk and Death: Body Symbols and Power of Regeneration among the Zaramo of Tanzania* (Westport: Bergin & Garvey, 1995).

22. Haynes, *Religion and Development*, p. 11.
23. S. Aigbe, *Theory of Social Involvement: A Case Study in the Anthropology of Religion, State and Society* (Lanham, NY: University of America Press, 1993); N. Akinnasi, 'Bourdieu and the Diviner: Knowledge and Symbolic Power in Yoruba Divination', in W. James (ed.) *The Pursuit of Certainty: Religious and Cultural Formation* (London: Routledge, 1995); Angro, *The Culture of the Sacred*; K. Barber, 'How Man Makes God in West Africa: Yoruba Attitudes towards Orisa', *Africa*, 51 (3) 1981, pp. 724–45; C. Bennett, *In Search of the Sacred: Anthropology and the Study of Religions* (London: Cassell, 1996); A. Gold, *Fruitful Journeys: The Ways of Rajasthani Pilgrims* (Delhi: Open University Press, 1989); A. Gottlieb, *Under the Kapok Tree: Identity and Difference in Beng Thought* (Chicago: University of Chicago Press, 1992); C. Hirschkind, 'Civic Virtue and Religious Reason: An Islamic Counter-Public', *Cultural Anthropology*, 16 (1) 2001; W. James, *The Listening Ebony: Moral Knowledge, Religion and Power among the Uduk of Sudan* (Oxford: Oxford University Press, 1988); W. James (ed.) *The Pursuit of Certainty: Religious and Cultural Formations* (London: Routledge, 1995); B. Knauft, *Genealogies for the Present in Cultural Anthropology* (London: Routledge, 1996); Lambek, *Knowledge and Practice*; M-L. Swantz, 'Modernity, Wealth and Witchcraft in Tanzania', *Research in Economic Anthropology*, 20 (2) 1990, pp. 73–90; Swantz, *Blood, Milk and Death*.
24. Angro, *Culture of the Sacred*; J. R. Bowen, *Religions in Practice: An Approach to the Anthropology of Religion* (Boston: Allyn & Bacon, 2002); Bowie, *Anthropology of Religion*; R. H. Crapo, *Anthropology of Religion: The Unity and Diversity of Religions* (New York: McGraw Hill, 2003); Glaizer, *Selective Readings in the Anthropology of Religion*; Hicks, *Ritual and Belief*; Lambek, *Reader in the Anthropology of Religion*; R. Scupin, *Religion and Culture: An Anthropological Focus* (Upper Saddle River, NJ: Prentice Hall, 1999; H. Whitehouse and J. Laiulaw, *Ritual and Memory: Toward a Comparative Anthropology of Religion* (Walmtcreek, CA: Alta Mira Press, 2004).
25. A. Mandir, 'The Global Fiduciary: Mediating the Violence of Religion', in John R. Hinnells and Richard King (eds) *Religion and Violence in South Asia: Theory and Practice* (London: Routledge Taylor & Francis Group, 2007).
26. Juergensmeyer, 'Religion in the New Global Order'.
27. L. McKean, *Divine Enterprise: Gurus and the Hindu Nationalist Movement* (Chicago: University of Chicago Press, 1996).
28. Bowie, *Anthropology of Religion*.
29. T. Asad, *Genealogies of Religion: Discipline and Reasons of Power in Christianity and Islam* (Baltimore: Johns Hopkins University Press, 1993).

30. L. Reychler and T. Paffenholz, *Peace Building: A Field Guide* (Boulder, CO: Lynne Reinner, 2000).
31. R. Hefner, 'Multiple Modernities: Christianity, Islam and Hinduism in a Globalising Age', *Annual Review of Anthropology*, 27, 1998, pp. 83–104; T. Ranger, 'Religious Movements and Politics in Sub-Saharan Africa', *African Studies Review*, 29 (2) 1986, pp. 1–70; M. Shaharaw and R. Canfield, *Revolutions and Rebellions in Afghanistan: Anthropological Perspectives* (Berkeley: University of California Press, 1984); P. van der Veer, *Conversion to Modernities: The Globalization of Christianity* (New York: Routledge, 1996).
32. J. Contursi, 'Militant Hinduism and the Buddhist Dalits', *American Ethnologist*, 2 (3) 1989, pp. 234–51; T. Cunningham, 'The Ethnography of Transnational Social Activism', *Anthropological Enquiry*, 26 (1) 2000, pp. 34–48; James, *The Pursuit of Certainty*.
33. Van der Veer, *Conversion to Modernities*.

Chapter 3. Gender, Mothering and Development: Case Studies of Three Hindu Transnational Movements

1. R. Baird, 'Secular State and the Indian Constitution', in Robert D. Baird (ed.) *Religion in Modern India* (Delhi: Manohar, 1981) pp. 389–416; S. Jodhka and P. Bora, 'Mapping Faith-Based Development Activities in Maharashtra, India', *Working Paper*, 28, Religion and Development Research Programme, 2009, www.rad.bham.ac.uk; T. N. Madan, *Modern Myths, Locked Minds: Secularism and Fundamentalism in India* (Delhi: Oxford University Press, 1997).
2. G. Flood, *The Blackwell Companion to Hinduism* (Oxford: Blackwells, 2003); E. Tomalin, 'Background Paper on Hinduism and International Development', *RAD Working Paper*, 2009, www.rad.bham.ac.uk
3. For a more detailed comparison see D. Killingley, 'Varna and Caste in Hindu Apologetic', in D. Killingley (ed.) *Hindu Ritual and Society* (Newcastle upon Tyne: Grevatt & Grevatt, 1991) pp. 7–31.
4. See chapters in the next section and Bradley, *Challenging the NGOs*; T. Bradley, 'Physical Religious Spaces in the Lives of Rajasthani Village Women: Ethnographic study and Practice of Religion in Development', *Journal of Human Development and Capabilities*, 10 (1) 2009, pp. 43–62; L. Hess, 'Rejecting Sita: Indians Respond to the Ideal Man's Cruel Treatment of His Ideal Wife', *Journal of the American Academy of Religion*, 67 (1) 1999, pp. 1–32; V. Narayana Rao, 'When does Sita Cease to be Sita? Notes Towards a Cultural Grammar of Indian Narratives', in M. Bose (ed.) *The Ramayana Revisited* (Oxford: Oxford University Press, 2004); S. J. Sutherland, 'Sita and Draupadi: Aggressive Behaviour and Female Role-Models in the Sanskrit Epics', *Journal of the American Oriental Society*, 109 (1) 1989, pp. 63–79; J. Suthren Hirst, *Sita's Story* (Norwich: Religious and Moral Education Press, 1997).

5. H. Pauwels, 'Only You: The Wedding of Rama and Sita, Past and Present', in M. Bose (ed.) *The Ramayana Revisited* (Oxford: Oxford University Press, 2004).

6. J. D. Mlecko, 'The Guru in Hindu Tradition', *Numen*, 29 (1) 1982, pp. 33–61.

7. C. J. Fuller, *The Camphor Flame: Popular Hinduism and Society in India* (New Jersey: Princeton University Press, 1992).

8. See also D. Eck, *Darsan: Seeing the Divine Image in India* (Chambersburg: Anima Books, 1981); D. Eck, *Seeing the Divine Image in India* (Chambersburg: Anima Books, 1998).

9. Haynes, *Religion, Globalization and Political Culture in the Third World*.

10. For examples of Amma go to ⟨http://www.youtube.com/watch?v= 9lwTAYeyv9U; and Dada Vaswani http://www.youtube.com/watch?v= E0oTMdx2gEY⟩.

11. G. Beckerlegge *The Ramakrishna Mission: The Making of a Modern Hindu Movement* (Delhi: Oxford University Press, 2000).

12. http://www.belurmath.org

13. Swami Vivekananda, *Ramakrishna and his Message* (Kolkata: Ad Rasta, 2006) p. 25.

14. Tomalin, 'Background Paper on Hinduism and International Development', p. 28.

15. Swami Pavitrananda, *A Short Life of the Holy Mother* (Calcutta: Advaita Ashrama, 2006) p. 9.

16. S. Bharathi, *Educational Philosophy of Swami Vivekananda* (Bombay: Jaico Publishing House, 2005).

17. Swami Vivekananda, *Women of India* (Calcutta: Advaita Ashrama, 2007) p. 37.

18. Ibid., p. 81.

19. www.ammachi.org

20. M. Warrier, 'Processes of Secularization in Contemporary India: Guru Faith in the Mata Amritanandamayi Mission', *Modern Asian Studies*, 37, 2003, pp. 213–53.

21. See Swami Amritasvarupananda, *Mata Amritanandamayi: A Biography* (Kerala: Mata Amritasvarpananda Mission, 1988).

22. Quoted by Swamini Krishnamitra Prana, *Sacred Journey* (Kerala: Mata Amritasvarpananda Mission, 2005) p. 30.

23. Ibid., p. 32.

24. See section below for more details and also Amritasvarupananda, *Mata Amritanandamayi*; Sri Mata Amritanandamayi Devi, *From Amma's Heart* (Kerala: Mata Amritasvarpananda Mission, 2003); Samini Krishnamrita Prana, *Torrential Love* (Kerala: Mata Amritanandamayi Mission Trust, 2007).

25. Amritasvarupananda, *Mata Amritanandamayi*; Amritanandamayi Devi, *From Amma's Heart*; Krishnamrita Prana, *Torrential Love.*

26. K. Jones, 'The Mother and her Gift: Guru and Charity in Kerala', in M. Beryseth, I. Dahle and B. Dambo (eds) *Betwixt Between* (Oslo: University of Oslo, 2006) p. 52.

27. Amritanandamayi Devi, *From Amma's Heart*, p. 14.

28. McKean, *Divine Enterprise*, p. 277, cited by E. Tomalin, 'Buddhist Feminist Transnational Networks, Female Ordination and Women's Enpowerment', *Oxford Development Studies*, 31 (22) 2009, pp. 81–100.

29. Tomalin, 'Buddhist Feminist Transnational Networks'.

30. A. Rajagopal, *Politics after Television: Hindu Nationalism and the Reshaping of the Indian Public* (Cambridge: Cambridge University Press, 2001); T. Sarkar, *Hindu Wife, Hindu Nation: Community, Religion and Cultural Nationalism* (New Delhi: Permanent Black, 2002); T. Sarkar and U. Butalia, *Women and Right-wing Movements: Indian Experiences* (London: Zed Books, 1995).

31. S. Rege, 'Dalit Women Talk Differently: A Critique of Difference and Towards a Dalit Feminist Standpoint Position', in M. Chaudhuri (ed.) *Feminism in India* (London: Zed Books, 2005) pp. 211–25; Sarkar and Butalia, *Women and Right-wing Movements.*

32. Sadhu Vaswani Mission, *A Mission with a Vision* (Puna: Gita Publishing House, 2009); J. P. Vaswani, *Sadhu Vaswani: His Life and Teachings* (Delhi: Sterling Publishers, 2002); J. P. Vaswani, *Peace or Perish: There is no Other Choice* (Pune: Gita Publishing House, 2007).

33. Vaswani, *Peace or Perish.*

34. J. Chiriyankandath, 'Hindu Nationalism and Regional Political Culture in India: A study of Kerala', *Nationalism and Ethnic Politics*, 2 (1) 1996, pp. 44–66; C. Jaffrelot and T. Blom Hansen *Hindu Nationalism and Hindu Politics* (Delhi: Oxford University Press, 2004).

35. Sen, *Shiv Sena Women.*

36. Taken from website www.sadhuvaswanimission.org06/2009

37. J. Chatterji, *The Spoils of Partition: Bengal and India (1947–1967)* (Cambridge: Cambridge University Press, 2007); B. K. Singh, *Indian National Congress and the Partition of India, 1937–47* (Delhi: Capital Publishing House, 1990); L. Wolpert, *Six Impossible Things Before Breakfast: The Evolutionary Origins of Belief* (London: Faber & Faber, 2006).

38. J. Brockington, *The Sacred Thread: Hinduism in its Continuity and Diversity* (Edinburgh: Edinburgh University Press, 1981).

39. Vaswani, *Peace or Perish* p. 85.

40. D. Anand, 'Anxious Sexualities: Masculinities, Nationalisam and Violence', *British Journal of Politics and International Relations*, 9 (2) 2007, pp. 257–69; T. Blom Hansen, 'Recuperating Masculinity: Hindu

Nationalism, Violence and the Exorcism of the Muslim "Other"', *Critique of Anthropology*, 16 (2) 1996, pp. 137–72.

41. See also Sen, *Shiv Sena Women*.
42. Vaswani, *Peace or Perish*, p. 84.
43. www.sadhuvaswanimission.org
44. Vaswani, *Sadhu Vaswani*; Vaswani, *Peace or Perish*.
45. Quote from interview with headmistresses of Mira secondary school.
46. Vaswani, *Peace or Perish*, p. 82.
47. Ibid.
48. Ibid., p. 31.
49. Ibid.
50. Ibid., p. 70.
51. http://www.sadhuvaswani.org/svisgdelhi/
52. K. A. Jacobsen, *Hinduismen* (Oslo: Pax, 2003).
53. See Chapter 7 and R. Misra (ed.) *Gandhian Model of Development and World Peace* (New Delhi: Concept Publishing Company, 1989).
54. Letter to Akhandananda, March/April 1894, in *The Complete Works of Swami Vivikananda* (New Delhi: Vedanta Press) vol. 6, p. 288.
55. Swami Vivekananda, *Salvation and Service* (Calcutta: Advaita Ashrama, 1998) p. 37.
56. Amritanandamayi Devi, *From Amma's Heart*, p. 56.
57. Jones, 'The Mother and Her Gift', p. 52.
58. A. Appadurai, 'Gratitude as a Social Model in South India', *Ethnos*, 13 (3) 1985 pp. 236–45.
59. M. Mauss, *The Gift: Form and Reason for Exchange in Archaic Society* (London: Routledge, 2001)
60. See Bradley, *Challenging the NGOs*; R. L. Stirrat and H. Henkel, 'The Development Gift: The Problem of Reciprocity in the NGO World', *Annals of the American Academy of Political and Social Science*, 554 (1) 1997, pp. 66–80.
61. For details, see T. Bradley and Z. Ramsay, 'The People Know they Need Religion in Order to Develop: The Relationship between Hindu Religious Teachings, Values and Beliefs and Concepts of Development', *Working Paper*, Religions and Development Research Programme, forthcoming, www.rad.bham.ac.uk
62. See Sen, *Shiv Sena Women*.
63. See ibid. for more details.
64. Vivekananda, *Salvation and Service*, p. 17.
65. K. Knott, 'Hindu Women, Destiny and Stridharma', *Religion*, 26 (1) 1996, pp. 15–35; K. Knott, *Hinduism: A Very Short Introduction* (Oxford: Oxford University Press 1998); J. Leslie, *The Perfect Wife: The Orthodox Hindu Woman According to the Stridharmapaddhati of Tryambakayajvan* (Delhi: Oxford University Press 1989); J. Leslie (ed.) *Roles and Rituals*

for Hindu Women (London: Pinter Publishers, 1991); J. Leslie, 'Gender and Religion: Gender and Hinduism', in L. Jones (ed.) *The Encyclopaedia of Religion* (Detroit: Thomas Gale, 2005) vol. 5, pp. 3318–26; J. Leslie and M. McGee (eds) *Invented Identities: The Interplay of Gender, Religion and Politics in India* (Delhi: Oxford University Press, 2000); P. Richman (ed.) *Questioning Ramayanas: A South Asian Tradition* (Delhi: Oxford University Press, 2000); J. Suthren Hirst and L. Thomas (eds) *Playing for Real: Hindu Role Models, Religion and Gender* (Delhi: Oxford University Press, 2004).

66. A. Feldhaus (ed.) *Images of Women in Maharashtrian Society* (Albany, NY: State University of New York Press, 1995); A. Gold and G. Raheja, *Listen to the Heron's Words: Reimagining Gender and Kinship in North India* (Berkeley CA: University of California Press, 1994); A. Good, *The Female Bridegroom: A Comparative Study of Life-Crisis Rituals in South India and Sri Lanka* (Oxford: Clarendon Press, 1991); K. Kapadia, *Siva and her Sisters: Gender, Caste and Class in Rural South India* (Boulder, CO: Westview Press, 1995).

67. Swami Vivekananda, *My Idea of Education* (Calcutta: Advaita Ashrama, 2008).

68. www.ammachi.org

Part II. Faith-based Organizations and Dialogues in Development

1. G. Bond, *Buddhism at Work: Community Development, Social Empowerment and the Sarvodaya Movement* (Bloomfield: Kumarian Press, 2004); C. Candland, 'Faith as Social Capital: Religion and Community Development in South Asia', *Policy Sciences*, 33 (3–4) 2000, pp. 355–74; M. Harper, D. S. K. Rao and A. Kumar Sahu, *Development, Divinity and Dharma: The Role of Religion in Development and Micro Finance Institutions* (Rugby: Practical Action, 2008); Hefferan, *Twinning Faith and Development*; Tyndale, *Visions of Development*.

2. Clarke, 'Faith Matters'.

3. Hefferan, *Twinning Faith and Development*.

4. See Z. Ramsay and T. Bradley, 'This Religion is the First Step in our Struggle', *Caste and Buddhist Identity in the Development Context: Views from Pune*, Working Paper, Religion and Development Research Programme, forthcoming, www.rad.bham.ac.uk

5. Ibid.

Chapter 4. What is a Faith-based Organization?

1. D. Hulme and M. Edwards (eds) *NGOs, States and Donors: Too Close for Comfort* (Basingstoke: Macmillan, 1997).

2. www.wfdd.org.uk; www.rad.bham.ac.uk

3. Clarke, 'Faith-based Organizations', p. 78.
4. G. Clarke, 'Introduction', in G. Clarke and M. Jennings (eds) *Development, Civil Society and Faith-based Organizations: Bridging the Sacred and the Secular* (Basingstoke: Palgrave Macmillan, 2008).
5. Ibid., p. 25.
6. http://www.oxfam.org.uk/about_us/history/index.htm
7. S. Hopgood, *Keepers of the Flame: Understanding Amnesty International* (Ithaca, NY: Cornell University Press, 2006).
8. Bradley, *Challenging the NGOs*.
9. Ibid.
10. S. Morse and N. McNamara, 'Analysing Institutional Partnerships in Development: A Contract between Equals or a Loaded Process?' *Progress in Development Studies*, 6 (4) 1 October 2006, pp. 321–36.
11. Edelman and Haugerud, *The Anthropology of Development and Globalization*; E. O'Keefe, 'Equity, Democracy and Globalization', *Critical Public Health*, 10 (2) 2000, pp. 167–77.
12. Tyndale, *Visions of Development*, p. 154.
13. B. de Sousa Santos, 'On Oppostional Postmodernism', in R. Munck and D. O'Hearn (eds) *Critical Development Theory: Contributions to a New Paradigm* (London: Zed Books, 1999) pp. 29–34; Escobar, 'Reflections on 'Development'; Esteva, 'Development'; Hobart, *An Anthropological Critique of Development*.
14. R. Chambers, 'Rural Appraisal: Rapid, Relaxed and Participatory', *IDS Discussion Paper*, 31 (Brighton: International Development Studies, University of Sussex, 1991); Crewe and Harrison, *Whose Development?*; Gardner and Lewis, *Anthropology, Development and the Postmodern Challenge*; Pottier, *Practising Development*; Pottier et al., *Negotiating Local Knowledge*.
15. Hulme and Edwards, *NGOs, States and Donors*.
16. S. Kumar, 'Development and Religion: Cultivating a Sense of the Sacred', *Development*, 46 (4) 2003, pp. 15–21.
17. Interview with VDPJ volunteer.
18. M. Khandelwal, *Women in Ochre Robes: Gendering Hindu Renunciation* (New York: State University of New York Press, 2004).
19. See Chapter 10 for more details.
20. L. Harlan, *Religion and Rajput Women: The Ethic of Protection in Contemporary Narratives* (Berkeley: University of California Press, 1992); V. Joshi, *Polygamy and Purdah: Women and Society among Rajputs* (Jaipur: Rawat Publications, 1995).
21. See the next chapter for more details and analysis.
22. http://www.cafod.org.uk/about_cafod accessed 4 May 2007.
23. http://www.christian-aid.org.uk/aboutca/who/value.htm accessed 4 May 2007.

24. Morse and McNamara, Analysing Institutional Partnerships'.
25. Bradley, *Challenging the NGOs*.
26. Gold and Raheja, *Listen to the Heron's Words*.
27. Peace Plan website accessed 6 February 2007.
28. C. Zene, *The Rishi of Bangladesh: A History of Christian Dialogues* (London: Routledge, 2002).
29. Clarke, 'Faith Matters'.
30. Clarke, 'Faith-based Organizations'.

Chapter 5. Can Compassion Bring Results? Reflections on the Work of an Intermediary FBO

1. Crewe and Harrison, *Whose Development?*; Gardner and Lewis, *Anthropology, Development and the Postmodern Challenge*; Hobart, *An Anthropological Critique of Development*; Pottier, *Practising Development*; Sachs, *The Development Dictionary*.
2. Crewe and Harrison, *Whose Development?*
3. De Sousa Santos, 'On Oppositional Postmodernism', p. 30.
4. Pottier, *Practising Development*.
5. R. Chambers, *Whose Reality Counts? Putting the Last First* (London: Intermediate Technology Publications, 1997).
6. This study was conducted jointly by the University of Lampeter and the University of Swansea.
7. www.rad.bham.ac.uk
8. M. Taylor, *Not Angels but Agencies: The Ecumenical Response to Poverty: A Primer* (New York: Trinity Press International, 1995).
9. Tyndale, 'Idealism and Practicality', p. 26.
10. Please note I am using a fictitious name 'Water for Rajasthan' to describe the FBO I observed. I choose not to disclose its identity because I do not wish to inhibit donors from making pledges in support of its work. In addition, while I am critical, I also hold a great deal of respect for its commitment and achievements in a very poor area of Rajasthan.
11. W. Harcourt, 'Editorial: Clearing the Path for Collective Compassion', *Development*, 46 (4) 2003, pp. 3–4; Tyndale, 'Idealism and Practicality'; Tyndale, *Visions of Development*.
12. Clarke, 'Faith-based Organizations'.
13. E. Turner, *Christian Words* (Edinburgh: T. & T. Clark, 1980) p. 79.
14. D. Liddell and A. Scott, *Greek–English Lexicon* (Oxford: Oxford University Press, 1976) p. 646.
15. See Matthew 5 (12), 25 (25–40) for examples.
16. John, 2 (10). These quotations are taken from the *Holy Bible Standard and Revised Version*, 1995 edition.
17. B. McGinn, *Christian Spirituality* (London: Routledge & Kegan Paul, 1985). 'Spirit' refers to the incarnation of the Holy Ghost believed by

Christians to be present in all human beings, who are thought to have
come from God and therefore represent part of his creation.

18. Ibid., p. 27. Biblical examples can be seen in Acts 2 (17).
19. *Holy Bible* 1 Cor 8 (7–13), 10 (29), 2 Cor 5 (11).
20. The example was accessed on 4 April 2005 by the author at http//www.
christinaid.org.uk/worship/040/welcome/reflect.htm
21. Stirrat and Henkel, 'The Development Gift', p. 72.
22. See also Zene, *The Rishi of Bangladesh*.
23. M. Godelier, *The Enigma of the Gift* (Cambridge: Polity Press, 1999)
gives a useful outline of Mauss's work, *The Gift*, in which Mauss does
not describe gift giving in terms of laws; rather, he believes that a spirit
exists within the system of gift giving that compels the recipient to
return the gift.
24. Cited by Stirrat and Henkel, 'The Development Gift'.
25. See Chapter 6 for details of the evolution of this organization.
26. See Chapter 6 for more details.
27. Gold and Raheja, *Listen to the Heron's Words*; Harlan, *Religion and
Rajput Women*; Joshi, *Polygamy and Purdah*; and W. S. Sax, *Mountain
Goddess: Gender and Politics in a Himalayan Pilgrimage* (Oxford: Oxford
University Press 1991).
28. Bradley, *Challenging the NGOs*; Gold and Raheja, *Listen to the Heron's
Words*.
29. Eck, *Darsan*; G. Flood, *Introduction to Hinduism* (Cambridge:
Cambridge University Press, 1996); Flood, *The Blackwell Companion to
Hinduism*; Knott, *Hinduism*.
30. Bradley, *Challenging the NGOs*.
31. F. Saeed, *Taboo! The Hidden Culture of the Red Light Area* (Oxford:
Oxford University Press, 2001).
32. J. Ferguson, *The Anti-Politics Machine: Development, Depoliticization and
Bureaucratic Power in Lesotho* (New York: Cambridge University Press,
1990).

Chapter 6. Competing Visions of Development: The Story of a Faith-based Partnership

1. I neither name the organizations nor give information about them that
may reveal their identities. I do this because the arguments I make take
a critical perspective on their work. However, this critical view should
not be taken to mean that I do not respect or value the work they do.
2. Mauss, *The Gift*.
3. Stirrat and Hinkel, The Development Gift'.
4. Quarles van Ufford and Schoffeleers, *Religion and Development*.
5. Harvey, *A Brief History of Neoliberalism*, p. 5.
6. 'Partnership' is a popular term in development that attempts to signify

an equal relationship between two organizations/levels in the aid chain. The term has been criticized for concealing the power relationship that still divides donors from recipients. On this subject, see J. Brinkerhoff, *Partnerships for International Development: Rhetoric or Results?* (Boulder, CO: Lynne Rienner Publishers, 2002); M. Erikson Baaz, *The Paternalism of Partnership: A Postcolonial Reading of Identity in Development Aid* (London: Zed Books, 2005); and J. Riley, *Stakeholders in Rural Development: Critical Collaboration in State–NGO Partnerships* (New Delhi: Sage, 2002). I use this term to describe the relationship between my two case studies simply because they used the term to describe their positioning in relation to each other.

7. Deuteronomy 26 v10.
8. N. Botting, *The Complete Fundraising Handbook* (London: Directory of Social Change in Association with the Institute of Charity Fundraising Managers, 2001); M. Edwards and A. Fowler (eds) *Earthscan Reader on NGO Management* (London: Earthscan, 2002); J. Flanagan, *Successful Fundraising: A Complete Handbook for Volunteers and Professionals* (Chicago: Contemporary Books, 1991); L. Jordan and P. van Tuijl (eds) *NGO Accountability: Politics, Principles and Innovations* (London: Earthscan, 2006); J. L. Lant, *Development Today: A Fund Raising Guide for Nonprofit Organizations* (Cambridge, MA: JLA Publications, 1988); J. Mordaunt and R. Paton, *Thoughtful Fundraising: Concepts, Issues and Perspectives* (Abingdon: Routledge, 2007).
9. Bradley, *Challenging the NGOs*.
10. M. Daly, *The Church and the Second Sex* (New York: Harper & Row, 1975); M. Daly, *Beyond God the Father: Towards a Philosophy of Women's Liberation* (London: Women's Press, 1986); D. Hampson, *Theology and Feminism* (Oxford: Basil Blackwell, 1990); D. Hampson, 'On Being All of a Piece/At Peace', in T. Elwes (ed.) *Women's Voices: Essays in Contemporary Feminist Theology* (London: Marshall Pickering, 1991); D. Hampson, *After Christianity* (Valley Forge, PA: Trinity Press International, 1996); A. Loades (ed.) *Feminist Theology: A Reader* (Louisville, KY: Westminster/John Knox Press, 1990); E. Schüssler Fiorenza, *Bread Not Stone: The Challenge of Feminist Biblical Interpretation* (Boston: Beacon Press, 1984).
11. Kwok Pui-lan, 'Unbinding Our Feet: Saving Brown Women and Feminist Religious Discourse', in Laura E. Donaldson and Kwok Pui-lan (eds) *Postcolonialism, Feminism and Religious Discourse* (London: Routledge, 2000); Kwok Pui-lan, *Introducing Asian Feminist Theology* (Sheffield: Sheffield Academic Press, 2002).
12. C. Mohanty, 'Under Western Eyes', in C. Mohanty and A. Russo (eds) *Third World Women and the Politics of Feminism* (Bloomington: Indiana

University Press, 1988); U. Narayan, *Dislocating Cultures: Identities, Tradition and Third World Feminism* (New York: Routledge, 1997).

13. B. Ruether, *Women/Church: Theology and Practice* (San Francisco: Harper, 1984); B. Ruether, *Sexism and God Talk: Towards a Feminist Theology* (Boston: Beacon Press, 1990); Schüssler Fiorenza, *Bread Not Stone*.

14. Bradley, *Challenging the NGOs*; K. Erndl, 'The Play of the Mother: Possession and Power in Hindu Women's Goddess Rituals', in T. Pintchman (ed.) *Women's Lives, Women's Rituals in the Hindu Tradition* (Oxford: Oxford University Press, 2007); Gold and Raheja, *Listen to the Heron's Words*; L. Harlan, 'Words that Breach Walls: Women's Rituals in Rajasthan', in T. Pintchman (ed.) *Women's Lives, Women's Rituals in the Hindu Tradition* (Oxford: Oxford University Press, 2007); M. Kishwar, 'Yes to Sita, No to Ram! The Continuing Popularity of Sita in India', *Manushi*, 98, January–February 1996, pp. 20–31.

15. A. Cornwall, E. Harrison and A. Whitehead (eds) *Feminisms in Development: Contradictions, Contestations and Challenges* (London: Zed Books, 2007).

16. R. Eyben, 'Battles over Booklets: Gender Myths in the British Aid Programme', in A. Cornwall, E. Harrison and A. Whitehead (eds) *Feminisms in Development: Contradictions, Contestations and Challenges* (London: Zed Books, 2007) p. 76.

17. Cornwall et al., *Feminisms in Development*, p. 150.

18. Kumar, 'Development and Religion'.

19. L. Rudolph and S. Hoeber Rudolph, *Postmodern Gandhi and other Essays: Gandhi in the World and at Home* (Delhi: Oxford University Press, 2006) p. 216.

20. B. C. Parekh, *Gandhi* (New York: Oxford University Press, 1997) p. 157.

21. K. Mathur, *Countering Gender Violence: Initiatives Towards Collective Action in Rajasthan* (New Delhi: Sage, 2004); K. Mathur, 'Body as Site, Body as Space: Bodily Integrity and Women's Empowerment in India', *IDSJ Working Paper*, Series no. 148, 2007.

22. See Kishwar, Yes to Sita, No to Ram!'; and Chapter 9.

23. V. Joshi and R. Hooja, 'Popular Vrats and Vrat Kathas: Women and Patriarchy', *IDSJ Working Paper*, Series no 079, 1997; Mathur, *Countering Gender Violence*; Mathur, 'Body as Site'.

24. Hess, 'Rejecting Sita'; Sutherland, 'Sita and Draupadi'; S. J. Sutherland, *Bridging Worlds: Studies on Women in South Asia* (Delhi: Oxford University Press, 1992) S. J. Sutherland, 'The Voice of Sita in Valimiki's Sundarakanda', in P. Richman (ed.) *Questioning Ramayanas: A South Asian Tradition* (Delhi: Oxford University Press, 2000); Suthren Hirst, *Sita's Story*.

25. Rudolph and Hoeber Rudolph, *Postmodern Gandhi and other Essays*, p. 158.

26. D. Kinsley, *Hindu Goddesses: Visions of the Divine Feminine in the Hindu Religious Tradition* (Delhi: Motilal Banarsidass, 1986).

27. See Chapters 4 and 5 for more detail.
28. D. Mosse, *Cultivating Development: An Ethnography of Aid Policy and Practice* (London: Pluto Press, 2005) p. 239.
29. O. Olivier de Sardan (ed.) *Anthropology and Development: Understanding Contemporary Social Change* (London: Zed Books, 2005).
30. S. George, *Another World is Possible if* ... (London: Verso, 2004); Harvey, *A Brief History of Neoliberalism*; Peet, *Geography of Power*.
31. Harvey, *A Brief History of Neoliberalism*, p. 3.
32. O'Keefe, 'Equity, Democracy and Globalization'.
33. Bradley, 'Physical Religious Spaces in the Lives of Rajasthani Village Women'; and Chapter 4.

Chapter 7. Gender, Gandhi and Community Organizations

1. M. Kishwar, 'Gandhi on Women', *Race and Class*, 28, 1985, pp. 43–61; S. Patel, 'Construction and Reconstruction of Women in Gandhi', *Economic and Political Weekly*, 23 (8) 1988, pp. 377–87.
2. E. Zelliot, *Gandhi and Ambedkar: A Study in Leadership* (Pune: Jambhala Books, 2005).
3. Cited by R. Saxena, 'Gandhi's Feminist Politics, Gender Equity and Patriarchal Values', in R. Johnson, 'Gandhi and Feminisms: Towards Women-Affirming Cultures of Peace', *Gandhi Marg*, 22 (1) April–June 2001, p. 105.
4. M. K. Gandhi, 'Women and Social Injustice', *Young India* (Ahmedabad: Navajiran Publishing House, 1947) p. 38.
5. Kishwar, 'Gandhi on Women'.
6. Gandhi, 'Women and Social Injustice', p. 36.
7. Patel, 'Construction and Reconstruction of Women in Gandhi'.
8. Gandhi, 'Women and Social Injustice', p. 33.
9. M. K. Gandhi, *From Yeravda Mandir* (Ahmedabad: Navajivan Publishing House, 1932) p. 3.
10. Ibid., p. 3.
11. Ibid., p. 6.
12. Ibid., p. 32.
13. Ibid., p. 35.
14. M. Kishwar, 'A Horror of 'Isms: Why I Do Not Call Myself a Feminist, *Off the Beaten Track* (New Dehli: Oxford University Press, 1999) pp. 269–90.
15. Ibid., p. 277.
16. Ibid., pp. 289–90.
17. J. Jain and A. V. Singh (eds) *Indian Feminisms* (New Delhi: Creative Books, 2001).

Part III. Religion as a Feminist Resource
1. Tomalin, Religion as a Rights-based Approach to Development'.

Chapter 8. Physical Religious Spaces in the Lives of Rajasthani Village Women
1. Knott, *Hinduism*.
2. Bowie, *The Anthropology of Religion*; Glaizer, *Selective Readings in the Anthropology of Religion*; Lambek, *A Reader in the Anthropology of Religion*.
3. Contursi, 'Militant Hinduism and the Buddhist Dalits'; E. V. Daniel, *Charred Lullabies: Chapters in an Anthropology of Violence* (Princeton, NJ: University of Princeton Press, 1996); C. Mahmood, *Fighting for Faith and the Nation: Dialogues with Sikh Militants* (Philadelphia: University of Pennsylvania Press, 1991); P. van der Veer, *Religious Nationalism: Hindus and Muslims in India* (Berkeley: University of California Press, 1994).
4. B. Agarwal, 'Two Poems on Sita', in P. Richman (ed.) *Questioning Ramayana: A South Asian Tradition* (Delhi: Oxford University Press, 2000); Kishwar, 'Yes to Sita, No to Ram!'; Sutherland, 'The Voice of Sita in Valimiki's Sundarakanda'.
5. Cooke and Kothari, *Participation*; Crewe and Harrison, *Whose Development?*; Gardner and Lewis, *Anthropology, Development and the Postmodern Challenge*; Hobart, *An Anthropological Critique of Development*; Mosse, *Cultivating Development*; Pottier, *Practising Development*; and Pottier et al., *Negotiating Local Knowledge*.
6. Laws, *Research for Development*.
7. M. C. Nussbaum, *Women and Human Development: The Capabilities Approach* (Cambridge: Cambridge University Press, 2000).
8. Asad, *Genealogies of Religion*; Chambers, *Whose Reality Counts?*; Esteva, 'Development'; Gardner and Lewis, *Anthropology, Development and the Postmodern Challenge*; Hobart, *An Anthropological Critique of Development*; Olivier de Sardan, *Anthropology and Development*; Pottier, *Practising Development*; Pottier et al., *Negotiating Local Knowledge*; Stirrat and Henkel, 'The Development Gift'; I. Tinker, 'The Myth of Development: A Critique of a Eurocentric Discourse', in R. Munck and D. O'Hearn (eds) *Critical Development Theory Contributions to a New Paradigm* (London: Zed Books, 1999).
9. Edited volumes on anthropology of religion include Angro, *The Culture of the Sacred*; Bennett, *In Search of the Sacred*; Bowen, *Religions in Practice*; Bowie, *The Anthropology of Religion*; Crapo, *Anthropology of Religion*; Glaizier, *Selective Readings in the Anthropology of Religion*; Hicks, *Ritual and Belief*; Lambek, *A Reader in the Anthropology of Religion*; Scupin, *Religion and Culture*; and Whitehouse and Laiulaw, *Ritual and Memory*.

10. Aigbe, *Theory of Social Involvement*; Akinnasi, 'Bourdieu and the Diviner'; Angro, *The Culture of the Sacred*; Barber, 'How Man Makes God in West Africa'; Bennett, *In Search of the Sacred*; Gold, *Fruitful Journeys*; Gottlieb, *Under the Kapok Tree*; Hirschkind, 'Civic Virtue and Religious Reason'; James, *The Listening Ebony*; James, *The Pursuit of Certainty*; Knauft, *Genealogies for the Present*; Lambek, *Knowledge and Practice in Mayotte*; R. Rappaport, *Ritual and Religion in the Making of Humanity* (Cambridge: Cambridge University Press, 1999); T. Sanders, 'Modernity, Wealth and Witchcraft in Tanzania', in B. Isaac (ed.) *Research in Economic Anthropology* (Stamford: JAI Press, 1999) vol. 20; Swantz, *Blood, Milk and Death*.

11. P. Cooey, W. Eakin and J. McDaniel, *After Patriarchy: Feminist Transformations in World Religions* (New York: Orbis Books, 1991); U. King, *Religion and Gender* (Oxford: Wiley Blackwell, 1995); King and Beattie, *Gender, Religion and Diversity*; A. Sharma (ed.) *Women in World Religions* (New York: State University of New York Press, 1987).

12. A. Ashforth *Witchcraft, Violence and Democracy in South Africa* (Chicago: University of Chicago Press, 2005); M. Auslander, 'Open the Wombs! The Symbolic Politics of Modern Ngoni Witch Finding', in J. Comaroff and J. Comaroff (eds) *Modernity and its Malcontents: Ritual and Power in Postcolonial Africa* (Chicago: University of Chicago Press, 1993); Geschiere and Cyprian, 'Domesticating Personal Violence'; S. Mesaki, 'Witchcraft and Witch-Killings in Tanzania: Paradox and Dilemma', unpublished Ph.D. thesis, University of Minnesota, 1994.

13. Brain, 'Witchcraft and Development'; T. J. Csordas, 'Health and the Body in African and Afro American Spirit Possession', *Social Science and Medicine*, 24 (1) 1987, pp. 1–11; R. R. Des Jarlais, *Body and Emotion: The Aesthetics of Illness and Healing in the Nepal Himalayas* (Philadelphia: University of Philadelphia Press, 1992); J. Erdtsieck, *In the Spirit of Uganga: Inspired Healing and Healership in Tanzania* (Amsterdam: AGIDS, 2003); Gessler, 'Traditional Healers in Tanzania'; Janzen, *Discourses of Healing in Central and Southern Africa*; Kendall, *Shamans, Housewives and Other Restless Spirits*; C. A. Kratz, *Affecting Performance: Meaning, Movement and Experience in Women's Initiation* (Washingdon, DC: Smithsonian Institution Press, 1994); P. Kumar, *Folk Icons and Rituals in Tribal Life* (Delhi: Albinav, 1984); Manji, *Magic Faith and Healing*; Marwick, *Witchcraft and Sorcery*; Masquelier, 'Lightning, Death and the Avenging Spirits'; Pool, *Dialogue and the Interpretation of Illness*; Rekdal, 'Cross-cultural Healing in East African Ethnography'; E. Turner, *Experiencing Ritual: A New Interpretation of African Healing* (Philadelphia: University of Pennsylvania Press, 1992).

14. Gold and Raheja, *Listen to the Heron's Words*.

15. U. von Mitzlaff, *Maasai Women: Life in a Patriarchal Society: Field Research among the Parakuyo, Tanzania* (Munich: Trickster Verlag, 1988).
16. Erndl, 'The Play of the Mother'.
17. M. Chatterjee, *Gandhi's Religious Thought* (Basingstoke: Palgrave Macmillan, 1983); J. T. F. Jordens, *Gandhi's Religion: A Homespun Shawl* (Basingstoke: Palgrave Macmillan, 1998); V. N. Rao, 'A Ramayana of their Own: Women's Oral Tradition in Telugu', in P. Richman (ed.) *Many Ramayanas: The Diversity of a Narrative Tradition in South Asia* (New Delhi: Oxford University Press, 1991).
18. See Chapter 10 for more details.
19. L. Bennett, *Dangerous Wives and Sacred Sisters: Social and Symbolic Roles of High Caste Women in Nepal* (New York: Columbia University Press, 1983); Fuller, *The Camphor Flame*.
20. Fuller, *The Camphor Flame*.
21. Agarwal, 'Two Poems on Sita'; A. Diesel, 'Tales of Women's Suffering: Draupadi and other Amman Goddesses as Role Models for Women', *Journal of Contemporary Religion*, 17 (1) 2002, pp. 5–20; L. Fruzzetti, *The Gift of a Virgin: Women, Marriage and Ritual in a Bengali Society* (Delhi: Oxford University Press, 1990).
22. M. Kishwar, 'Who am I? Living Identities vs Acquired Ones', *Manushi*, May–June 1996.
23. Sutherland, 'The Voice of Sita in Valimiki's Sundarakanda'.
24. J. Leslie, *Authority and Meaning in Indian Religions: Hinduism and the Case for Valmiki* (London: Ashgate, 2003) p. 61.
25. Other literature that makes links between women's rituals and the articulation and/or expression of personhood include Diesel, 'Tales of Women's Suffering'; A. Gold, 'Khyal: Changing Yearnings in Rajasthani Songs', *Manushi*, 95, July–August 1996; B. Lincoln, *Emerging from the Chrysalis: Studies in Rituals of Women's Initiation* (Oxford: Oxford University Press, 1981); A. I. Richards, *Chisungu: A Girls' Initiation Ceremony Among the Bemba of Zambia* (London: Tavistock, 1982); M. Udvardy, 'Kifudu: A Female Fertility Cult among the Girama', in A. Jacabson Widding and W. van Beck (eds) *The Creative Communion: African Folk Models of Fertility and the Regeneration of Life* (Uppsala: Acta Universitatis, 1990); von Mitzlaff, *Maasai Women*.

Chapter 9. Positioning Religion in Research and Activism to End Domestic Violence in Rajasthan

1. I do not name these activists, organizations or women. Domestic violence is a sensitive and delicate issue, so the anonymity of both activists and the victims of the violence must be assured. Furthermore, my work is meant to support the important work of activists and I do not want readers to misinterpret my analysis as criticism of the

approaches taken. To safeguard against this I have chosen to keep my informants and their organizations anonymous.

2. Mathur, *Countering Gender Violence*; Mathur, 'Body as Site, Body as Space'; K. Mathur, K. Shivastava and S. Jain, 'Exploring Possibilities: A Review of the Women's Development Programme Rajasthan', *IDS Paper*, Jaipur, December 1996; R. S. Rajan, 'Rethinking Law and the Violence: The Domestic Violence (Prevention) Bill in India', *Gender and History*, 16 (3) 2002, pp. 769–93; M. Unnithan and K. Srivastava, 'Gender Politics, Development and Women's Agency in Rajasthan', in R. D. Grillo and R. L. Stirrat (eds) *Discourses on Development: Anthropological Perspectives* (Oxford: Berg, 1997) pp. 157–81.

3. B. D. Miller, *The Endangered Sex: Neglect of Female Children in Rural North India* (New York: Cornell University Press, 1981); L. Minturn, *Sita's Daughters: Coming Out of Purdah* (Oxford: Oxford University Press, 1993); S. S. Mitter, *Dharma's Daughters: Contemporary Indian Women and Hindu Culture* (Brunswick, NJ: Rutgers University Press, 1991); J. Sagade, *Child Marriage in India: Socio-Legal and Human Rights Dimensions* (Oxford: Oxford University Press, 2005); H. C. Upreti, *The Myth of Sati: Some Dimensions of Widow Burning* (New Delhi: Himalaya Press, 1991).

4. A point also noted by T. Abraham, *Women and the Politics of Violence* (New Delhi: Shakti Books, 2002); F. Agnes, 'The Anti-Rape Campaign: The Struggle and the Setback', in C. Datar (ed.) *Struggle against Violence* (Calcutta: Stree Publications, 1992); H. Ahmed-Ghosh, 'Chattels of Society: Domestic Violence in India', *Violence against Women*, 10 (1) 2004, pp. 94–118; R. E. Emerson Dobash and R. P. Dobash, *Rethinking Violence against Women* (London: Sage, 1998); S. Engla and S. Merry, 'Rights, Religion and Community Approaches to Violence against Women in the Context of Globalization', *Law and Society Review*, 35 (1) 2001, pp. 39–88; S. French, W. Teays and L. Purdy, *Violence against Women: Philosophical Perspectives* (Ithaca, NY: Cornell University Press, 1998); K. Kapadia (ed.) *The Violence of Development: The Politics of Identity, Gender and Social Inequalities in India* (London: Zed Books, 2002); M. Macey, 'Religion, Male Violence and the Control of Women: Pakistan Muslim Men in Bradford, UK', in C. Sweetman (ed.) *Gender, Religion and Spirituality* (Oxford: Oxfam, 1999); Mathur, *Countering Gender Violence*; Mathur, 'Body as Site, Body as Space'; M. Nayak, C. Byrne, M. Martin and A. Abraham, 'Attitudes Towards Violence against Women: A Cross-nation Study', *Sex Roles*, 49 (7/8) 2003, pp. 333–42.

5. K. Mathur, 'Violence against Women: The Rajasthan Scenario', *IDS Working Paper*, 088, Jaipur, n.d.

6. J. Jain, *Women's Writing: Text and Context* (Jaipur: Rawat Publications, 1996); Mathur, 'Violence against Women'; K. Mathur, 'Assessing the

Impact of the WDP', *IDS Working Paper*, Jaipur, n.d.; Mathur et al., 'Exploring Possibilities'; S. Mayaram, 'The Politics of Women's Reservation: Women Panchayat Representatives in Rajasthan Performance, Problems and Potential', *IDS Working Paper*, Jaipur (074) n.d.

7. S. Srinivasan and A. Bedi, 'Domestic Violence and Dowry: Evidence from a South Indian Village', *World Development*, 35 (5) 2007, pp. 857–80.
8. UNIFEM, *Support Services to Counter Violence against Women in Rajasthan* (Geneva: United Nations Development Fund for Women, 2002).
9. L. Minturn, *Sita's Daughters: Coming Out of Purdah: The Rajput Women of Khalapur Revisited* (Oxford: Oxford University Press, 1993).
10. T. Bradley and E. Tomalin (eds) *Dowry: Bridging the Gap between Theory and Practice* (New Delhi: Women Unlimited, 2009)
11. Miller, *The Endangered Sex*; Sagade, *Child Marriage in India*.
12. Recorded during an interview with the director at the organization's office in Jaipur, 19 October 2007.
13. UNIFEM, *Support Services to Counter Violence*, p. 11.
14. Bowie, *The Anthropology of Religion*.
15. Narayan, *Dislocating Cultures*, p. 113.
16. King, *Religion and Gender*; King, 'Religion and Gender'.
17. Also King and Beattie, *Gender, Religion and Diversity*.
18. R. Parliwala, 'Reaffirming the Anti-Dowry Struggle', in S. Basu (ed.) *Dowry and Inheritance* (Delhi: Women Unlimited, 2005); R. Parliwala, 'The Spider's Web: Seeing Dowry, Fighting Dowry', in T. Bradley and E. Tomalin (eds) *Dowry: Bridging the Gap between Theory and Practice* (New Delhi: Women Unlimited, 2009).
19. S. Basu (ed.) *Dowry and Inheritance* (Delhi: Women Unlimited, 2005); S. Basu, 'Legacies of the Dowry Prohibition Act in India: Marriage Practices and Feminist Discourses', in T. Bradley and E. Tomalin (eds) *Dowry: Bridging the Gap between Theory and Practice* (New Delhi: Women Unlimited, 2009).
20. Flood, *Introduction to Hinduism*; Knott, *Hinduism*; Tomalin, 'Background Paper on Hinduism'.
21. Eck, *Darsan*; Eck, *Seeing the Divine Image in India*.
22. C. Bell, *Ritual Perspectives and Dimensions* (Oxford: Oxford University Press, 1997).
23. Kinsley, *Hindu Goddesses*.
24. Diesel, 'Tales of Women's Suffering'; K. Erndl, *Victory to the Mother: The Hindu Goddess of North West India in Myth, Ritual and Symbol* (New York: Oxford University Press, 1992); Fruzetti, *The Gift of a Virgin*; Hess, 'Rejecting Sita'; A. Hiltebeitel and K. Erndl, *Is the Goddess a*

Feminist? The Politics of South Asian Goddesses (New York: New York University Press, 2000); Kishwar, 'Who am I?; Kishwar, 'Yes to Sita, No to Ram!'; Knott, 'Hindu Women, Destiny and Stridharma'; T. Pinchman (ed.) *Women's Lives: Women's Rituals in the Hindu Tradition* (Oxford: Oxford University Press, 2007); Suthren Hirst, *Sita's Story*; Suthren Hirst and Thomas, *Playing for Real.*

25. Joshi and Hooja, 'Popular Vrats and Vrat Kathas', p. 12.
26. A. Pearson, *'Because it Gives me Peace of Mind': Ritual Fasts in the Religious Lives of Hindu Women* (New York: State University of New York Press, 1996).
27. Bradley, Challenging the NGOs.
28. Mathur, 'Body as Site, Body as Space', p. 3.
29. K. Mathur and S. Rajan 'Gender Training: Potential and Limitations', *IDS Working Paper*, 2000; Mathur, *Countering Gender Violence.*
30. Mathur, *Countering Gender Violence*, p. 139.
31. See also A. Garg, 'Countering Violence against Women in Rajasthan: Problems, Strategies and Hazards', *Development*, 44, 2001, pp. 111–13.
32. Mathur, 'Body as Site, Body as Space', p. 10.
33. S. R. Rajan and S. Sharma, 'Mahila Shikaha Karmis in the Shikaha Karmi Programme: A Study', *IDS Working Paper*, Jaipur, April 1995; M. Subramaniam, *The Power of Women's Organizing: Gender, Caste, and Class in India* (Lanham, MD: Lexington Books, 2006).
34. Mathur, 'Body as Site, Body as Space', p. 17.
35. Mathur, *Countering Gender Violence*, p. 1.
36. S. Basu, *She Comes to Take Her Rights: Indian Women, Property and Propriety* (New Delhi: Kali for Women, 2001).
37. Bell, *Ritual Perspectives and Dimensions.*
38. Bradley, *Challenging the NGOs.*
39. Harlan, 'Words that Breach Walls'.
40. Suthren Hirst and Thomas, *Playing for Real.*
41. D. T. Meyers, *Gender in the Mirror: Cultural Imagery and Women's Agency* (Oxford: Oxford University Press, 2002).
42. See also C. Datar, 'Reflections on the Anti-rape Campaign in Bombay', in S. Wieringa (ed.) *Women's Struggles and Strategies* (The Hague: Institute of Social Studies, 1998); G. Kelkar, 'Stopping the Violence against Women: Fifteen Years of Activism in India', in M. Schuler (ed.) *Freedom from Violence: Women's Strategies from around the World* (Washington, DC: Open Estonia Foundation International, 1992) pp. 5–99; G. Misra and R. Chandiramani (eds) *Sexuality, Gender and Rights: Exploring Theory and Practice in South and Southeast Asia* (New Delhi: Sage Publications, 2005); R. Perez, 'Practising Theory through Women's Bodies: Public Violence and Women's Strategies of Power and Place', in K. Saunders (ed.) *Feminist Post-development Thought: Rethinking*

Modernity, Post-colonialism and Representation (London: Zed Books, 2002) pp. 263–80; F. Pickup, *Ending Violence against Women: A Challenge for Development and Humanitarian Work* (Oxford: Oxfam, 2001).

Chapter 10. *Puja* as an Approach to Health Care

1. Eck, *Darsan*; Eck, *Seeing the Divine Image in India.*
2. Chapter 1 and see also T. Bradley, 'Does Compassion Bring Results', *Culture and Religion*, 6 (3) 2005, pp. 337–51; Eade, *Development and Culture*; Tomalin, 'Religion as a Rights-based Approach to Development'; Tyndale, *Visions of Development.*
3. This project coincided with a national campaign running throughout India in 1995 to reduce the average family size to 2.5 children per couple.
4. This was the response given by Deepak director of VSR when I asked him why he appointed female health professionals.
5. Knott, *Hinduism.*
6. Gold and Raheja, *Listen to the Heron's Words.*
7. See also S. Batliwala and D. Dhanraj, 'Revisiting the Gender Agenda', *IDS Bulletin*, 38 (2) 2007.
8. Harlan, *Religion and Rajput Women*; Joshi, *Polygamy and Purdah*; Mathur, *Countering Gender Violence.*
9. Fuller, *The Camphor Flame.*
10. C. M. Bell, *Ritual Theory, Ritual Practice* (Oxford: Oxford University Press, 1992).
11. Harlan, 'Words that Breach Walls'.
12. Ibid.

Conclusion

1. Benthall, *Returning to Religion.*
2. Quarles van Ufford and Schoffeleers, *Religion and Development.*
3. P. Bourdieu, *Outline of a Theory of Practice* (Cambridge: Cambridge University Press, 1977).
4. M. Weber, *The Sociology of Religion* (Boston: Beacon Press, 1993).
5. See also C. Geertz, *The Interpretation of Cultures: Selected Essays by Clifford Geertz* (London: Lawrence & Wishart, 1975).
6. DFID, *Building a Common Future* (London: UK Department for International Development's White Paper, 2009).

References

Abraham, T. (ed.) (2002) *Women and the Politics of Violence* (New Delhi: Shakti Books)

Agarwal, B. (2000) 'Two Poems on Sita', in P. Richman (ed.) *Questioning Ramayana: A South Asian Tradition* (Delhi: Oxford University Press)

Agnes, F. (1992) 'The Anti-Rape Campaign: The Struggle and the Setback', in C. Datar. (ed.) *Struggle against Violence* (Calcutta: Stree Publications)

Ahmed-Ghosh, H. (2004) 'Chattels of Society: Domestic Violence in India', *Violence against Women*, 10 (1) pp. 94–118

Aigbe, S. (1993) *Theory of Social Involvement: A Case Study in the Anthropology of Religion, State and Society* (Lanham, NY: University of America Press)

Akinnasi, N. (1995) 'Bourdieu and the Diviner: Knowledge and Symbolic Power in Yoruba Divination', in W. James (ed.) *The Pursuit of Certainty: Religious and Cultural Formation* (London: Routledge)

Alkire, S. (2006) 'Religion and Development', in D. A. Clark (ed.) *The Elgar Companion to Development Studies* (Cheltenham: Edward Elgar) pp. 502–10

Alkire, S. and E. Newell (2005) *What Can One Person Do? Faith to Heal a Broken World?* (London: Darton, Longman & Todd)

Alvarez, S., E. Dagnino and A. Escobar (eds) (1998) *Cultures of Politics/Politics of Cultures: Re-visioning Latin American Social Movements* (Boulder, CO: Westview Press)

Amritanandamayi, Swami (1988) *Mata Amritanandamayi: A Biography* (Kerala: Mata Amritasvarpananda Mission)

Amritanandamayi Devi, Sri Mata (1991) *From Amma's Heart* (Kerala: Mata Amritanandamayi Mission Trust)

Anand, D. (2007) 'Anxious Sexualities: Masculinities, Nationalism and Violence', *British Journal of Politics and International Relations*, 9 (2) pp. 257–69

Angro, M. (ed.) (2004) *The Culture of the Sacred: Exploring the Anthropology of Religion* (Prospect Heights: Waveland Press)

Appadurai, A. (1985) 'Gratitude as a Social Model in South India', *Ethnos*, 13 (3) pp. 236–45

Asad, T. (1993) *Genealogies of Religion: Discipline and Reasons of Power in Christianity and Islam* (Baltimore: Johns Hopkins University Press)

Ashforth, A (2005) *Witchcraft, Violence and Democracy in South Africa* (Chicago: University of Chicago Press)

Auslander, M. (1993) 'Open the Wombs! The Symbolic Politics of Modern Ngoni Witch Finding', in J. Comaroff and J. Comaroff (eds) *Modernity and its Malcontents: Ritual and Power in Postcolonial Africa* (Chicago: University of Chicago Press) pp. 167–92

Baird, R. (1981) 'Secular State and the Indian Constitution', in Robert D. Baird (ed.) *Religion in Modern India* (Delhi: Manohar) pp. 389–416

Barber, K. (1981) 'How Man Makes God in West Africa: Yoruba Attitudes towards Orisa', *Africa*, 51 (3) pp. 724–45

Basu, S. (2001) *She Comes to Take Her Rights: Indian Women, Property and Propriety* (New Delhi: Kali for Women)

Basu, S. (ed.) (2005) *Dowry and Inheritance* (Delhi: Women Unlimited)

Basu, S. (2009) 'Legacies of the Dowry Prohibition Act in India: Marriage Practices and Feminist Discourses', in T. Bradley and E. Tomalin (eds) *Dowry: Bridging the Gap between Theory and Practice* (New Delhi: Women Unlimited)

Batliwala, S. and D. Dhanraj (2007) 'Revisiting the Gender Agenda', *IDS Bulletin*, 38 (2)

Beckerlegge, G. (2000) *The Ramakrishna Mission: The Making of a Modern Hindu Movement* (Delhi: Oxford University Press)

Bell, C. M. (1992) *Ritual Theory, Ritual Practice* (Oxford: Oxford University Press)

Bell, C. M. (1997) *Ritual Perspectives and Dimensions* (Oxford: Oxford University Press)

Bennett, C. (ed.) (1996) *In Search of the Sacred: Anthropology and the Study of Religions* (London: Cassell)

Bennett, L. (1983) *Dangerous Wives and Sacred Sisters: Social and Symbolic Roles of High Caste Women in Nepal* (New York: Columbia University Press)

Benthall, J. (1991) 'The Middle East', *Anthropology Today*, 7 (2) pp. 11–15.

Benthall, J. (2008) *Returning to Religion: Why a Secular Age is Haunted by Faith* (London: IB.Tauris)

Beyer, P. (1994) *Religion and Globalization* (London: Sage)

Beyer, P. and C. Beaman (eds) (2007) *Religion, Globalization and Culture* (Leiden: Brill)

Bharathi, S. (2005) *Educational Philosophy of Swami Vivekananda* (Bombay: Jaico Publishing House)

Birkeflet, S. (1991) *Latin American Liberation Theology: A Bibliography on Essential Writing* (Oslo: Faculty of Theology)

Blom Hansen, T. (1996) 'Recuperating Masculinity: Hindu Nationalism, Violence and the Exorcism of the Muslim "Other"', *Critique of Anthropology*, 16 (2) pp. 137–72

Bond, G. (2004) *Buddhism at Work: Community Development, Social Empowerment and the Sarvodaya Movement* (Bloomfield: Kumarian Press)

Botting, N. (2001) *The Complete Fundraising Handbook* (London: Directory of Social Change in Association with the Institute of Charity Fundraising Managers)

Bourdieu, P. (1977) *Outline of a Theory of Practice* (Cambridge: Cambridge University Press)

Bowen, J. R. (2002) *Religions in Practice: An Approach to the Anthropology of Religion* (Boston: Allyn & Bacon)

Bowie, F. (2000) *The Anthropology of Religion: An Introduction* (Oxford: Blackwell)

Bradley, T. (2005) 'Does Compassion Bring Results', *Culture and Religion*, 6 (3) pp. 337–51

Bradley, T. (2006) *Challenging the NGOs: Women, Religion and Western Dialogues in India* (London: Tauris Academic Studies)

Bradley, T. (2009) 'Physical Religious Spaces in the Lives of Rajasthani Village Women: Ethnographic study and Practice of Religion in Development', *Journal of Human Development and Capabilities*, 10 (1) pp. 43–62

Bradley, T. and E. Tomalin (eds) (2009) *Dowry: Bridging the Gap between Theory and Practice* (New Delhi: Women Unlimited)

Bradley, T and Z. Ramsay (forthcoming) 'The People Know they Need Religion in Order to Develop: The Relationship between Hindu Religious Teachings, Values and Beliefs and Concepts of Development', *Working Paper*, Religions and Development Research Programme www.rad.bham.ac.uk.

Brain, J. L. (1982) 'Witchcraft and Development', *African Affairs*, 81 (324) pp. 371–84

Brinkerhoff, J. (2002) *Partnerships for International Development: Rhetoric or Results?* (Boulder, CO: Lynne Rienner Publishers)

Brockington, J. (1981) *The Sacred Thread: Hinduism in its Continuity and Diversity* (Edinburgh: Edinburgh University Press)

Bruneau, T. (1980) 'The Catholic Church and Development in Latin America: The Role of the Basic Christian Communities', *World Development*, 8 (7/11)

Burdick, J. (1991) *Looking for God in Brazil: The Progressive Catholic Church in Urban Brazil's Religious Arena* (Berkeley: University of California Press)

Candland, C. (2000) 'Faith as Social Capital: Religion and Community Development in South Asia', *Policy Sciences*, 33 (3–4) pp. 355–74

Carlos, P. (1994) *Jesus and Liberation: A Critical Analysis of the Christology of Latin American Liberation Theology* (New York: P. Lang)

Chambers, R. (1991) 'Rural Appraisal: Rapid, Relaxed and Participatory', *IDS Discussion Paper*, 31 (Brighton: International Development Studies, University of Sussex)

Chambers, R. (1997) *Whose Reality Counts? Putting the Last First* (London: Intermediate Technology Publications)

Chatterjee, M. (1983) *Gandhi's Religious Thought* (Basingstoke: Palgrave Macmillan)

Chatterji, J. (2007) *The Spoils of Partition: Bengal and India, 1947–1967* (Cambridge: Cambridge University Press)

Chiriyankandath, J. (1996) 'Hindu Nationalism and Regional Political Culture in India: A study of Kerala', *Nationalism and Ethnic Politics*, 2 (1) pp. 44–66

Clarke, G. (2006) 'Faith Matters: Faith-based Organisations, Civil Society and International Development', *Journal of International Development*, 18 (6) pp. 835–48

Clarke, G. (2008) 'Faith-based Organizations: An Overview', in G. Clarke and M. Jennings (eds) *Development, Civil Society and Faith-based Organizations: Bridging the Sacred and the Secular* (Basingstoke: Palgrave Macmillan)

Clarke, G. (2008) 'Introduction', in G. Clarke and M. Jennings (eds) *Development, Civil Society and Faith-based Organizations: Bridging the Sacred and the Secular* (Basingstoke: Palgrave Macmillan)

Coleman, S. (2000) *The Globalisation of Charismatic Christianity* (Cambridge: Cambridge University Press)

Contursi, J. (1989) 'Militant Hinduism and the Buddhist Dalits', *American Ethnologist*, 2 (3) pp. 234–51

Cooey, P., W. Eakin and J. McDaniel (1991) *After Patriarchy: Feminist Transformations in World Religions* (New York: Orbis Books)

Cooke, B. and U. Kothari (eds) (2001) *Participation: The New Tyranny?* (London: Zed Books)

Cornwall, A., E. Harrison and A. Whitehead (eds) (2007) *Feminisms in Development: Contradictions, Contestations and Challenges* (London: Zed Books)

Crapo, R. H. (2003) *Anthropology of Religion: The Unity and Diversity of Religions* (New York: McGraw Hill)

Crewe, E., and Harrison, E. (1998) *Whose Development? An Ethnography of Aid* (London: Zed Books)

Csordas, T. J. (1987) 'Health and the Body in African and Afro American Spirit Possession', *Social Science and Medicine*, 24 (1) pp. 1–11

Csordas, T. J. (1994) *The Sacred Self: A Cultural Phenomenology of Charismatic Healing* (Berkeley: University of California Press)

Cunningham, T. (2000) 'The Ethnography of Transnational Social Activism', *Anthropological Enquiry*, 26 (1) pp. 34–48

Daly, M. (1975) *The Church and the Second Sex* (New York: Harper & Row)

Daly, M. (1986) *Beyond God the Father: Towards a Philosophy of Women's Liberation* (London: Women's Press)

Daniel, E. V. (1996) *Charred Lullabies: Chapters in an Anthropology of Violence* (Princeton, NJ: University of Princeton Press)

Datar, C. (1998) 'Reflections on the Anti-rape Campaign in Bombay', in S. Wieringa (ed.) *Women's Struggles and Strategies* (The Hague: Institute of Social Studies)

Deneulin, S. (2006) 'Development as Freedom and the Costa Rican Human Development Story', *Oxford Development Studies*, 33 (3/4) pp. 493–510

Deneulin, S. with M. Bano (2009) *Religion in Development: Rewriting the Secular Script* (London: Zed Books)

de Rivero, C. (2001) *The Myth of Development: The Non Viable Economies of the 21st Century* (London: Zed Books)

Desai, V. and R. Potter (eds) (2002) *The Companion to Development Studies* (London: Arnold Publications, 2002)

Des Jarlais, R. R. (1992) *Body and Emotion: The Aesthetics of Illness and Healing in the Nepal Himalayas* (Philadelphia: University of Philadelphia Press)

de Sousa Santos, B. (1999) 'On Oppositional Postmodernism', in R. Munck and D. O'Hearn (eds) *Critical Development Theory: Contributions to a New Paradigm* (London: Zed Books) pp. 29–34

DFID (2009) *Building a Common Future* (London: UK Department for International Development's White Paper)

Diesel, A. (2002) 'Tales of Women's Suffering: Draupadi and other Amman Goddesses as Role Models for Women', *Journal of Contemporary Religion*, 17 (1) pp. 5–20

Eade, D. (ed.) (2002) *Development and Culture* (Oxford: Oxfam)

Eck, D. L. (1981) *Darsan: Seeing the Divine Image in India* (Chambersburg: Anima Books)

Eck, D. L. (1988) *Seeing the Divine Image in India* (Chambersburg: Anima Books)

Edelman, M. and A. Haugerud (eds) (2005) *The Anthropology of Development and Globalization: From Classical Political Economy to Contemporary Neoliberalism* (Oxford: Blackwell)

Edwards, M. and A. Fowler (eds) (2002) *Earthscan Reader on NGO Management* (London: Earthscan)

Elliott, C. (ed.) (2007) *Global Empowerment of Women: Responses to Globalization and Politicised Religions* (London: Routledge)

Emerson Dobash, R. E. and R. P. Dobash (1998) *Rethinking Violence against Women* (London: Sage)

Engla, S. and S. Merry (2001) 'Rights, Religion and Community Approaches to Violence against Women in the Context of Globalization', *Law and Society Review*, 35 (1) pp. 39–88

Erdtsieck, J. (2003) *In the Spirit of Uganga: Inspired Healing and Healership in Tanzania* (Amsterdam: AGIDS)

253

Erikson Baaz, M. (2005) *The Paternalism of Partnership: A Postcolonial Reading of Identity in Development Aid* (London: Zed Books)

Erndl, K. (1992) *Victory to the Mother: The Hindu Goddess of North West India in Myth, Ritual and Symbol* (New York: Oxford University Press)

Erndl, K. (2007) 'The Play of the Mother: Possession and Power in Hindu Women's Goddess Rituals', in T. Pintchman (ed.) *Women's Lives, Women's Rituals in the Hindu Tradition* (Oxford: Oxford University Press)

Escobar, A. (1992) 'Reflections on 'Development': Grassroots Approaches and Alternative Politics in the Third World', *Futures*, 24

Escobar, A. (1995) *Encountering Development: The Making and Unmaking of the Third World* (New York: Prinkel)

Esteva, G. (1993) 'Development', in W. Sachs (ed.) *The Development Dictionary: A Guide to Knowledge as Power* (London: Zed Books)

Eyben, R. (2007) 'Battles over Booklets: Gender Myths in the British Aid Programme', in A. Cornwall, E. Harrison and A. Whitehead (eds) *Feminisms in Development: Contradictions, Contestations and Challenges* (London: Zed Books) pp. 65–78.

Feiderman, S. (1985) 'Struggles for Control: The Roots of Health and Healing in Modern Africa', *The African Studies Review*, 28 (2/3) pp. 43–57

Feldhaus, A. (ed.) (1995) *Images of Women in Maharashtrian Society* (Albany, NY: State University of New York Press)

Ferguson, J. (1990) *The Anti-Politics Machine: 'Development', Depoliticization and Bureaucratic Power in Lesotho* (New York: Cambridge University Press, 1990)

Ferguson, J. (2008) 'Means and Ends of Development: The Uses of Neoliberalism', keynote conference paper for conference, The Ends of Development: Market, Morality, Religion, Political Theory, VU University Amsterdam 19–20 June

Flanagan, J. (1991) *Successful Fundraising: A Complete Handbook for Volunteers and Professionals* (Chicago: Contemporary Books)

Flood, G. (1996) *Introduction to Hinduism* (Cambridge: University of Cambridge Press)

Flood, G. (2003) *The Blackwell Companion to Hinduism* (Oxford: Blackwells)

Fox, J. (2001) 'Religion as an Overlooked Element of International Relations', *International Studies Review*, 3 (2) pp. 53–73

French, S., W. Teays and L. Purdy (1998) *Violence against Women: Philosophical Perspectives* (Ithaca, NY: Cornell University Press)

Fruzzetti, L. (1990) *The Gift of a Virgin: Women, Marriage and Ritual in a Bengali Society* (Delhi: Oxford University Press)

Fuller, C. J. (1992) *The Camphor Flame: Popular Hinduism and Society in India* (New Jersey: Princeton University Press)

Gandhi, M. K. (1932) *From Yeravda Mandir* (Ahmedabad: Navajivan Publishing House)

Gandhi, M. K. (1947) 'Women and Social Injustice', in M. K. Gandhi, *Young India* (Ahmedabad: Navajivan Publishing House)

Gardner, K. and D. Lewis (1996) *Anthropology, Development and the Postmodern Challenge* (London: Pluto Press)

Garg, A. (2001) 'Countering Violence against Women in Rajasthan: Problems, Strategies and Hazards', *Development*, 44, pp. 111–13

Geertz, C. (1975) *The Interpretation of Cultures: Selected Essays by Clifford Geertz* (London: Lawrence & Wishart)

George, S. (2004) *Another World is Possible if …* (London: Verso)

Gessler, M. C. (1995) 'Traditional Healers in Tanzania: The Treatment of Malaria with Plant Remedies', *Journal of Ethnopharmacology*, 48 (3) 3 November, pp. 131–44

Geschiere, P. and F. Cyprian (1994) 'Domesticating Personal Violence: Witchcraft, Courts and Confessions in Cameroon', *Africa*, 64 (3) pp. 323–41

Ghatak, A. (2006) 'Faith, Work and Women in a Changing World: The Influence of Religion in the Lives of Beedi Rollers in West Bengal', *Gender and Development*, 14 (3) pp. 375–83

Glaizer, S. (2003) *Selective Readings in the Anthropology of Religion: Theoretical and Methodological Essays* (Westport CT: Praeger)

Godelier, M. (1999) *The Enigma of the Gift* (Cambridge: Polity Press)

Gold, A. (1989) *Fruitful Journeys: The Ways of Rajasthani Pilgrims* (Delhi: Open University Press)

Gold, A. (1996) 'Khyal: Changing Yearnings in Rajasthani Songs', *Manushi*, 95, July–August

Gold, A. and G. Raheja (1994) *Listen to the Heron's Words: Reimagining Gender and Kinship in North India* (Berkeley CA: University of California Press)

Good, A. (1991) *The Female Bridegroom: A Comparative Study of Life-Crisis Rituals in South India and Sri Lanka* (Oxford: Clarendon Press)

Gottlieb, A. (1992) *Under the Kapok Tree: Identity and Difference in Beng Thought* (Chicago: University of Chicago Press)

Hampson, D. (1990) *Theology and Feminism* (Oxford: Basil Blackwell)

Hampson, D. (1991) 'On Being All of a Piece/At Peace', in T. Elwes (ed.) *Women's Voices: Essays in Contemporary Feminist Theology* (London: Marshall Pickering) pp. 131–45

Hampson, D. (1996) *After Christianity* (Valley Forge, PA: Trinity Press International)

Harcourt, W. (2003) 'Editorial: Clearing the Path for Collective Compassion', *Development*, 46 (4) 2003, pp. 3–5

Harlan, L. (1992) *Religion and Rajput Women: The Ethic of Protection in Contemporary Narratives* (Berkeley: University of California Press)

Harlan, L. (2007) 'Words that Breach Walls: Women's Rituals in Rajasthan', in T. Pintchman (ed.) *Women's Lives, Women's Rituals in the Hindu Tradition* (Oxford: Oxford University Press)

Harper, M., D. S. K. Rao and A. Kumar Sahu (2008) *Development, Divinity and Dharma: The Role of Religion in Development and Micro Finance Institutions* (Rugby: Practical Action)

Harper, S. (ed.) (2000) *The Lab, the Temple and the Market: Reflections at the Intersection of Science, Religion and Development* (Bloomfield, CT: Kumarian Press)

Harvey, D. (2005) *A Brief History of Neoliberalism* (Oxford: Oxford University Press)

Haynes, J. (1993) *Religion in Third World Politics* (Buckingham: Open University Press)

Haynes, J. (1998) *Religion in Global Politics* (Harlow: Longman)

Haynes, J. (ed.) (1999) *Religion, Globalization and Political Culture in the Third World* (Basingstoke: Macmillan)

Haynes, J. (ed.) (2006) *The Politics of Religion: A Survey* (London: Routledge)

Haynes, J. (2007) *Religion and Development: Conflict or Cooperation?* (Basingstoke: Palgrave Macmillan)

Hefferan, T. (2007) *Twinning Faith and Development: Catholic Parish Partnering in the US and Haiti* (Bloomfield: Kumarian Press)

Hefner, R. (1998) 'Multiple Modernities: Christianity, Islam and Hinduism in a Globalising Age', *Annual Review of Anthropology*, 27, pp. 83–104

Hess, L. (1999) 'Rejecting Sita: Indians Respond to the Ideal Man's Cruel Treatment of His Ideal Wife', *Journal of the American Academy of Religion*, 67 (1) pp. 1–32

Hicks, D. (ed.) (2002) *Ritual and Belief: Readings in the Anthropology of Religion* (Boston: McGraw Hill)

Hiltebeitel, A. and K. Erndl (2000) *Is the Goddess a Feminist? The Politics of South Asian Goddesses* (New York: New York University Press)

Hirschkind, C. (2001) 'Civic Virtue and Religious Reason: An Islamic Counter-Public', *Cultural Anthropology*, 16 (1) pp. 3–34

Hobart, M. (ed.) (1993) *An Anthropological Critique of Development: The Growth of Ignorance* (New York: Oxford University Press)

Hopgood, S. (2006) *Keepers of the Flame: Understanding Amnesty International* (Ithaca, NY: Cornell University Press)

Hopkins, D., L. Lorentzen and E. Mendieta (2002) *Religions/Globalizations: Theories and Cases* (Durham, NC: Duke University Press)

Howell, J and J. Pearce (2002) *Civil Society and Development: A Critical Exploration* (Boulder, CO: Lynne Rienner Publishers)

Hulme, D. and M. Edwards (eds) (1997) *NGOs, States and Donors: Too Close for Comfort* (Basingstoke: Macmillan)

Jacobsen, K. A. (2003) *Hinduismen* (Oslo: Pax)

Jaffrelot, C. and T. Blom Hansen (2004) *Hindu Nationalism and Hindu Politics* (Delhi: Oxford University Press)

Jain, J. (1996) *Women's Writing: Text and Context* (Jaipur: Rawat Publications)

Jain, J. and A. V. Singh (eds) (2001) *Indian Feminisms* (New Delhi: Creative Books)

James, W. (1988) *The Listening Ebony: Moral Knowledge, Religion and Power among the Uduk of Sudan* (Oxford: Oxford University Press)

James, W. (ed.) (1995) *The Pursuit of Certainty: Religious and Cultural Formations* (London: Routledge)

Janzen, J. (1992) *Discourses of Healing in Central and Southern Africa* (Berkeley: University of California Press)

Jenkins, A. B. and N. Alexander (2007) 'Who Rules the World Bank', bank information center http://www.bicusa.org/EN/Article.3327.aspx

Jodkha, S and P. Bora (2009) 'Mapping Faith-Based Development Activities in Maharashtra, India', *Working Paper*, 28, Religion and Development Research Programme, www.rad.bham.ac.uk

Jones, K. (2006) 'The Mother and Her Gift: Guru and Charity in Kerala', in M. D. Bergseth, I. Dahle and B. Dambo (eds) *Betwixt Between* (Oslo: University of Oslo)

Jordan, L. and P. van Tuijl (eds) (2006) *NGO Accountability: Politics, Principles and Innovations* (London: Earthscan)

Jordens, J. T. F. (1998) *Gandhi's Religion: A Homespun Shawl* (Basingstoke: Palgrave Macmillan)

Joshi, V. (1995) *Polygamy and Purdah: Women and Society among Rajputs* (Jaipur: Rawat Publications)

Joshi, V. and R. Hooja (1997) 'Popular Vrats and Vrat Kathas: Women and Patriarchy', *IDSJ Working Paper*, Series no 079

Juergensmeyer, M. (2005) 'Religion in the New Global Order', http//www. maxwell.syr.edu/Moynihan/programs/sac/paper_20pdfs/marks_20paper

Kamat, V. (2004) *Negotiating Illness and Misfortune in Post Socialist Tanzania: An Ethnographic Study in Temeke District Dar es Salaam*, Ph.D., Emory University, Department of Anthropology, University Microfilms International

Kapadia, K. (1995) *Siva and her Sisters: Gender, Caste and Class in Rural South India* (Boulder, CO: Westview Press)

Kapadia, K. (ed.) (2002) *The Violence of Development: The Politics of Identity, Gender and Social Inequalities in India* (London: Zed Books)

Kapur, D. (2000) 'Who Gets to Run the World? *Foreign Policy*, 121.

Kapur, D., J. Lewis and R. Webb (eds) (1997) *The World Bank: Its First Half Century* (Washington: Brookings Institution Press)

257

Kelkar, G. (1992) 'Stopping the Violence against Women: Fifteen Years of Activism in India', in M. Schuler (ed.) *Freedom from Violence: Women's Strategies from around the World* (Washington, DC: Open Estonia Foundation International) pp. 5–99

Kendall, L. (1985) *Shamans, Housewives and Other Restless Spirits: Women in Ritual Life* (Honolulu: University of Hawaii Press)

Khandelwal, M. (2004) *Women in Ochre Robes: Gendering Hindu Renunciation* (New York: State University of New York Press)

Killingley, D. (1991) 'Varna and Caste in Hindu Apologetic', in D. Killingley (ed.) *Hindu Ritual and Society* (Newcastle upon Tyne: Grevatt & Grevatt) pp. 7–31

King, R. (1999) *Orientalism and Religion: Postcolonial Theory, India and the Mystic East* (London: Routledge)

King, U. (ed.)(1995) *Religion and Gender* (Oxford: Wiley Blackwell)

King, U. (2005) 'Religion and Gender', in Ursula King and Tina Beattie (eds) *Encyclopaedia of Religion* (New York: Macmillan)

King, U and T. Beattie (eds) (2004) *Gender, Religion and Diversity: Cross Cultural Perspectives* (London: Continuum)

Kinsley, D. (1986) *Hindu Goddesses: Visions of the Divine Feminine in the Hindu Religious Tradition* (Delhi: Motilal Banarsidass)

Kishwar, M. (1985) 'Gandhi on Women', *Race and Class*, 28, pp. 43–61

Kishwar, M. (1996) 'Who am I? Living Identities vs Acquired Ones', *Manushi*, May–June

Kishwar, M. (1996) 'Yes to Sita, No to Ram! The Continuing Popularity of Sita in India', *Manushi*, 98, January–February, pp. 20–31

Kishwar, M. (1999) 'A Horror of 'Isms: Why I Do Not Call Myself a Feminist, in M. Kishwar, *Off the Beaten Track* (New Dehli: Oxford University Press) pp. 269–90

Knauft, B. (1996) *Genealogies for the Present in Cultural Anthropology* (London: Routledge)

Knott, K. (1996) 'Hindu Women, Destiny and Stridharma', *Religion*, 26 (1) pp. 15–35

Knott, K. (1998) *Hinduism: A Very Short Introduction* (Oxford: Oxford University Press)

Kothari, U. (ed.) (2005) *A Radical History of Development Studies: Individuals, Institutions and Ideologies* (London: Zed Books)

Kramer, F. (1993) *The Red Fez: Art and Spirit Possession in Africa* (London: Verso)

Kratz, C. A. (1994) *Affecting Performance: Meaning, Movement and Experience in Women's Initiation* (Washingdon, DC: Smithsonian Institution Press)

Krishnamrita Prana, Swamini (2005) *Sacred Journey* (Kerala: Mata Amritasvarpananda Mission)

Krishnamrita Prana, Swamini (2007) *Torrential Love* (Kerala: Mata Amritasvarpananda Mission)

Kumar, P. (1984) *Folk Icons and Rituals in Tribal Life* (Delhi: Albinav)

Kumar, S. (2003) 'Development and Religion: Cultivating a Sense of the Sacred', *Development*, 46 (4) pp. 15–21

Kumar Giri, A. (2002) *Conversations and Transformations: Toward a New Ethics of Self and Society* (Maryland: Lexington Books)

Kwok Pui-lan (2000) *Introducing Asian Feminist Theology* (Sheffield: Sheffield Academic Press)

Kwok Pui-lan (2002) 'Unbinding Our Feet: Saving Brown Women and Feminist Religious Discourse', in Laura E. Donaldson and Kwok Pui-lan (eds) *Postcolonialism, Feminism and Religious Discourse* (London: Routledge) pp. 62–81

Lambek, M. (1993) *Knowledge and Practice in Mayotte: Local Discourses of Islam, Sorcery and Spirit Possession* (Toronto: University of Toronto Press)

Lambek, M. (ed.) (2002) *A Reader in the Anthropology of Religion* (Oxford: Blackwell)

Lant, J. L. (1988) *Development Today: A Fund Raising Guide for Nonprofit Organizations* (Cambridge, MA: JLA Publications)

Laws, S. (2003) *Research for Development: A Practical Guide* (London: Sage and Save the Children)

Leach, M. and I. Scoones (2007) 'Mobilising Citizens: Social Movements and the Politics of Knowledge', *IDS Working Paper Series*, 276, Brighton: Institute of Development Studies

Legerwerf, L. (1987) *Witchcraft, Sorcery and Spirit Possession: Pastoral Responses in Africa* (Gweru: Mambo Press)

Leslie, J. (1989) *The Perfect Wife: The Orthodox Hindu Woman According to the Stridharmapaddhati of Tryambakayajvan* (Delhi: Oxford University Press)

Leslie, J. (ed.) (1991) *Roles and Rituals for Hindu Women* (London: Pinter Publishers)

Leslie, J. (2003) *Authority and Meaning in Indian Religions: Hinduism and the Case for Valmiki* (London: Ashgate)

Leslie, J. (2005) 'Gender and Religion: Gender and Hinduism', in L. Jones (ed.) *The Encyclopaedia of Religion* (Detroit: Thomas Gale) vol. 5, pp. 3318–26

Leslie, J and M. McGee (eds) (2000) *Invented Identities: The Interplay of Gender, Religion and Politics in India* (Delhi: Oxford University Press)

Liddell, D. and A. Scott (1976) *Greek–English Lexicon* (Oxford: Oxford University Press)

Lincoln, B. (1981) *Emerging from the Chrysalis: Studies in Rituals of Women's Initiation* (Oxford: Oxford University Press)

Linden, I. (2003) *A New Map of the World* (London: Darton, Longman & Todd)

Ling, T. (1980) 'Buddhist Values and Development Problems: A Case Study of Sri Lanka', *World Development*, 8 (7/11)

Loades, A. (ed.) (1990) *Feminist Theology: A Reader* (Louisville, KY: Westminster/John Knox Press)

Macey, M. (1999) 'Religion, Male Violence and the Control of Women: Pakistan Muslim Men in Bradford, UK', in C. Sweetman (ed.) *Gender, Religion and Spirituality* (Oxford: Oxfam)

McGinn, B. (1985) *Christian Spirituality* (London: Routledge & Kegan Paul)

McKean, L. (1996) *Divine Enterprise: Gurus and the Hindu Nationalist Movement* (Chicago: University of Chicago Press)

Madan, T. N. (1997) *Modern Myths, Locked Minds: Secularism and Fundamentalism in India* (Delhi: Oxford University Press)

Mahmood, C. (1991) *Fighting for Faith and the Nation: Dialogues with Sikh Militants* (Philadelphia: University of Pennsylvania Press)

Mandir, A. (2007) 'The Global Fiduciary: Mediating the Violence of Religion', in John R. Hinnells and Richard King (eds) *Religion and Violence in South Asia: Theory and Practice* (London: Routledge Taylor & Francis Group)

Manji, A. (2003) *Magic, Faith and Healing: Mysteries of Africa* (Pittsburgh: Sterling House)

Marshall, K. (1998) 'Development and Religion: A Different Lens on Development Debates', *Peabody Journal of Education*, 76 (3–4) pp. 339–75

Marshall, K. and L. Keough (2004) *Mind, Heart and Soul in the Fight against Poverty* (Washington, DC: World Bank)

Marwick, M. (ed.) (1982) *Witchcraft and Sorcery* (Harmondsworth: Penguin)

Masquelier, A. (1994) 'Lightning, Death and the Avenging Spirits: Bori Values in a Muslim World', *Journal of Religion in Africa*, 24 (1) pp. 2–51

Mathur, K. (n.d.) 'Violence against Women: The Rajasthan Scenario', *IDS Working Paper*, 088, Jaipur

Mathur, K. (n.d.) 'Assessing the Impact of the WDP', *IDS Working Paper*, Jaipur

Mathur, K. (2004) *Countering Gender Violence: Initiatives Towards Collective Action in Rajasthan* (New Delhi: Sage)

Mathur, K. (2007) 'Body as Site, Body as Space: Bodily Integrity and Women's Empowerment in India', *IDSJ Working Paper*, Series no. 148

Mathur, K. and S. Rajan (2000) 'Gender Training: Potential and Limitations', *IDS Working Paper*

Mathur, K., K. Shivastava and S. Jain (1996) 'Exploring Possibilities: A Review of the Women's Development Programme Rajasthan', *IDS Paper*, Jaipur, December

Mauss, M. (2001) *The Gift: Form and Reason for Exchange in Archaic Society* (London: Routledge)

Mayaram, S. (n.d.) 'The Politics of Women's Reservation: Women Panchayat Representatives in Rajasthan Performance, Problems and Potential', *IDS Working Paper*, Jaipur (074)

Mesaki, S. (1994) 'Witchcraft and Witch-Killings in Tanzania: Paradox and Dilemma', unpublished Ph.D. thesis, University of Minnesota

Meyer, D. and S. Staggenborg (1996) 'Movements, Countermovements and the Structure of Political Opportunity', *Amercian Journal of Sociology*, 101 (6) May, pp. 1628–60

Meyers, D. T. (2002) *Gender in the Mirror: Cultural Imagery and Women's Agency* (Oxford: Oxford University Press)

Miller, B. D. (1981) *The Endangered Sex: Neglect of Female Children in Rural North India* (Ithaca, NY: Cornell University Press)

Minturn, L. (1993) *Sita's Daughters: Coming Out of Purdah: The Rajput Women of Khalapur Revisited* (Oxford: Oxford University Press)

Misra, G. and R. Chandiramani (eds) (2005) *Sexuality, Gender and Rights: Exploring Theory and Practice in South and Southeast Asia* (New Delhi: Sage Publications)

Misra, R. (ed.) (1989) *Gandhian Model of Development and World Peace* (New Delhi: Concept Publishing Company)

Mitter, S. S. (1991) *Dharma's Daughters: Contemporary Indian Women and Hindu Culture* (Brunswick, NJ: Rutgers University Press)

Mlecko, J. D. (1982) 'The Guru in Hindu Tradition', *Numen*, 29 (1) pp. 33–61

Mohanty, C. (1988) 'Under Western Eyes', in C. Mohanty and A. Russo (eds) *Third World Women and the Politics of Feminism* (Bloomington: Indiana University Press)

Molyneux, M. and S. Razavi (2006) *Beijing Plus Ten: An Ambivalent Record on Gender Justice* (Geneva: UNRISD)

Mordaunt, J. and R. Paton (2007) *Thoughtful Fundraising: Concepts, Issues and Perspectives* (Abingdon: Routledge)

Morse, S. and N. McNamara (2006) 'Analysing Institutional Partnerships in Development: A Contract between Equals or a Loaded Process?' *Progress in Development Studies*, 6 (4) 1 October, pp. 321–36

Mosse, D. (2005) *Cultivating Development: An Ethnography of Aid Policy and Practice* (London: Pluto Press)

Narayan, U. (1997) *Dislocating Cultures: Identities, Tradition and Third World Feminism* (New York: Routledge)

Narayana Rao, V. (2004) 'When does Sita Cease to be Sita? Notes Towards a Cultural Grammar of Indian Narratives', in M. Bose (ed.) *The Ramayana Revisited* (Oxford: Oxford University Press)

Nayak, M., C. Bryne, M. Martin and A. Abraham (2003) 'Attitudes Towards Violence against Women: A Cross-nation Study', *Sex Roles*, 49 (7/8) pp. 333–42

Norget, K. (1999) 'Progressive Theology and Popular Religiosity in Oaxaca', in C Smith and J. Prokoopy (eds) *Latin America in Motion* (New York: Routledge)

Nussbaum, M. C. (2000) *Women and Human Development: The Capabilities Approach* (Cambridge: Cambridge University Press)

O'Keefe, E. (2000) 'Equity, Democracy and Globalization', *Critical Public Health*, 10 (2) pp. 167–77

Olivier de Sardan, J. P. (ed.) (2005) *Anthropology and Development: Understanding Contemporary Social Change* (London: Zed Books)

Parekh, B. C. (1997) *Gandhi* (New York: Oxford University Press)

Parliwala R. (2005) 'Reaffirming the Anti-Dowry Struggle', in S. Basu (ed.) *Dowry and Inheritance* (Delhi: Women Unlimited)

Parliwala R. (2009) 'The Spider's Web: Seeing Dowry, Fighting Dowry', in T. Bradley and E. Tomalin (eds) *Dowry: Bridging the Gap between Theory and Practice* (New Delhi: Women Unlimited)

Patel, S. (1988) 'Construction and Reconstruction of Women in Gandhi', *Economic and Political Weekly*, 23 (8) pp. 377–87

Pauwels, H. (2004) 'Only You: The Wedding of Rama and Sita, Past and Present', in M. Bose (ed.) *The Ramayana Revisited* (Oxford: Oxford University Press)

Pavitrananda, Swami (2006) *A Short Life of the Holy Mother* (Calcutta: Advaita Ashrama)

Peach, L. J. (2000) 'Human Rights, Religion and (Sexual) Slavery', *Annual of the Society of Christian Ethics*, 20, pp. 65–87

Pearson, A. (1996) *'Because it Gives me Peace of Mind': Ritual Fasts in the Religious Lives of Hindu Women* (New York: State University of New York Press)

Pearson, R. and E. Tomalin (2008) 'Intelligent Design? A Gender Sensitive Interrogation of Religion and Development', in G. Clarke and M. Jennings (eds) *Development, Civil Society and Faith-based Organizations: Bridging the Sacred and the Secular* (Basingstoke: Palgrave Macmillan)

Peet, R. (2007) *Geography of Power: The Makings of Global Economic Power* (London: Zed Books)

Perez, R. (2002) 'Practising Theory through Women's Bodies: Public Violence and Women's Strategies of Power and Place', in K. Saunders (ed.) *Feminist Post-Development Thought: Rethinking Modernity, Post-Colonialism and Representation* (London: Zed Books) pp. 263–80

Pickup, F. (2001) *Ending Violence against Women: A Challenge for Development and Humanitarian Work* (Oxford: Oxfam)

Pinchman, T. (ed.) (2007) *Women's Lives: Women's Rituals in the Hindu Tradition* (Oxford: Oxford University Press)

Pool, R. (1994) *Dialogue and the Interpretation of Illness: Conversations in a Cameroon Village* (Oxford: Berg)

Pottier, J. (ed.) (1993) *Practising Development: Social Science Perspectives* (London: Routledge)

Pottier, J., A. Bicker and P. Stilloe (eds) (2003) *Negotiating Local Knowledge: Power and Identity in Development* (London: Pluto Press)

Pratt, J. (2003) *Class, Nation, Identity: The Anthropology of Political Movements* (London: Pluto Press)

Quarles van Ufford, P. and A. Kumar Giri (eds) (2003) *A Moral Critique of Development: In Search of Global Answers* (New York: Routledge)

Quarles van Ufford, P. and M. Schoffeleers (eds) (1998) *Religion and Development: Towards an Integrated Approach* (Amsterdam: Free University Press)

Qureshi, S. (1980) 'Islam and Development: The Zia Regime in Pakistan', *World Development*, 8 (7/11)

Rahnema, M. and V. Bawtree (eds) *The Post-development Reader* (London: Zed Books, 1997)

Rajagopal, A. (2001) *Politics after Television: Hindu Nationalism and the Reshaping of the Indian Public* (Cambridge: Cambridge University Press)

Rajan, R. S. (2002) 'Rethinking Law and the Violence: The Domestic Violence (Prevention) Bill in India', *Gender and History*, 16 (3) pp. 769–93

Rajan, S. R. and S. Sharma (1995) 'Mahila Shikaha Karmis in the Shikaha Karmi Programme – A Study', *IDS Working Paper*, Jaipur. April

Rakodi, C. (2007) 'Understanding the Role of Religions in Development: The Approach of the Religion and Development Research Programme', *Working Paper 9*, www.rad.bham.ac.uk

Ramsay, Z. and T. Bradley (forthcoming) 'This Religion is the First Step in our Struggle', *Caste and Buddhist Identity in the Development Context: Views from Pune*, Working Paper, Religion and Development Research Programme, www.rad.bham.ac.uk

Ranger, T. (1985) 'Religious Movements and Politics in Sub-Saharan Africa', *African Studies Review*, 29 (2) pp. 1–70

Rao, V. N. (1991) 'A Ramayana of their Own: Women's Oral Tradition in Telugu', in P. Richman (ed.) *Many Ramayanas: The Diversity of a Narrative Tradition in South Asia* (New Delhi: Oxford University Press)

Rappaport, R. (1999) *Ritual and Religion in the Making of Humanity* (Cambridge: Cambridge University Press)

Rege, S. (2005) 'Dalit Women Talk Differently: A Critique of Difference and Towards a Dalit Feminist Standpoint Position', in M. Chaudhuri (ed.) *Feminism in India* (London: Zed Books) pp. 211–25

Rekdal, O. B. (1999) 'Cross-cultural Healing in East African Ethnography', *Medical Anthropology Quarterly*, 13 (4) pp. 458–82

Rew, A. (2004) 'Samen op Weg? Travelling Together? Religious Reform and Female Empowerment in Northern Orissa', in O. Salemink, A. van

Harskamp and A. Kumar Giri (eds) *The Development of Religion/The Religion of Development* (Delft: Eburon)

Reychler, L. and T. Paffenholz (eds) (2000) *Peace Building: A Field Guide* (Boulder, CO: Lynne Reinner)

Richards, A. I. (1982) *Chisungu: A Girls' Initiation Ceremony Among the Bemba of Zambia* (London: Tavistock)

Richman, P. (ed.) (2000) *Questioning Ramayanas: A South Asian Tradition* (Delhi: Oxford University Press)

Riley, J. (2002) *Stakeholders in Rural Development: Critical Collaboration in State–NGO Partnerships* (New Delhi: Sage)

Robertson, R. (1992) *Globalization: Social Theory and Global Culture* (London: Sage)

Rudolph, L. and S. Heober Rudolph (2006) *Postmodern Gandhi and other Essays: Gandhi in the World and at Home* (Delhi: Oxford University Press)

Ruether, B. (1984) *Women/Church: Theology and Practice* (San Francisco: Harper)

Ruether, B. (1990) *Sexism and God Talk: Towards a Feminist Theology* (Boston: Beacon Press)

Sachs, J. (1992) *The Development Dictionary: A Guide to Knowledge as Power* (London: Zed Books)

Sadhu Vaswani Mission (2009) *A Mission with a Vision* (Puna: Gita Publishing House)

Saeed, F. (2001) *Taboo! The Hidden Culture of the Red Light Area* (Oxford: Oxford University Press)

Sagade, J. (2005) *Child Marriage in India: Socio-Legal and Human Rights Dimensions* (Oxford: Oxford University Press)

Sanders, T. (1999) 'Modernity, Wealth and Witchcraft in Tanzania', in B. Isaac (ed.) *Research in Economic Anthropology*, vol. 20 (Stamford: JAI Press)

Sarkar, T. (2002) *Hindu Wife, Hindu Nation: Community, Religion and Cultural Nationalism* (New Delhi: Permanent Black)

Sarkar, T. and U. Butalia (1995) *Women and Right-wing Movements: Indian Experiences* (London: Zed Books)

Sax, W. S. (1991) *Mountain Goddess: Gender and Politics in a Himalayan Pilgrimage* (Oxford: Oxford University Press)

Saxena, R. (2001) 'Gandhi's Feminist Politics, Gender Equity and Patriarchal Values', in R. Johnson, 'Gandhi and Feminisms: Towards Women-Affirming Cultures of Peace', *Gandhi Marg*, 22 (1) April–June, pp. 113–28

Schech, S. B. and J. Haggis (2002) *Culture and Development: A Critical Introduction* (Oxford: Blackwell)

Schüssler Fiorenza, E. (1984) *Bread Not Stone: The Challenge of Feminist Biblical Interpretation* (Boston: Beacon Press)

Scupin, R. (1999) *Religion and Culture: An Anthropological Focus* (Upper Saddle River, NJ: Prentice Hall)

Sen, A. (2004) *Development as Freedom* (New Delhi: Oxford University Press)

Sen, A. (2007) *Shiv Sena Women: Violence and Communalism in a Bombay Slum* (London: C. Hurst & Company)

Shaharaw, M and R. Cranfield (1984) *Revolutions and Rebellions in Afghanistan: Anthropological Perspectives* (Berkeley: University of California Press)

Sharma, A. (ed.) (1987) *Women in World Religions* (New York: State University of New York Press)

Singh, B. K. (1990) *Indian National Congress and the Partition of India, 1937–1947* (Delhi: Capital Publishing House)

Solle, D. (1993) *Celebrating Resistance: The Way of the Cross in Latin America* (London: Mowbray)

Srinivasan, S. and A. Bedi (2007) 'Domestic Violence and Dowry: Evidence from a South Indian Village', *World Development*, 35 (5) pp. 857–80

Stirrat, R. L. and H. Henkel (1997) 'The Development Gift: The Problem of Reciprocity in the NGO World', *Annals of the American Academy of Political and Social Science*, 554 (1) pp. 66–80

Subramaniam, M. (2006) *The Power of Women's Organizing: Gender, Caste, and Class in India* (Lanham, MD: Lexington Books)

Sutherland, S. J. (1989) 'Sita and Draupadi: Aggressive Behaviour and Female Role-Models in the Sanskrit Epics', *Journal of the American Oriental Society*, 109 (1) pp. 63–79

Sutherland, S. J. (1992) *Bridging Worlds: Studies on Women in South Asia* (Delhi: Oxford University Press)

Sutherland, S. J. (2000) 'The Voice of Sita in Valimiki's Sundarakanda', in P. Richman (ed.) *Questioning Ramayanas: A South Asian Tradition* (Delhi: Oxford University Press)

Suthren Hirst, J. (1997) *Sita's Story* (Norwich: Religious and Moral Education Press)

Suthren Hirst, J. and L. Thomas (eds) (2004) *Playing for Real: Hindu Role Models, Religion and Gender* (Delhi: Oxford University Press)

Swantz, M.-L. (1990) 'Modernity, Wealth and Witchcraft in Tanzania', *Research in Economic Anthropology*, 20 (2) pp. 73–90

Swantz, M.-L. (1995) *Blood, Milk and Death: Body Symbols and Power of Regeneration among the Zaramo of Tanzania* (Westport: Bergin & Garvey)

Taylor, M. (1995) *Not Angels but Agencies: The Ecumenical Response to Poverty: A Primer* (New York: Trinity Press International)

Tehranian, M. and J. B. Lum (2006) *Globalization and Identity: Cultural Diversity, Religion and Citizenship* (Piscatawy, NJ: Transaction Publications)

Ter Haar, G and S. Ellis (2006) 'The Role of Religion in Development: Towards a New Religion between the European Union and Africa', *The European Journal of Development Research*, 18 (3) pp. 351–67

Thomas, S. (2005) *The Global Resurgence of Religion and the Transformation of International Relations* (New York: Palgrave Macmillan)

Tinker, I. (1999) 'The Myth of Development: A Critique of a Eurocentric Discourse', in R. Munck and D. O'Hearn (eds) *Critical Development Theory Contributions to a New Paradigm* (London: Zed Books)

Tomalin, E. (2006) 'Religion as a Rights-based Approach to Development', *Progress in Development Studies*, 6 (2) pp. 93–108

Tomalin, E. (2006) 'The Thai Bhikkhuni Movement and Women's Empowerment', *Gender and Development*, 14 (3) pp. 385–97.

Tomalin, E. (2009) 'Buddhist Feminist Transnational Networks, Female Ordination and Women's Enpowerment', *Oxford Development Studies*, 31 (22) pp. 81–100

Tomalin, E. (2009) 'Background Paper on Hinduism and International Development', *RAD Working Paper*, www.rad.bham.ac.uk

Tombs, D. (2002) *Latin America Liberation Theology* (Leiden: Brill)

Turner, E. (1980) *Christian Words* (Edinburgh: T. & T. Clark)

Turner, E. (1992) *Experiencing Ritual: A New Interpretation of African Healing* (Philadelphia: University of Pennsylvania Press)

Tucker, V. (1996) 'Introduction: A Cultural Perspective on Development', *European Journal of Development Research*, 8 (2) pp. 1–21

Tyndale, W. (2003) 'Idealism and Practicality: The Role of Religion and Development', *Development*, 46 (4) pp. 22–8

Tyndale, W. (ed.) (2006) *Visions of Development: Faith-Based Initiatives* (Aldershot: Ashgate)

Udvardy, M. (1990) 'Kifudu: A Female Fertility Cult among the Girama', in A. Jacabson Widding and W. van Beck (eds) *The Creative Communion: African Folk Models of Fertility and the Regeneration of Life* (Uppsala: Acta Universitatis)

UNIFEM (2002) *Support Services to Counter Violence against Women in Rajasthan* (Geneva: United Nations Development Fund for Women)

Unnithan, M. and K. Srivastava (1997) 'Gender Politics, Development and Women's Agency in Rajasthan', in R. D. Grillo and R. L. Stirrat (eds) *Discourses on Development: Anthropological Perspectives* (Oxford: Berg) pp. 157–81

Upreti, H. C. (1991) *The Myth of Sati: Some Dimensions of Widow Burning* (New Delhi: Himalaya Press)

van der Veer, P. (1994) *Religious Nationalism: Hindus and Muslims in India* (Berkeley: University of California Press)

van der Veer, P. (1996) *Conversion to Modernities: The Globalization of Christianity* (New York: Routledge)

Vaswani, J. P. (2002) *Sadhu Vaswani: His Life and Teachings* (Delhi: Sterling Publishers)

Vaswani, J. P. (2007) *Peace or Perish: There is no Other Choice* (Pune: Gita)

Ver Beek, K. A. (2000) 'Spirituality: A Development Taboo', *Development in Practice*, 10 (1) 1 February, pp. 31–43

Vivekananda, Swami (2006) *Ramakrishna and his Message* (Kolkata: Ad Rasta)

Vivekananda, Swami (2007) *Women of India* (Calcutta: Advaita Ashrama)

Vivekananda, Swami (1998) *Salvation and Service* (Calcutta: Advaita Ashrama)

Vivekananda, Swami (2008) *My Idea of Education* (Calcutta: Advaita Ashrama)

von der Mehden, F. (1980) 'Religion and Development in Southeast Asia: A Comparative Study', *World Development*, 8 (7/11)

von Mitzlaff, U. (1988) *Maasai Women: Life in a Patriarchal Society: Field Research among the Parakuyo, Tanzania* (Munich: Trickster Verlag)

Warburg, M., A Hvithamar and A. Wasmind (eds) (2005) *Baha'i and Globalisation* (Aarhus: Aarhus University Press)

Warrier, M. (2003) 'Processes of Secularization in Contemporary India: Guru Faith in the Mata Amritanandamayi Mission', *Modern Asian Studies*, 37 (1) pp. 213–53.

Weber, M. (1993) *The Sociology of Religion* (Boston: Beacon Press)

Whitehouse, H. and J. Laiulaw (2004) *Ritual and Memory: Toward a Comparative Anthropology of Religion* (Walmtcreek, CA: Alta Mira Press)

White, S. and R. Tiongco (1997) *Doing Theology and Development: Meeting the Challenge of Poverty* (St Andrews: St Andrews Press)

Wilber, C. K. and K. P. Jameson (1980) 'Religious Values and Social Limits to Development', *World Development*, Elsevier, 8 (7–8) pp. 467–79

Wolpert, L. (2006) *Six Impossible Things Before Breakfast: The Evolutionary Origins of Belief* (London: Faber & Faber)

Woods, N. (2001) 'Making the IMF and World Bank more Accountable', *International Affairs*, 77 (1) pp. 83–100

Zelliot, E. (2005) *Gandhi and Ambedkar: A Study in Leadership* (Pune: Jambhala Books)

Zene, C. (2002) *The Rishi of Bangladesh: A History of Christian Dialogues* (London: Routledge)

Index

269